D0929904

Infertility
and Pregnancy Loss

Constance Hoenk Shapiro

Infertility
and Pregnancy Loss

A Guide for
Helping Professionals

Jossey-Bass Publishers

San Francisco • London • 1988

INFERTILITY AND PREGNANCY LOSS
A Guide for Helping Professionals
 by Constance Hoenk Shapiro

Copyright © 1988 by: Jossey-Bass Inc., Publishers
350 Sansome Street
San Francisco, California 94104
&
Jossey-Bass Limited
28 Banner Street
London EC1Y 8QE

Copyright under International, Pan American, and
Universal Copyright Conventions. All rights
reserved. No part of this book may be reproduced
in any form—except for brief quotation (not to
exceed 1,000 words) in a review or professional
work—without permission in writing from the publishers.

Excerpts from an article entitled "The Impact of Infertility on the
Marital Relationship" by Constance Hoenk Shapiro are reprinted in
Chapters Two and Four with permission from *Social Casework*,
1982, *63*, 387–393. Copyright © 1982 by Family Service America.

Excerpts from an article entitled "Is Pregnancy After Infertility a
Dubious Joy?" by Constance Hoenk Shapiro are reprinted in Chapter
Nine with permission from *Social Casework*, 1986, *67*, 306–313.
Copyright © 1986 by Family Service America.

Library of Congress Cataloging-in-Publication Data

Shapiro, Constance Hoenk.
  Infertility and pregnancy loss.

  (A Joint publication in the Jossey-Bass social and
behavioral science series and the Jossey-Bass health
series)
  Includes bibliographies and index.
  1. Infertility—Psychological aspects. 2. Fetal
death—Psychological aspects. 3. Loss (Psychology)
I. Title. II. Series: Jossey-Bass social and behavioral
science series. III. Series: Jossey-Bass health series.
[DNLM: 1. Counseling. 2. Infertility—psychology.
3. Pregnancy Outcome—psychology. WP 570 S529i]
RC889.S48   1988   155.9'16   88-42800
ISBN 1-55542-121-0 (alk. paper)

Manufactured in the United States of America

JACKET DESIGN BY WILLI BAUM
FIRST EDITION

Code 8854

A joint publication in
The Jossey-Bass
Social and Behavioral Science Series
and
The Jossey-Bass Health Series

Contents

Part Three: Special Counseling Issues

10. Ectopic Pregnancy and Miscarriage   148

11. Stillbirth   165

12. Conclusion: The Persistent Legacy of Infertility   187

     Resource A: Glossary   201

     Resource B: Bibliography of Infertility
     Publications   216

     Resource C: Educational, Self-Help, and
     Support Group Resources   232

     References   235

     Index   243

Preface

Adoption: Our lives are empty without a child of
our own. We have much love and happiness to share
with your newborn. Let us put you at ease. Legal
and medical expenses paid, confidential. Call collect, anytime.

Behind this newspaper classified ad lies the heartache of infertility. Some infertile couples seek a child through adoption, while
others will explore different ways of becoming parents: artificial insemination, in vitro fertilization, gamete intrafallopian
transfer (GIFT), or a surrogate mother. Still other couples will
choose to remain childfree when their infertility prevents them
from having children. However, in order to come to a decision
about whether or how to bring a child into their lives, most infertile individuals must do complex emotional work on the feelings precipitated by the knowledge that they are infertile.

Infertility is the inability to conceive a pregnancy after a
year or more of regular sexual relations without contraception
or the incapacity to carry pregnancies to a live birth, according
to the American Fertility Society. In 1982, the rate of infertility of American couples of childbearing age was 14 percent
(Mosher and Pratt, 1985); however, the actual rate of infertility
is undoubtedly higher, considering the number of infertile men
and women who are unaware of their condition because they
have not yet tried to have a child (Andrews, 1984). Many of
these couples have carefully practiced birth control for years, so
that they could raise their families when their lives were most

secure. The realization that they are infertile comes as a brutal and unanticipated shock.

Recent media attention given to the problem of infertility and to the medical technologies that offer new hope to infertile couples tempts the public to associate infertility primarily with the inability to conceive. Yet infertility also means the inability to carry a pregnancy to a healthy birth because of an ectopic pregnancy, a miscarriage, or a stillbirth. Unfortunately, pregnancy loss affects a substantial number of American couples. Approximately one in five women suffers a miscarriage, one in eighty pregnancies ends in the birth of a stillborn child, and 1 to 2 percent of all pregnancies are ectopic. All told, approximately one million women a year in this country have an unsuccessful pregnancy (Friedman and Gradstein, 1982, p. xvii).

The infertility experience is likely to bring the couple to the attention of a number of professionals who are in a position to help them with the emotional turmoil that is an integral component of the infertility experience. However, relatively little has been written for helping professionals concerning the unique problems faced by couples who are unsuccessful in their efforts to become birth parents. In *Infertility and Pregnancy Loss*, I have tried to fill that gap in the literature. The book is based in large part on my counseling experiences with over one hundred infertile individuals and couples. The variety of issues presented in counseling sessions, combined with the courage and resilience shown by many infertile people once they received emotional support, convinced me that a book of this scope could be immensely valuable to the many professionals with whom infertile people come into contact during their struggle to become parents. Too often the urgency of a couple's medical needs has eclipsed the equally important emotional dimension that accompanies the infertility experience. Professionals are often reluctant to respond to the emotional needs of infertile people partly because they do not know what interventions could prove most helpful. After all, infertility counseling is a relatively recent area of expertise and is continually developing as the options for couples evolve and change.

A generation ago, adoption was perceived as the most

salient outcome to the struggle with infertility—in part because medical technology offered relatively little hope to infertile couples and also because a large number of healthy infants were available for adoption. Adoption still remains an option for many couples, but the wait is often long, and the professional never should assume that adoption is a pat answer to the devastating blow caused by infertility. In this book, adoption is presented in the context of the decision-making process that couples must work through. The professional wanting more in-depth information on adoption issues and procedures should refer to the books and articles contained in Resource B and the references section at the end of the book. *Infertility and Pregnancy Loss* presents a balance between theory and practice to help the professional assess the needs of the couple or individual and offer support ranging from counseling to education. Case vignettes are provided throughout the book to illustrate the dilemmas that couples face and the ways in which the professional can intervene. Although based on my counseling experiences, the case situations have been altered to preserve client confidentiality.

Who Should Read This Book?

Many different helping professionals could potentially become involved in offering emotional support to infertile individuals. Social workers, psychologists, psychiatrists, family counselors, adoption counselors, and genetics counselors are likely to be consulted as infertile people mourn their losses, try to deal with the narcissistic blow they have sustained, contemplate the implications of their infertility, and confront the decisions that must be made. Clergy of all faiths are in a special position to offer both support and solace when infertile people turn to them during times of despair, loss of faith, and anger that their prayers are not being heard. Certainly, nurses, midwives, and physicians will encounter the sadness of a couple's infertility at many times throughout diagnostic workups and treatments, during and after pregnancy losses, and, if a fragile pregnancy is achieved, during the long nine-month wait ahead. Although the purpose for professional intervention with an infertile couple will differ according to circumstances, all professionals must be sensitive to the couple's need to mourn their losses and must appreciate the couple's courage as they undertake the difficult grief work precipitated by their infertility.

Overview of the Contents

The book is organized in three parts. The first part (Chapters One through Four) provides an in-depth view of the infertility experience.

Chapter One, "The Complex Dimensions of Infertility," defines infertility, details its prevalence, provides information on contributing factors, and introduces the concepts of attachment and loss that are referred to in later chapters. An overview of the impact of diagnosis and treatment is presented, with an emphasis on the emotional component of these experiences.

Chapter Two, "Confronting Infertility as a Crisis," explains that infertility is a life event that few people anticipate they will need to face. When a diagnosis of infertility is given, couples may face a period of crisis where they have few adequate coping mechanisms to muster. Crisis theory is detailed as it applies to the unique needs of infertile people, and counseling strategies are suggested as the professional helps the client come to terms with the crisis of infertility.

Chapter Three, "Confronting Infertility over Time," discusses the chronic grief that many infertile couples suffer as the diagnosis or treatment proves inconclusive and they are offered neither closure nor hope. Couples most likely to experience chronic grief are those with unexplained infertility, women with endometriosis, men with low sperm counts, and couples committed to lengthy treatments that require repeated efforts, such as artificial insemination and in vitro fertilization. This chapter offers information about chronic conditions and the unique issues of unresolved mourning that the professional must recognize.

Chapter Four, "Mourning the Many Losses of Infertility," offers a theoretical framework of the mourning process that is appropriate for use with infertile clients whose treatment is unsuccessful. It also provides specific suggestions for ways in which the professional can be responsive to the emotional needs of clients as they mourn the losses associated with their infertility.

The second part (Chapters Five through Eight) provides ideas for specific strategies.

Chapter Five, "Teaching Assertive Coping Skills," offers strategies that professionals can use to help infertile clients be appropriately assertive with medical professionals, employers, friends, and family members who may make ignorant or insensitive remarks about their infertility. It discusses the goals of and the barriers to assertive communication and contrasts assertiveness with two undesirable characteristics, aggressiveness and nonassertion.

Chapter Six, "Conducting Support Groups," describes the help that members of a support group can offer to one another in times of difficulty. The chapter covers such topics as the first meeting and the initial stages of group development, themes that emerge as the group sessions proceed, and the emotions among group members as termination of the group approaches.

Chapter Seven, "Helping Clients Cope with Ongoing Sources of Stress," details some common sources of stress (emotional isolation, the sexual relationship, holidays) and provides practical coping strategies that professionals can encourage infertile individuals to use as an antidote to stress.

Chapter Eight, "Helping Clients Handle Infertility Decisions," discusses common infertility decisions, such as whom to tell, what to tell, whether to pursue treatment, which treatment to pursue (artificial insemination, GIFT, in vitro fertilization), when to discontinue treatment, and whether to pursue other options (surrogate mothers, adoption, childfree living). Included are several theoretical frameworks that the professional may want to use in decision making with infertile couples and individuals.

The third part (Chapters Nine through Twelve) contains chapters that address special circumstances.

Chapter Nine, "Pregnancy After Infertility: A Dubious Joy?," examines pregnancy by trimesters to highlight the specific sources of stress that couples who achieve a pregnancy after a history of infertility may encounter. Attention is also given to the postpartum experience and the unique adjustments faced by the previously infertile couple.

Chapter Ten, "Ectopic Pregnancy and Miscarriage," emphasizes that the failure to carry a pregnancy to a healthy delivery can be a devastating blow to a couple. At the time of an ectopic pregnancy or a miscarriage, the attention of most helping professionals is on the medical well-being of the woman. This chapter focuses on the emotional dimensions of pregnancy loss for both the male and the female in the couple and suggests specific ways in which the professional can help the couple cope with the loss of their pregnancy.

Chapter Eleven, "Stillbirth," details the issues faced by parents and family members of a stillborn baby, suggesting ways in which the professional can best provide comfort, information, and advocacy services, both in the hospital and after the woman's discharge. Special attention is given to decisions that the couple must make: whether to name the baby, whether to hold the baby, whether to have a service, whether to send out birth and death announcements, how to help other children in the family understand the death, and what to do in the difficult months ahead.

Chapter Twelve, the concluding chapter, discusses "The Persistent Legacy of Infertility." Even when couples have come to terms with infertility (whether through having a birth child, adopting a child, or opting for childfree living), there are predictable times when infertility issues will reemerge. For example, couples with children may be faced with special challenges when their children reach adolescence and enter their own childbearing years. Similarly, the onset of menopause may revive in infertile women the feelings of hopelessness that they encountered in their earlier struggles with infertility. Couples without children are likely to experience some sadness as the children of their friends achieve milestones or as these couples face the loneliness of old age without the comfort of adult children. This chapter helps the professional appreciate the lifelong issues associated with infertility, even after infertile couples have "resolved" the most pressing problems associated with their childbearing years.

This book focuses heavily on the psychosocial needs of infertile individuals and emphasizes the importance of working with the couple as a unit whenever possible. Because ample literature exists on the physiological causes of infertility, readers who want to know more about specific conditions may refer to the bibliography in Resource B and to the references section. In addition, the glossary in Resource A provides definitions of the most common medical terms pertaining to infertility, and the list of organizations and materials in Resource C can be utilized for educational and support purposes by professionals and their clients.

Acknowledgments

Many people have helped me in my efforts to write this book. My clients have been my best teachers over the years as they have shared their concerns with me and we have worked together to find comfort and solutions to their infertility struggles. My professional colleagues at Ferre Institute, Jean Morris and Luba Djurdjinovic, have always been available to discuss infertility concerns, to provide technical material, to read rough drafts of chapters, and to suggest changes that would enhance the book as a whole. My friend Susan Lang drew upon her own struggle with infertility to offer sensitive and incisive editorial suggestions. I am indebted to RESOLVE, Inc., for providing the bibliography that appears as Resource B and the list of organizations in Resource C. Likewise, the glossary of infertility terms provided by Serono Symposia, USA, (Resource A) has added to the scope of this book. Yvonne Sterling, who has extended herself beyond her role of secretary and computer whiz, has been a constant source of encouragement in my four years of work on this book. And to Stuart, my husband, I owe special thanks for his computer instruction, his tolerance for the clutter my manuscript produced for months on end, and his support in making final decisions on the book.

Ithaca, New York   Constance Hoenk Shapiro
August 1988

To My Precious Children
Adrienne and Daniel

The Author

Constance Hoenk Shapiro is an associate professor in the Department of Human Service Studies in the New York State College of Human Ecology at Cornell University. She received her B.A. degree (1969) in sociology from Wellesley College, her M.S. degree (1971) from the Columbia University School of Social Work, and her Ph.D. degree (1978) in education from Cornell University.

Shapiro's main research activities have been in the area of human sexuality, with particular focus on adolescent pregnancy, sex education, and adult infertility. In 1983 she received the State University of New York's Chancellor's Award for Excellence in Teaching. She has published numerous articles in professional journals and is the author of *Adolescent Pregnancy Prevention* (1981).

Shapiro has been director of the social work program at Cornell University since 1986. She is on the board of directors of the Ferre Institute in Utica, New York; is a founding member of the Central New York chapter of RESOLVE, Inc.; and serves as a consultant to federal, state, and local organizations on issues relating to human sexuality. In addition to teaching, consulting, and research, Shapiro maintains a private practice for infertile individuals and couples.

Infertility
and Pregnancy Loss

1

The Complex Dimensions
of Infertility

Couples who cope with infertility often speak of its intrusiveness into many areas of their lives. They must contend not only with the disruptive medical issues of diagnosis and treatment but also with the personal psychological pain of being an infertile person in a predominantly fertile world. Added to the personal struggle are the various social relationships affected by infertility—relationships with parents, in-laws, siblings, friends, relatives, neighbors, and co-workers, most of whom are unaware of the pain the infertile person is trying to overcome. And most important is the couple's own relationship, which can serve both as a buttress against the insensitivity of the fertile world and also as a source of stress when partners cannot understand or reach out to comfort each other.

Attachment and Loss

The concepts of attachment and loss are integral to the infertility struggle. Although most people think that attachment occurs in relationship to another living person, one can also become attached to a fantasy baby or to a fetus in utero. For couples who decide to try to conceive a pregnancy, the attachment to a dream child begins as they contemplate the ways that the baby will alter their lifestyle, envision the physical attributes that their baby may have, and anticipate the special talents or interests that they will encourage their little one to develop.

Prospective parents also begin to think about themselves differently. If this is their first child, they begin to think about themselves as parents, about their parents as grandparents, and about their siblings as aunts and uncles. If they already have children, as in the situation of secondary infertility or a remarriage, the addition of the new baby represents a shift in the relationships that currently exist in the family. All this before the baby is even conceived!

> Even while we were trying to conceive, I found myself pretending that I was already pregnant. I'd go window shopping for maternity clothes, and I even picked up a couple of little outfits and a teddy bear for the baby. I found myself lingering in the infant section of department stores, mentally furnishing the nursery. When the doctor diagnosed our infertility, I had to stop all that pretending. Now I don't even go into any section of a store that reminds me of babies.

The infertility experience abruptly interrupts these forming attachments. Perhaps there is difficulty in conceiving the dream child; maybe the pregnancy is lost through miscarriage, ectopic (or tubal) pregnancy, or stillbirth. The interruption of the emotional attachment to a dream child or to a developing baby can present a devastating blow to the couple and their family members who shared in the anticipation of a new baby.

Yet the loss of fertility or the loss of an unborn child is, for the most part, an unrecognized event in society. No rituals exist to legitimize the grief of the infertile couple who mourn the baby they never conceived or gave birth to. In a sense, infertility is a silent and unrecognized loss, one that many couples struggle to resolve in lonely isolation. Friedman and Gradstein (1982) differentiate the mourning that accompanies infertility from the mourning that occurs after the death of a loved one. When a pregnancy is lost or a dream child not conceived, there is no tangible "outside" person to mourn, and grieving for someone who is not physically present is awkward. Also, because there are no memories or shared life experiences, the loss often has a feeling of unreality about it. Contributing to this sense of unreality is the commonly described experience of finding that the attachment to the unconceived or unborn child may not be shared by anyone else. The loss of fertility or a pregnancy is often met with comments such as "It's important not to give up" or "You can try again"; both of these statements minimize the couple's feelings that the loss is very real. With the realization that infertility is a serious problem, many couples begin a process of anticipatory mourning for the child they fear they may never have. There is an ambivalence in this mourning; for just as they are emotionally in touch with their grief, they also are actively involved in treatments that they hope will cure their infertility. Anticipatory mourning represents an emotional distancing from the initial attachment they had to their fantasy child.

For couples who try to conceive a child soon after their marriage, the diagnosis and treatment of infertility may represent the first crisis of the marriage. This crisis presents the newly married couple with many emotional challenges: not only must they face the threat to an important shared hope, but they also must learn quickly how to comfort each other and how to express their need for emotional support. Thus, infertility may test the resilience of their relationship at a time when both partners are also preoccupied with their individual emotional needs.

All couples undergoing infertility treatment are likely to be involved in some aspect of the mourning process. Because their efforts to resolve feelings of grief rarely are synchronized, the couple often feel emotionally out of step as they individually struggle with the issues that treatment presents. Jack explained the discontinuity in their grieving this way:

> I find myself furious at the world. I'm short-tempered with doctors, with well-meaning friends, and even with Louise—especially with Louise, I suppose, because all she ever does is dissolve in tears. She can't seem to mobilize herself out of her sadness even to decide whether we should give up the

treatments we've been involved in for the past
three years. And, of course, she gets even more
withdrawn when I'm exploding with frustration.

As the following chapters point out, the process of
mourning is highly individual for each person, and it depends on
many factors: experiences with previous losses, methods for
coping and managing stress, the support offered by the partner
and by significant others, other life events occurring simultaneously, the extent of emotional investment in the pregnancy or
in the hope of becoming pregnant, the length of time the couple
have been trying to conceive, and the prognosis for future success in childbearing. Initially, the couple may regard the experience of infertility as a crisis. They may feel unable to cope with
the unfamiliar and unexpected emotions that emerge as they try
to integrate the losses associated with their infertility. It is
usually at this time that the couple are especially open to input
from helping professionals, both on the medical and the emotional fronts. Their quest for coping mechanisms to surmount
and overcome this initial crisis presents the helping professional
with a unique opportunity to offer both emotional support and
concrete information.

If the crisis period passes with one or both partners still
not coping adequately, or if the initial experience with infertility leads into subsequent diagnostic workups and treatments,
the couple may find themselves confronting a number of losses
(Mahlstedt, 1985). The loss of their dream child is often the
most frightening one, but the couple also may lose their role as
birth parents, their trust in their reproductive capacities, their
sense of control over life plans, and their feelings of normality
in a predominantly fertile world. These losses will need to be
mourned, and the readiness to undertake this difficult emotional work differs with each individual. The helping professional
can be especially supportive in enabling the couple to articulate
the specific losses that are causing pain; the professional also
can validate their feelings of sadness and offer support as they
mourn their losses.

Couples who have come to terms with many of the losses

of infertility, but who still continue the struggle for a birth child despite the uncertainty of this struggle, will experience chronic mourning. In limbo with their infertility, these couples must learn to cope week to week, month to month, and year to year. For these individuals, periodic support is likely to be most appropriate, particularly at times made more difficult by medical interventions, health problems, or emotional low points. Some of these couples may be actively seeking to adopt a child, but the anxiety connected with the long waiting process, combined with their ongoing medical problems, may prompt them to seek support to shore up their flagging emotional resources.

Infertile individuals and the professionals helping them can benefit greatly from the many services of RESOLVE, Inc., located at 5 Water Street, Arlington, Mass. 02174 (617/643-2424). This national nonprofit organization for infertile men and women has chapters in over forty-five cities throughout the United States. RESOLVE provides telephone counseling, referral to medical and related services, support groups, and public education through newsletters, fact sheets, and chapter meetings.

Prevalence of Infertility

In their first year of trying to achieve a pregnancy, about 80 percent of sexually active couples will conceive; in a second year, perhaps as many as 15 percent will conceive (Mazor, 1984, p. xvi). During the third year, a yet smaller group will achieve pregnancy, resulting in an overall inclusive accumulative percentage of 9 percent for the second and third years. The remainder—approximately 11 percent—have an infertility problem; their chances of conceiving decrease over time in the absence of treatment.

According to Mazor (1984, p. 25), about 50 percent of all infertility problems are related to factors in the female (mainly, problems in tubal patency or problems in ovulation). Approximately 30 percent of the problems can be traced to the male partner, and these problems are, generally, less amenable to treatment. For 20 percent of infertile couples, the diagnostic workup reveals that both partners contribute to the infertility problem (Menning, 1977). For such couples, infertility indeed represents a challenge, both medically and emotionally. In some cases, one or both individuals have a borderline problem resulting in subfertility; in other cases, both partners have infertility problems; and, in still other cases, the shared problem is one that relates to coital technique and can be helped by education and counseling rather than by medical intervention. Finally, in a small percentage of cases, the infertility is classified as "unexplained."

Among those couples who submit to a proper investigation of their problem, 50 percent will respond to treatment and can be helped to conceive. In contrast, only 5 percent of infertile couples who do not seek medical intervention will subsequently conceive (Menning, 1977, p. 5). The impression that adoption will enhance a couple's chances of subsequently conceiving is not based in fact; adoptive parents achieve a pregnancy at the same 5 percent rate as those couples who do not seek medical intervention for their infertility (Lamb and Leurgans, 1979).

Much more recognition is being given to the problem of infertility than was given even a decade ago—partly because sexual issues are now discussed more openly. In addition, the dearth of healthy infants available for adoption has caused many couples to take advantage of the medical treatments now available, whereas a generation ago most infertile couples chose to enlarge their families through adoption, keeping their infertility a private matter.

Contributing Factors

The actual number of infertile couples is at its highest point in history—partly because an increasing number of couples have decided to delay childbearing until they are in their thirties and forties, a period of less fertility than the twenties. An infertility problem that is more prevalent among women past their thirties is endometriosis, a condition in which the lining of the uterus migrates to other parts of the abdominal cavity. The uterine tissue bleeds and sheds at the time of menstruation, resulting for many women in pain, scarring, and cyst formation.

Between one-fourth and one-third of all infertile women have endometriosis.

In addition, the increase in sexually transmitted diseases has resulted in scarring and adhesions in the reproductive tracts of many males and females. Besides contributing to difficulty in conceiving, reproductive adhesions in women may be responsible for the recent rise in the incidence of ectopic pregnancies. Certain forms of birth control have also contributed to infertility: the intrauterine device (IUD) has been found to be a source of pelvic inflammatory disease, which, in turn, can scar the Fallopian tubes; a small number of women who use birth control pills experience difficulties in ovulation after they discontinue the pill. In addition, some individuals, for a variety of reasons, are seeking reversal of earlier sterilization procedures as life goals change in previously unanticipated ways. Substances such as Agent Orange (a defoliant used during the Vietnam War), diethylstilbestrol (DES, a drug taken to prevent miscarriages), and radiation are emerging as important to the population of childbearing age, even though exposure to these substances may have occurred years ago. Current factors, such as toxins in the workplace, substance abuse, nutrition, and excessively vigorous exercise, may also play a role in infertility.

The function of stress in infertility is not yet clearly understood, but over the past two decades less and less emphasis has been placed on psychogenic factors as causes of infertility. As elaborate theories about the psychodynamics of infertile people remained unconfirmed by rigorous research, and as advances in medical technology have led to improved diagnostic techniques and a better understanding of reproductive physiology, a diagnosis can now be established for more than 90 percent of infertile cases (Mazor, 1984, p. 24). In the remaining 10 percent, the difficulty in obtaining an accurate diagnosis may be attributed to inadequate technology.

Stress may affect the hypothalamus, thus contributing to infertility by inhibiting ovulation; or stress may cause a woman's tubes to clamp down in spasm, thus preventing the migration of sperm. In males, research with both animals and humans has shown that extreme emotional or physical stress can impair spermatogenesis; the effect of stress, however, appears to be reversible once the stress element is removed. Stress also can cause erectile dysfunction, usually a temporary difficulty that can be relieved by counseling.

The Impact of Diagnosis

Some couples are infertile because of identified problems in the male or in the female. Others are infertile because of their unique reproductive factors in combination; with a more fertile partner, either person might have little or no difficulty conceiving. Regardless of which partner is physiologically responsible for the infertility, both partners must grapple with the psychological impact of their inability to conceive a baby or carry a pregnancy successfully to term. This is a devastating blow to couples who had looked forward to beginning a family and who subsequently feel that their dreams have been shattered. Sometimes an infertile partner fears actual or emotional abandonment by the fertile partner; some will continually test and provoke the mate with comments like "If you had married someone else, you would have a family by now" (Mazor, 1984). Although some authors report an increased incidence of extramarital affairs (Walker, 1978), others cite the more frequent loss of libido and depression (Mazor, 1984; Mahlstedt, 1985; Menning, 1977). The couple's ability to come to terms with the crisis of infertility will greatly influence their relationship as a couple; their social interactions with friends, co-workers, and extended family members; and their capacity to look ahead to life options that may or may not include enlarging their family.

The Diagnostic Workup

Since many females are accustomed to receiving reproductive health care (pelvic and breast examinations, Pap smears, and the like), they usually are able to tolerate the initial procedures of an infertility workup without undue psychological difficulty, although the procedures themselves may be uncomfortable. However, as the effort to reach a diagnosis requires more tests, additional expenses, and perhaps hospitalization, the woman's anxiety is likely to build. She may worry about being found defective and may harbor the fear that she does not deserve to have a child (Mazor, 1984; Mahlstedt, 1985).

> Even though I know our infertility is a medical problem, I keep asking "Why us?" Is there something about us that would make us bad parents? If everyone else can conceive so easily, there must be a reason that we've been singled out to be infertile. If we weren't meant to be parents, then what's the point in even pursuing medical treatment?

Since the diagnostic process involves a range of procedures, the woman is likely to feel probed and manipulated physically, and psychologically she is likely to feel the stress associated with revealing intimate details of her sexual life, with charting her basal body temperature daily, and with having intercourse on a schedule that coincides with ovulation (Lalos and others, 1985b). Some women feel apprehensive when they ask their male partners to participate in the diagnostic procedure, especially if they want children more than their partner does.

A diagnostic workup can continue for months and sometimes years, and the length of time the couple must spend in this process can be anxiety provoking. The woman feels anger and sadness each month as the beginning of her period indicates that, once again, she is not pregnant; the couple face decisions about the risks and costs and intrusiveness of each new procedure; and, if the woman is in her thirties or forties, she feels strong pressure to reach a diagnosis, thereby not wasting precious months in her quest to achieve a pregnancy.

Males are less accustomed than females to seeking routine medical care for their reproductive health; therefore, many males feel highly apprehensive at the prospect of seeing a physician. This apprehension is often exacerbated by the need to produce a semen sample by masturbation, a process that may arouse feelings of guilt, inadequacy, and anxiety in the male (Lalos and others, 1985b). A semen analysis must be made at an early stage of the diagnostic workup; it is an important diagnostic procedure in evaluating male infertility, and several samples may be needed during the course of several months, depending on the findings. In contrast to many of the procedures used to diagnose infertility in the female, semen analysis is an inexpensive and nonintrusive procedure.

Since many males attach feelings of self-worth and virility to the outcome of the semen analysis, the results can have an impact on the male's self-esteem and his general feelings of adequacy (Mahlstedt, 1985). The process of having his sperm counted and scored can be threatening to even the most secure male's ego (Menning, 1977). One diagnostic procedure in particular, the postcoital test, can be highly stressful for males. One or two days prior to ovulation, the woman must visit her physician a few hours after having intercourse, so that the physician can examine her cervical mucus to determine how sperm interact with the vaginal and cervical environment. With the doctor's appointment looming, the male is truly required to perform on command, and the consequent tension may cause him to experience temporary impotence (Rosenfeld and Mitchell, 1979; Lalos and others, 1985b). The same reaction may occur when the couple have charted the woman's basal body temperature in an effort to determine the day on which she ovulates. This problem presents itself as a mid-cycle pattern of sexual dysfunction (Drake and Grunert, 1979). Once again the male is required to have intercourse on a schedule unrelated to his own sexual urges. For a male who has never experienced temporary impotence, the entire diagnostic workup may call into question some basic assumptions about his virility.

If the couple are pursuing an initial infertility workup in their local community, the woman usually will be seen by her gynecologist and the male will be evaluated by a urologist. Diagnostic impressions usually are offered individually to the female or to the male, leaving the partner with the task of remembering the information accurately and conveying it to his or her mate. This diagnostic division often contributes to the couple's difficulty in viewing infertility as a shared problem and intensifies the likelihood that one partner will carry an inordinate feeling of guilt or blame (Mahlstedt, 1985). If the couple are being evaluated in an infertility clinic, both partners probably will have been seen by specialists in the clinic and told together of the outcome of their infertility workup. These couples find it easier to share the burden of infertility, since both partners are informed about their own and the other's condition.

During this period, the couple can benefit greatly from psychological support (Mahlstedt, 1985). Whatever the outcome of diagnosis, the couple have new information to process and a pressing need to weigh future options. Couples who have been in suspense for weeks or months of diagnostic tests often need help in understanding the implications of the diagnosis for future life plans, so that they can make decisions with full understanding of the available options. A professional familiar with issues such as infertility treatment, grief, loss, and adoption can be of great help to the couple who are trying to integrate diagnostic information with future life goals.

Outcome of Diagnosis

It may be months before any diagnostic impression can be reached. In the doctor's office, one of three scenarios may occur: the couple may be told that they have a problem for which there is no medical cure; they may be told that they have a problem for which treatment is available; or they may be told that they have idiopathic (unexplained) infertility. The psychological response of infertile couples will differ according to which of these three diagnoses they receive.

Untreatable Infertility. If the couple are told that their infertility is caused by a problem for which there is no medical cure, their psychological response almost universally resembles that of mourning a death (Rosenfeld and Mitchell, 1979; Menning, 1977; Shapiro, 1982). The very fact that they have invested in an infertility workup indicates the importance their fertility holds for them. To learn that they are infertile and that they will never conceive a child catapults them into a mourning process for the several losses they have sustained. First and foremost is the loss of the child they hoped to have, around whom they may already have begun to build fantasies and form an elusive attachment; second is the loss of reproductive health, which may translate into a feeling of body betrayal; and third is the loss associated with the hopes of experiencing pregnancy and childbirth and perhaps breastfeeding a baby. Some of these losses will be more compelling for one partner than for the other; the pace of the mourning process also is likely to differ for each partner.

Treatable Infertility. When a couple receive the information that there is treatment available for their infertility, they probably will have an ambivalent response. On one level, they feel relieved and hopeful that one day they will give birth to a healthy baby. On another level, they feel apprehensive as they anticipate difficult decisions, particularly if they have limited financial resources, must travel a long distance to receive treatment, or must weigh the risks associated with various medical interventions. Finally, there is likely to be a residue of fear and apprehension as they realize that the treatment may not be successful and that they may never give birth to a child. The couple now must decide whether to embark on what may be a costly, disruptive, and psychologically stressful undertaking.

> We don't have much time or much money. I can't afford to miss much work for our infertility treatments, and we're in our late thirties, so adoption agencies won't be willing to consider us much longer. So we have to decide. Do we gamble on treatment and put our savings into that? Or do we move ahead with adoption?

Idiopathic (Unexplained) Infertility. The couple who receive a diagnosis of unexplained infertility carry a unique emotional burden. They are plunged into a psychological limbo in which neither they nor their physicians know what more to do to enhance their chances of becoming birth parents. For some of these couples, the diagnosis of idiopathic infertility will be the beginning of a series of visits to infertility specialists; for others, it will represent the beginning of the mourning process, in which they experience denial, anger, bargaining, and grief without being able to move into the final stage of acceptance. Essentially, the couple feel that they no longer have control over their life plans to have a baby; and with medical professionals also baffled about the cause of their infertility, the couple enter what is often a lengthy period of chronic mourning.

Secondary Infertility. Secondary infertility is the inability to conceive again after one or more successful pregnancies. The causes of secondary infertility are the same as those associated with primary infertility. Secondary infertility is cured at the same success rate as primary infertility, in about 50 percent of cases (Menning, 1977, p. 137). Such conditions presumably have developed or worsened between the birth of an earlier child and the current wish to conceive again. The emotions associated with secondary infertility often include surprise followed by frustration, as the couple once in control of their reproduction find that fertility eludes them (Menning, 1977). Couples with secondary infertility face pressures to have more children from friends, family, and their own child. When such couples express sadness or grief about their inability to conceive future children, other people often discount their pain, reminding them that they are, in fact, already parents. Despite the pleasure they take in parenthood, couples with secondary infertility may find themselves overattentive to the needs of their child. They may become overprotective, and they may set unrealistic goals for the child, since all their hopes rest on this child's accomplishments and good health (Menning, 1977).

The Impact of Treatment

The beginning of treatment for infertility represents both a confirmation of infertility and the hope that the problem can be cured. In both the male and the female, the psychological impact of treatment will be affected by a variety of factors: how they feel about the intrusiveness of medical treatments, what potential side effects are associated with specific treatments, how flexible their personal and work lives are to the carefully timed nature of some treatments, and what level of success they have been led to associate with the particular treatments they will be undergoing.

Treatment often is given at infertility clinics many miles from the couple's home. In that case, the woman may be separated from family and friends just when they might be most helpful in offering emotional support. Even the male partner may be unable to remain at the infertility clinic beyond a few days, since the economic or professional strains of missing work may be more compelling than his partner's need for his physical presence. The period of waiting during recovery or during ongoing treatment procedures is often immensely stressful for the woman, who must find other sources of support if family and friends are not accessible.

The couple involved in infertility treatment are in a period of anxious waiting. If the couple have unexplained infertility or if both partners have problems contributing to their infertility, each partner may be experiencing a variety of treatments in a close time span. Thus, each partner may be so immersed in his or her own emotional problems that there is less support to offer the other. These couples will need help in looking outside their relationship for the emotional support they both need. By sharing the problem of infertility, the couple may come to have more empathy for each other and may find that they grow closer through the experience of their infertility. However, infertility is a major focus of these couples' lives, and it is often very difficult for them to think of themselves except in their roles as infertile people (Mazor, 1984; Mahlstedt, 1985).

Long-Term Consequences

Each couple will face unique long-term consequences of their infertility, depending on the conditions contributing to the infertility and the solutions they find as they confront their inability to give birth to a child.

Inability to Conceive. Couples who have been unable to conceive will need to come to terms with the specific losses represented by their infertility. Grieving for these losses, although most intense in the months immediately following the diagnosis, may reemerge from time to time as they face their loss of control over life hopes. For some couples who choose to exert control by pursuing adoption, artificial insemination, gamete intrafallopian transfer (GIFT), or in vitro fertilization, the pain of infertility may recede as they concentrate on new options. On the other hand, all these options involve waiting periods, feelings of being evaluated, and chances of not succeeding; therefore, the raw feelings aroused by infertility will likely be in the forefront until the couple have a child.

Pregnancy Loss. For couples whose infertility is caused by their inability to carry a pregnancy to term, the issues are more complex. The couple know that they can conceive; yet efforts at conception have brought them heartbreak as they experience miscarriages, ectopic pregnancies, and stillbirths.

> When the doctor diagnosed my missed abortion, I knew I had hit the depths. Here was this baby I tried ten years to conceive, and suddenly she dies and a whole part of me dies with her. The doctor encouraged me to carry my dead baby until labor began spontaneously. I became a recluse. I couldn't even bear to go to the store for milk. And after the baby was delivered the agony didn't stop. People who had known me while I was pregnant would inquire happily about the baby when it was obvious I was no longer pregnant.

The level of attachment that the couple allow themselves during a pregnancy will influence the extent to which they feel a sense of loss, and their feelings about their losses will, in turn, influence their willingness to undertake another pregnancy. In a miscarriage, the loss is primarily an emotional one, as the couple question whether they will ever be able to have a healthy pregnancy (Pizer and Palinski, 1980; Borg and Lasker, 1981). When an ectopic pregnancy occurs, there are the more concrete fears of risks to the woman's life and of the possibility that one of her tubes may burst or need to be removed, thereby impairing future fertility (Friedman and Gradstein, 1982). Couples who have experienced the tragedy of a stillbirth want to have a healthy baby and, at the same time, fear that their reproductive capabilities are fragile and that a future pregnancy, too, could be lost (DeFrain, 1986). So couples who have suffered a pregnancy loss are, foremost, highly aware of their reproductive fragility and subsequently are both hopeful and hesitant about the prospect of achieving another pregnancy. These couples must be helped to mourn the losses associated with the lost pregnancy, so that they can invest in a subsequent pregnancy for its own sake and not be plagued with unresolved issues at a time when they are entitled to feel more hopeful (Shapiro, 1986).

Artificial Insemination. The couple found to be eligible for artificial insemination must deal with their feelings about achieving a pregnancy in a noncoital way. The clinical atmosphere surrounding the insemination experience can be unsettling for couples, although some physicians encourage mutual involvement by asking the male to carry the semen to the person who will perform the insemination or by encouraging the couple to partake of some wine or champagne after the insemination has been accomplished. Couples who are participating in artificial insemination with the husband's sperm (AIH) face the pressures of having the male producing a specimen while the woman waits to be inseminated. In such situations, the male may be unable to provide the specimen, because the anxiety attached to his role in the procedure renders him temporarily impotent. The woman is often concerned that she may not be ovulating on the day of the insemination, in spite of efforts to use home ovulation test kits accurately. Since about 50 percent of infertility clinics do not do inseminations on weekends, some couples feel frustrated that they have missed a potential insemination because of the rigidity of the clinic's schedule (B. Freeman, former executive director of RESOLVE, personal communication, Aug. 1986).

When the male is sterile or has a low sperm count, or when the male is fertile but at serious risk of passing on a congenital disease to genetic offspring, the choice is usually to use donor sperm. Couples choosing artificial insemination by donor (AID) face all the problems of couples undergoing AIH, as well as some unique problems. The Roman Catholic Church and Orthodox Judaic practice forbid its use; some couples have concerns about the female's carrying "another man's baby"; the couple must decide whether they will share news about the insemination and, if so, with whom; the couple may be concerned about health problems of the donor and, more abstractly, may wonder whether their capacity for emotional attachment to a child conceived with donor sperm will be different from their attachment to a child that shares both of their genes (Andrews, 1984).

In Vitro Fertilization (IVF). With in vitro fertilization, a doctor performs a laparoscopy to remove an egg (or eggs) from the woman's ovary. The egg is then placed in a petri dish filled with a medium conducive to growth. Next, some of the male partner's sperm are added. After the egg is fertilized, the doctor inserts it, by means of a tube that passes through the woman's vagina, into the uterus. Once in the uterus, the embryo can implant itself and begin to grow like any other embryo.

For couples who select in vitro fertilization as a method of pursuing their quest for a child, a number of different questions arise. First, the couple must be prepared to accept the relatively low success rate of 13 percent or less that most clinics offer (Soules, 1985); they must be prepared to cover the costs of the in vitro program that are not reimbursable by insurance (Andrews, 1984); they must tolerate the medication prescribed for the woman; they must be able to travel to the in vitro clinic they have selected and to bear the expenses associated with absence from work, travel, and hotel stays; and they must confront the immense anxiety they will face each month as they wait to see whether the fertilization has been successful. Ironically, the couple must also be prepared for the possibility of multiple births, with both the risks and potential joys of having more than one baby at a time. Finally, they will need to accept the emotional stress that may ensue during the pregnancy, if a pregnancy is achieved (Shapiro, 1986). The couple must ultimately decide how open to be about the method by which the woman has become pregnant; and, if a healthy baby is born, they will need to discuss whether or how and when to tell their child of his or her special way of being conceived. The couple may ultimately explore whether to have a subsequent in vitro fertilization in their efforts to enlarge their family further, and at this time they are likely, once again, to be thrown back into some of the emotional issues confronted at the time of their initial in vitro experience.

Gamete Intrafallopian Transfer (GIFT). In the gamete intrafallopian transfer procedure, ripe egg cells are retrieved from the follicles in the ovary and are immediately mixed with about 100,000 sperm from the male partner and reinserted by means of a catheter into each of the woman's Fallopian tubes. As opposed to IVF, fertilization and cell division occur in the woman's body, without need for laboratory culturing. GIFT mimics the way a normally fertilized egg would begin its journey to the uterus for implantation. Eligible patients must have at least one normal patent Fallopian tube.

Many couples are intrigued by the GIFT procedure because of the natural environment in which conception occurs. However, because of the involvement of the woman's Fallopian tubes, there still remains the risk of an ectopic pregnancy. Statistics of success since GIFT was developed in 1984 vary by clinic and by the infertility problems of the patients being treated. Success rates of 38.6 percent (Guastella and others, 1986), 27 percent (Malloy and others, 1987), and 40 percent (Matson and others, 1987) have been achieved.

The emotional response to the GIFT procedure is likely to be similar to that of patients undergoing in vitro fertilization, given the parallels in the procedures. The experience of hormone therapy for the female, careful monitoring by laboratory tests, ultrasound scans, and pelvic exams, and the expectation that the male partner will produce a semen sample a few hours before the procedure—all contribute to the stress of the couple.

Adoption. Couples who are unable to give birth to children or who have unexplained infertility are faced with important decisions to make about enlarging their families. Many such couples decide to adopt a child, even though they are aware that an agency adoption requires a home study of the couple and that couples hoping to adopt a healthy white infant are likely to have a long wait. A couple wishing to hasten the process may explore independent adoption or may consider adopting a child from another country, a child with special needs, an older child, or a sibling group. Minority or biracial couples applying through an agency also will need to undergo a home study, although the waiting period they face will not be as lengthy, given the greater number of minority children available for adoption. The evaluation process is difficult for many couples, who recognize that birth parents never need to be under agency scrutiny or to confront other problems associated with agency adoption (Ginsburg, 1984).

Surrogate Mothers. A surrogate mother is a woman who is inseminated with the sperm of a man whose own partner is not able to conceive or carry a pregnancy to term. After the surrogate mother gives birth, the child is adopted by the couple.

The prospect of using a surrogate mother is a complicated option for most couples. The publicity surrounding the Baby M case emphasized the considerable risks involved. Couples need to be aware of the laws in their state, which might prohibit the use of a surrogate mother. In addition, the couple must decide whether they will recruit a surrogate themselves or use one of the increasing number of agencies that match prospective surrogates with infertile couples. The couple using a surrogate will be faced with many decisions, many of which are outlined in Chapter Eight. Questions of involvement and autonomy are present from the time the surrogate is identified until she surrenders the child. In addition to normal concerns about the pregnancy itself, the infertile couple will be preoccupied with the fear that the surrogate might change her mind during the pregnancy or after delivery and decide to keep the baby. However, for some infertile couples, the joys of a child that is genetically related to the male outweigh the risks associated with the decision to use a surrogate mother.

Childfree Living. Some couples, confronted with the rather narrow options by which they can enlarge their families, make the conscious choice to live their lives without children, perhaps deciding to channel their energies into work, pleasure, or substitute nurturing experiences such as volunteer work, creative endeavors, or philanthropic efforts. In spite of the conscious decision not to add children to their family, the childfree couple may sometimes regret that they do not have children. Mazor (1984) reports that concerns of generational identity are common. Many individuals worry about forever remaining the child of their parents, never fully achieving adult status. Some talk about feeling "old," about being confronted prematurely with a sense of their own mortality, about being the last of their genetic line. Leitko and Greil (1985) suggest that childlessness disappears as a source of emotional distress during midlife and does not appear again as a distinct deprivation until the late elderly years, and then as a resource deficit rather than as part of an identity crisis.

Summary

Infertility is truly a bio-psycho-social condition. As such, it presents several challenges to the professional working with infertile people. First is the challenge of inquiring about and acknowledging the intrusiveness of infertility into many areas of the individual's life. The complex interactions among medical disruptions, psychological pain, and social relationships can be difficult to sort out and work through. Second is the challenge of working with other professionals concerned with the well-being of the infertile person; teamwork among professionals concerned with the individual's emotional, medical, and spiritual health is crucial in this area. Third is the challenge of conceptualizing infertility as something that affects the *couple*, even though only one partner may be diagnosed as infertile. As individuals involve, blame, rage at, protect, withdraw from, and support their partners, their relationship alternately deepens and is strained by their efforts to come to terms with the impact of their infertility. The professional who recognizes this delicate balance is in the best position to help both partners articulate their needs and extend support to one another.

2

Confronting Infertility
as a Crisis

As pointed out in the development and life-span literature, a crisis is a turning point that offers the opportunity for either regression or growth. Foreseeable crises in the family life span are organized traditionally around events that initially focus on the couple's relationship and subsequently on child-parent interactions (Rhodes, 1977). Most couples preparing for a pregnancy are unprepared to experience problems in conceiving or in carrying a pregnancy to term. Since infertility is usually an unanticipated crisis, most couples have not developed coping mechanisms to respond to the narcissistic hurt that accompanies the fruitless effort to conceive or bear a child. Infertility therefore represents a crisis situation—a problem perceived as a threat, a loss, or a challenge (Rapaport, 1962).

Before the crisis, most couples are involved in a period of planning for children. They may have explored their financial and personal readiness to begin a family, their educational and career needs, their ability as a couple to share their lives with a child, and the role that children would play in their lives. The planning undoubtedly assumed new aspects as the couple's relationship matured and the partners shared new experiences. Some couples may have observed siblings and friends begin to raise families and confront the changes that occur with pregnancy and parenthood. Parents and in-laws may have dropped hints or spoken openly about their wish to become grandparents. And, most important, the couple may have begun to share their fantasies about how it will feel to be parents and what their unborn child will be like. Will it have its father's curly hair? Its mother's dimples? The musical talent of both parents-to-be? Will it do well in school and ultimately in college?

The most striking aspect of this conscious and subconscious planning is the assumption that the couple will, of course, be able to conceive a baby and that the woman will have an uncomplicated pregnancy and deliver a healthy infant. The couple are aware that problems can occur, but they probably have never considered what they would do if faced with infertility. When they suddenly encounter the unexpected dimension of infertility in their efforts to build a family, their planning, optimism, and anticipation come to a crashing halt.

Although some individuals and couples may experience a crisis at the time infertility is diagnosed, others cope well with the infertility workup and diagnosis, only to fall apart emotionally at a later stage in the infertility experience. Since many diagnosed conditions are treatable, infertile people often cope initially by clinging to the hope that a specific treatment will be successful. Depending on the infertile person's emotional resilience, the importance attached to having a child, and the other life satisfactions available, an individual may cope quite adequately with the ups and downs of infertility treatment. However, for many individuals and couples, hope begins to wear thin when month after month passes without a healthy pregnancy.

> It's been six years since we began trying. Jack has had an operation to correct a varicocele, and I have had five operations to correct problems contributing to my infertility. Our last doctor told us that in vitro fertilization would really offer us the only hope, since my tubes are so badly scarred. Even though Jack and I had spent lots of money already on our infertility, we thought we could scrimp and maybe borrow to meet the costs of IVF not covered by our insurance. We applied to several IVF programs a few months ago, and each of them has rejected us because of our age. They were our last

hope! Now we're left with nothing—all those years of struggle and now it's worse than ever. We're emotionally battered, surgically probed, and financially drained. I'm constantly on the verge of tears —or hysterical. We just can't go on like this.

Sometimes one partner may feel unable to cope, whereas the mate's functioning appears relatively unimpaired. Even when only one partner claims to be in crisis, the helping professional should view the crisis as affecting the couple's relationship, since the functioning partner will undoubtedly feel powerless to help his or her mate. Whether the crisis is specifically precipitated by infertility, or whether it occurs because the couple are emotionally drained by their infertility and unable to weather other life tensions, the indicators of crisis are the same: an inability to cope; feelings of being confused and out of control; and—in some cases—a readiness to reach out for help, perhaps to family and friends but very likely to medical professionals. The quality of support that a couple seek and receive at this time of crisis has a significant impact on their capacity to surmount the crisis and develop effective means of coping with the struggle that infertility will present in the months ahead.

The Onset of Crisis

At the time of crisis, the person actively seeks a satisfactory method of coping with the shock. Those facing infertility often struggle to reach out to others, although they often are reluctant to seek medical assistance for fear that the diagnosis will somehow confirm infertility. For some couples, the finality of a diagnosis can precipitate a crisis. One man relates this experience:

We're still in a state of shock. When the doctor finished our tests and invited us to meet with him to discuss the results, we expected to learn what we could do to be more successful in conceiving. Instead, his news devastated us. I learned that I am sterile and nothing can be done to improve my infertility. Frankly, I didn't hear a thing he said after that. I can remember struggling not to scream or cry or put my fist through a wall. After we got home I couldn't even talk to Betsy, and I could tell she didn't know what to say to me. Even now, a week after the diagnosis, our conversation goes in circles. We cry, we lose our tempers, but we can't make any sense out of this awful news and what we're going to do with our lives now.

If a physician is consulted and a diagnosis determined, the couple face choices ranging from medical intervention to adoption or childfree living, depending on the finality of the diagnosis. When no diagnosis emerges from the preliminary medical workup, couples encounter a unique emotional challenge. They may embark on a series of visits to infertility specialists, or they may enter what is often a lengthy period of chronic mourning.

If the crisis involves pregnancy loss, rather than the inability to conceive, the couple will be highly dependent on their physician and hospital personnel in the initial stages of crisis resolution. Later stages, which involve mourning their loss and accepting support from family and friends, are both physically and emotionally draining. The exhaustion of resolving a pregnancy loss is in part attributable to society's unwillingness to view a miscarriage, ectopic pregnancy, missed abortion, or stillbirth as an event that deserves all the compassion and concern attendant on the death of a loved one. The awkwardness of family and friends, coupled with encouragement to "put it behind you and try again soon," can prevent the crisis from becoming a growth experience and, instead, can leave the couple feeling powerless and bereft in the face of their unacknowledged loss.

Confusion and Disorganization

During the initial stage of a crisis, the helping professional will want to work actively with the individual or couple. Since the infertile individual probably has had little previous experience in this area, the professional can encourage discussion about the unexpectedness of the loss. Most likely, the individual will manifest intense feelings and disorganized thoughts—a general sense of being out of control. The helping professional, while encouraging the individual to verbalize feelings, can offer realistic reassurance that he or she is not going crazy but, rather, is struggling to make sense of a loss for which no one can be prepared. Labeling the experience as a loss may enable the individual to redefine the experience in a framework that makes sense; for, after all, people who have endured a loss are rarely expected to cope in a totally functional way.

Once the infertile person appreciates that disorganization is an expected reaction to the loss recently experienced, the helping professional can give the person credit for seeking help at such a difficult time. Even in this period of upset, the individual's capacity to reach out for help indicates that he or she is beginning to try to cope. The professional will want to reassure the infertile person that resources for coping with the current crisis are available, even though the feelings associated with the loss may not disappear altogether. Most such crises will be resolved within six to eight weeks. During the first two or three weeks, however, it may be more productive for the professional to see the individual for short periods (about half an hour each) two or three times a week, rather than adhering to the more traditional counseling framework of seeing clients for an hour each week. The reason for a shorter and more frequent time frame is twofold: first, the individual may need to feel that the helping professional is easily accessible, and frequently scheduled appointments convey this reassuringly; second, lengthy discussions are rarely productive because of the individual's emotional disorganization and, in many cases, actually contribute to the person's sense of confusion.

In the brief meetings, the professional should ask the individual to share the most immediate feelings that are causing discomfort; at the same time, the professional should encourage the individual to undertake certain specific tasks (perhaps in partnership with the professional) in the next few days. Tasks should be oriented toward gaining control and mastery over the recent events. For example, an infertile woman may be asked to read about the specific issue of infertility that she is grappling with, undertake relaxation exercises to reduce feelings of stress, find specific ways to nurture and pamper herself, share feelings with an understanding confidante, or make lists of questions that she would like to ask other professionals who are familiar with the particular infertility issue that precipitated the crisis.

> Nancy, even though you're feeling completely over-whelmed, you've taken an important step by reach-ing out for help at this difficult time. I believe we can work together to find some new ways of help-ing you cope—both with your painful emotions and with the concrete situation of your recent diagnosis. One of the most important places for us to begin is with your physical health, because the kind of stress you are experiencing can be so dis-tracting that you forget to take good care of your-self. So we'll begin by having you concentrate in the next few days on healthy nutrition, pampering yourself, and daily exercise. Let's talk together now about what activities you'll structure into each day that will ensure attention to each of these areas. When you see me in a few days, we'll discuss whether these activities have been helpful, and then we'll also spend some time on how you can reach out to others for comfort.

The helping professional can expect a range of responses from the infertile person during this first stage of coping with the crisis. There is likely to be an upsurge of energy, which the individual can channel into productive means of gaining mastery over the crisis. As mentioned, the infertile person probably will feel confused and generally unprepared to deal with the recent events. For that reason, the professional's offer to help is likely to be especially welcome. If the assistance can include some reading material for the infertile person to review and discuss, the level of confusion will begin to diminish. During these early stages of crisis, the infertile person is also likely to feel very iso-lated with the problem that has precipitated the crisis. The professional's acceptance of the individual as someone who has sustained a loss and who deserves credit for reaching out for help at a difficult time will go a long way toward establishing initial trust while reassuring the individual that he does not need to cope with this crisis alone.

In the beginning stages of crisis, the infertile person also needs to exercise denial as he seeks to absorb the enormity of what the loss represents. The helping professional must be patient during this period, respecting the person's pace and being prepared to repeat information whenever necessary.

Reassessment

In the next stage of the crisis, the individual begins to come to terms with the loss, and conflicts with friends and other family members may become a focus of discussions with the helping professional. The disorganization engendered by the crisis becomes more apparent; and the infertile person may work through a period of reassessment, attempting to reorder his life in response to the crisis. The individual's reluctance to assume familiar roles may become a source of strain in relationships with family, friends, and colleagues, who fail to understand the individual's need to find new ways of coping. Nonetheless, some infertile individuals develop new perspectives on life during this reassessment period. Tom relates:

> You know, I used to be such a good teacher. I loved the kids in my class, and they felt a special relationship with me too—probably because lots of them are from homes without a father and they appreciated my attention. But now I feel myself pulling back from them as if I can't afford to extend myself emotionally anymore. I mean, after all, if I can't father a child of my own, what's the point in taking care of other people's kids?

This period of reassessment can be difficult for some people, particularly those who are careful planners and who pride themselves on being in control. The helping professional may want to reassure the individual that, by adopting new coping mechanisms, he can regain some measure of control. A discussion of the individual's past and present efforts to cope is especially appropriate at this time, because it allows the helping professional to suggest new methods of handling prevailing tensions. Most people at this stage of crisis are highly receptive to suggestions and are responsive to considering new ways to manage the chaos that has become uncomfortable and frightening. It is natural at this time to reach out to others for help and support, especially if the individual is besieged with feelings of inadequacy, uncertainty, and vulnerability.

The main problem that infertile individuals confront at this time—especially when one or both of the partners are undergoing medical tests or treatments—is how to protect their need for privacy in a highly personal and sensitive area and how to communicate their need for support. One of the most satisfactory coping mechanisms at this stage is intellectual mastery, gained by exhaustive research into infertility, particularly those aspects that are relevant to the couple's situation. Whether the couple choose to reach out to others for emotional support or to become familiar with the medical aspects of their infertility (and many couples do both), the need for support is pronounced during this time of reassessment.

Recovery

In the recovery stage, the person's new coping mechanisms, often derived in a trial-and-error fashion, have been evaluated for their effectiveness, and some have been incorporated into the individual's efforts to handle the crisis. The individual, recognizing the need for support from people who may not previously have been needed in this way, begins to discover new dimensions in old relationships and to develop new relationships. New roles may be gaining acceptance in relationships at home and at work, or there may be a continuing need to renegotiate these roles once the infertile person's needs are more clearly understood. The helping professional may now want to encourage the couple or the individual to learn and practice some assertive behavior.

Assertive behavior, discussed more thoroughly in Chapter Five, has several important dimensions that enable the individual to move from the stage of disorganization to a stage of reorganization, which can represent a higher level of functioning. First, assertive behavior enables individuals to identify their own needs. During a crisis, many infertile people are aware of pain and discomfort, but they are less clear about what they need in order to function more comfortably. With the assistance of the helping professional, the infertile person can acquire a clearer understanding of potential goals for meeting these newly identified needs. Tasks between the infertile person and professional then can be directed toward specific needs that the individual has expressed. Second, assertive behavior allows the individual to communicate clearly with others. During the period of disorganization, clarity of communication may have suffered just when the person most needed to have others understand the toll that the crisis had taken. Rebuilding lines of communication, with one's needs clearly in mind, is an important step for the infertile person to take. Third, assertive behavior enables individuals to respond straightforwardly to insensitive behavior, rather than seething with resentment, withdrawing, or exploding with anger.

Janice, you've spent a fair amount of time talking about your feelings of sadness and those circumstances in your life that are especially painful. I'm glad you are emotionally able to be in touch with your sadness, because it signifies that you are working on feelings associated with the losses involved in your infertility. But, at the same time, it is also important to begin to talk about how to bring more comfort into your life. Let's begin by discussing some of the interactions you've mentioned with Jeff. If I remember correctly, you've told me that you try to hide your tears from him because you don't want him to know how upset you're feeling these days. Yet, at the same time, you say you are angry at Jeff for not understanding your pain and for carrying on life as usual when you're so distressed. At this point, we must work to identify what you need in your relationship with Jeff and how you can communicate this to him in an effective way. I would prefer to have Jeff attend the sessions in which we discuss some of these new communication skills, since I suspect he may have some needs of his own that relate to your infertility experiences as a couple.

Reaching out to others and being clear about one's needs are major tasks to be encouraged as the infertile person moves from recovery to reorganization.

Reorganization

As the person in crisis experiences a diminution of anxiety and an increased understanding of the issues contributing to the crisis, she becomes able to respond to the professional's encouragement to take an active role in resolving the crisis. At this point, the person can use resources other than the professional to aid her in dealing constructively with the problem at hand. In a broader context, the reaching out to others represents a willingness to seek and utilize new coping mechanisms. Reorganization represents a time of consolidation as the infertile person discards dysfunctional coping efforts in favor of those that are more appropriate to the current situation. Also at this time, the individual will find herself increasingly able to view the earlier crisis in some sort of perspective. The pain of the ordeal will still be apparent, but the focus of life is no longer exclusively on the crisis.

People in crisis are often described as having "tunnel vision." In other words, they are so preoccupied with their problem that they lose perspective on the wide range of options for seeking and utilizing help. The professional can help the individual recognize the limitations of the tunnel vision perspective and consider new ways of developing and using resources. Once the tunnel vision expands, the infertile person is more able to look to the future and consider steps that she might take to move ahead with life plans. As the crisis is resolved, the infertile person ideally should develop new behaviors that allow flexible use of persons and resources, not only in crisis but also in ordinary situations. The professional's goal in crisis intervention is to help the infertile person through the crisis itself and to encourage her to emerge from that difficult period with more coping skills than were present at the precrisis level. Jane relates:

> I'm feeling much more in control than I did when I began coming for counseling two months ago. Then I felt as if all hope was gone, as if there was nowhere to go with our infertility. Now I still feel as if we have a long way to go in our struggle, but counseling has helped me regain some emotional stamina. Even though I'm still immensely sad about our infertility, I'm ready now to investigate adoption and to see whether that is something that Sam and I would want to consider as a way of bringing a child into our family. I know even that decision won't be easy, but at least now I feel more ready to begin the process and to think about it in a meaningful way.

Not all individuals will emerge at a higher level of reorganization after the crisis has been resolved. Several factors are associated with a person's capacity to be resilient when facing a crisis: (1) behavioral adaptability and flexibility within the family; (2) affection among family members; (3) good marital adjustment between husband and wife; (4) nonmarginal economic status; (5) the person's previous experience (direct or vicarious) with the type of crisis encountered; (6) objective knowledge of facets of a specific crisis before it occurs—which presupposes the individual's capacity to discuss feelings evoked by the crisis; and (7) established patterns of interaction with the extended family, neighbors, and friends.

A study of this list permits several conclusions. An individual can benefit from, and may even require, the involvement of others to work through the crisis. These people may be fam-

ily members, helping professionals, friends, or persons in a support group. The professional can help the infertile person consider which resources would be of greatest value and may offer
to be an advocate in obtaining relevant infertility literature, appropriate medical services, or prompt counseling for the individual. In addition to using the above factors to assess the resilience of the infertile person, the professional may also use the
list to consider other stressors that may hinder effective work
on infertility crisis resolution.

Summary

When intervening at a time of crisis, the helping professional has certain functions that are particularly noteworthy.
First, the professional assumes an active stance, helping the infertile person identify the actual precipitant of the crisis and
understand the meaning of that precipitant in his current life
circumstances.

Second, the professional helps the individual explore why
the previous efforts at problem solving proved unsatisfactory.
Once the individual is able to acknowledge a readiness for new
ways of coping, the professional must respond with concrete
suggestions that are at a level the individual is ready to try. A
task-centered approach, such as that pioneered by Reid and Epstein (1972), is particularly appropriate to helping clients in crisis. In addition, the professional must be prepared to be in contact with the individual on a fairly frequent basis during the
period of disorganization immediately following the crisis, because the individual will need constant input and reassurance
regarding his ability to work on the issues at hand.

Third, the professional must be careful to balance the infertile person's need to express or discharge feelings with some
efforts toward accomplishing tasks aimed at resolving the crisis.
The professional hopes that, in resolving the current crisis precipitated by infertility, the individual will have consolidated some
of the newly learned coping skills. The use of new skills—master-
ing relevant knowledge, recognizing one's needs, being assertive
in communication, and seeking emotional and medical support—
will be important in the ongoing quest for building a family.

3

Confronting Infertility
over Time

In the literature about mourning, a distinction is made between acute and chronic grief (Jackson, 1974). In observing the reactions of parents to the birth of a handicapped newborn, helping professionals noticed that the parents' initial grief was acute but that, in many situations, it was followed by a prolonged period of chronic grief. Though less intense, the chronic grief was a reflection of the parents' efforts to cope on a long-term basis.

Acute grief, the immediate response to a loss, is initially very intense as the person experiences the emotions associated with coming to terms with the loss. Various frameworks for acute grief have been postulated. Most notably, Elisabeth Kübler-Ross (1969) has identified the predictable stages of mourning as denial, anger, bargaining, grief, and acceptance. A person who is mourning will experience some or all of these stages, although some persons may not experience them sequentially and some may find particular stages more meaningful than others, depending on the individual's coping style and the particular loss endured. The initial intensity of acute grief eventually gives way to more measured emotions as the immediate crisis passes and the grieving person begins to establish some coping mechanisms. The finality of most losses enables the survivor to resolve the losses by learning that life can go on without the lost object and by finding ways to fill the void caused by the loss.

Chronic grief differs from acute grief in that the survivor is unable to fill the void. For the parents of a handicapped child, the initial mourning for the loss of the healthy child in the parents' fantasies gives way to the realities of living with the child, coping with the handicap, and being repeatedly reminded of what that child can never achieve. These feelings, which are most poignant as developmental milestones are passed without being achieved, last throughout the child's life and serve as a constant reminder to parents that their loss is ever present.

In the course of the initial infertility workup, a couple most likely will experience the stages associated with acute grief, detailed in Chapter Four. If a diagnosis is lacking or is not definitive, however, the couple may be plunged into years of exploratory efforts and treatments. Professionals often assume, incorrectly, that infertile people who come to terms with their acute grief have done their most important emotional work. Professionals and infertile couples alike must recognize and validate the chronic grief that will emerge as infertility stretches over time.

> We can't even get on with our lives. I still hope each month that Brenda won't get her period. I know her cycle better than she does, it seems. But I can always tell when her period has begun because even now, after all these years, her eyes are red and puffy from crying. It seems that we can't go on like this. Isn't there more to life than living from one menstrual period to the next?

Infertile couples live in a state of psychological limbo. On the one hand, they wish for a definitive end to their quest for a birth child; on the other, they hope beyond hope that the next test or treatment will be the successful one. Visits to physicians represent both the hope for fertility and the constant reminder of infertility.

Couples who are most likely to experience chronic grief are those with unexplained infertility; women with endometriosis, who must endure constant physical pain if they hope to preserve any remnants of fertility; men with low sperm counts who hope that they can father a birth child; and those immersed in lengthy treatments that require repeated efforts, such as artificial insemination, gamete intrafallopian transfer (GIFT), and in vitro fertilization. These infertile people probably have already experienced the stages of acute grief, but they are not able to achieve the final stage of acceptance; their infertility represents a partial loss more than a final one. Some couples actually admit that it would be far easier if a doctor could tell them that they will never give birth to a child, because this news would allow them to get on with their lives and the decisions that have been on hold for so long. Others doggedly pursue treatments, feeling that they cannot move beyond their infertility until they have "done everything possible."

Endometriosis as a Chronic Condition

Endometriosis is a painful disease in which tissue from the uterine lining is present in such abnormal locations as the tubes, ovaries, and peritoneal cavity. In these locations, the endometrial tissue develops into nodules, tumors, lesions, implants, or growths. Because the endometrial growths usually respond to the hormones of the menstrual cycle, they accumulate tissue, break down, and bleed each month. Endometrial tissue is outside the uterus, however, and has no way of leaving the body; the result is internal bleeding, degeneration of the blood and tissue shed from the growths, inflammation of the surrounding areas, and formation of scar tissue. Other complications, depending on the location of the growths, include rupture of growths (which can spread the endometriosis to new areas), the formation of adhesions, intestinal bleeding or obstruction (if the growths are in the intestines), interference with bladder function (if the growths are on or in the bladder), and the pain associated with these complications.

Endometriosis tends to worsen over the years, often causing infertility. Women with endometriosis, therefore, are placed at double jeopardy: they not only must cope with the sorrow of their infertility, but they also must endure very real physical pain and the frustration that there is yet no definitive cure, other than hysterectomy and removal of the ovaries. Some physicians prescribe hormonal treatment, including estrogen and progesterone, progesterone alone, or a testosterone derivative (Danazol, Cyclomen). Although hormones can sometimes force the endometriosis into remission for several months, the side effects can present problems. Ironically, physicians often advise a woman with endometriosis to get pregnant, because pregnancy and breastfeeding stop ovulation and subsequently prevent the monthly bleeding and shedding of uterine tissue. Many women with endometriosis are infertile, however, and are unable to get pregnant; life for these women becomes a succession of efforts to hold the pain of the disease at bay.

The chronic condition of endometriosis adds a special burden to coping with infertility. The woman who feels that her body has betrayed her will almost always have feelings of loss of control. The woman with endometriosis also is likely to be handicapped by her physical pain. Such a chronic condition has no resolution; the woman must face her endometriosis and its accompanying pain, learn to cope, and adapt to the havoc that the disease wreaks.

Jeanne Fleming (1984), who writes about infertility as a chronic illness, emphasizes the importance of adaptive coping. The first step is to understand the limitations of an illness such as endometriosis and then to assess the impact of the illness on long-term functioning. For some women, the uncertainty from month to month makes adaptive coping especially difficult; their challenge is to accept the fluctuation in functioning while trying to understand the extent of limitation as thoroughly as possible.

The range of feelings for the woman with painful endometriosis may resemble those associated with mourning: denial, anger, bargaining, grief, and acceptance. In addition to the grief associated with her infertility, the woman is also likely to grieve because she is different from the ideal adult whom she envisioned during her growing years. Instead of this ideal figure, she has become a woman who inconveniences her family by not functioning optimally, a woman who must depend on her family in areas where she would prefer to be more independent, or a woman who believes that her illness is destructively affecting her family's ability to communicate and to work out differences. Yet many women with endometriosis fail to realize that each family has its unique limitations, which were not caused by the woman's condition. It is far more constructive, therefore, to encourage the entire family to adopt a more functional method of coping. The goal then shifts from living up to one's ideal to resolving difficulties collectively as they arise. Successful recognition of difficulties and subsequent efforts at problem solving then can leave the door open for other shared family goals: acknowledging strengths and limitations and ways in which family members can work together to function effectively; having friends, especially those who understand the uncertainties that life can hold; enjoying life as fully as possible; and achieving as much as can be expected. Supportive and nurturing friends are especially important. Such friends can be good listeners, show their concern in helpful ways, and genuinely offer help when it is needed.

Active involvement with health care professionals will allow the woman some intellectual mastery over her illness as she becomes increasingly aware of her options and the consequences of her choices. It is vitally important for anyone with a chronic illness to feel nurtured medically, and the woman with endometriosis should be encouraged to seek health care providers who reduce her stress rather than add to it.

To help the family accommodate to the problems that endometriosis causes on a regular or a sporadic basis, the helping professional can encourage the family to appreciate the normalcy and strengths that it does have. The woman will feel most productive in this situation if she can acknowledge her feelings about the impact of the endometriosis on her and the family but, rather than dwelling on the disadvantages in detail, focus on the strengths that the family members can use as they cope collectively. The woman also can be helped to cope with her feeling that she lacks control over herself and her environment. She can be encouraged to try to understand the source of such feelings as she experiences them, rather than being overwhelmed by them. Such a procedure can allow the woman to solve the problem at hand and focus her energy on her strengths and potential. By regularly labeling the source of such feelings, the woman will begin to feel that she is exerting some control, if not over the unpredictability of life events, at least over her own emotions and her ability to make sense of them.

The Professional's Role

The professional who works with infertile people experiencing chronic grief has several challenges. First is how to make life meaningful during the quest for a baby. Many infertile people deny themselves life's pleasures "until we have a baby" and therefore face the double predicament of suffering with their infertility and having no daily enjoyments to sustain them during this difficult time. At some level, these people believe that perhaps they do not deserve to have children and, therefore, are also undeserving of the other joys that life could hold. Aware of the battered self-esteem that infertility can inflict on otherwise confident people, the helping professional needs to determine how the infertility has affected the individual's self-esteem and how his life has changed since infertility was diagnosed. Only then can the professional begin to appreciate what was normal for the infertile person and, subsequently, help the person look to past pleasures as models of what can still be possible. The helping professional can encourage the infertile person to move beyond the identity of victim to that of survivor.

Sometimes one partner is caught up in the grieving process while the other is moving ahead with life despite the infertility that they share. In these circumstances, the person who has already adopted the survivor role can help the other person regain a healthier perspective. The grieving partner, on the other hand, may feel a tremendous amount of anger toward the mate who is coping. This anger stems from the grieving person's belief that the partner does not want a baby as much and does not understand the depth of the mate's grief. Before the coping partner can help the grieving mate, the professional must help them both communicate about their different perceptions of the world and the effect of infertility on their lives, both separately and as a couple. Then the couple can begin to work together to restore some of the happier fragments of their times together before infertility permeated their lives.

A second challenge is to explore what the quest for a

baby represents for the couple. It surely embodies their wish to enlarge their family, but it also may provide clues about why the couple persist in their efforts to achieve a pregnancy, rather than considering other options. Discovering what the baby means to the couple can be complicated, and is likely to lead ultimately to some decision making, discussed in more detail in Chapter Eight. Prior to a decision, however, the couple must communicate openly about what they hope a baby will bring to their lives. The helping professional can expect a range of responses: the desire for a pregnancy, the wish to experience parenthood, the need to be seen by the world (and especially by one's own parents) as an adult, the wish to relive one's childhood, the need to provide a family experience better than one's own as a child, the desire to be loved by a little person, the need for a child to carry on one's genetic lineage, the need for a child as the confirmation of one's fertility, the opportunity to consolidate the relationship with one's mate, and, perhaps, the need to fill a void that exists in the couple's relationship. It may be especially important to help the partners differentiate between realistic and unrealistic expectations that they attach to having a baby. If achieving autonomy from one's parents, for example, is a strong motivation, the professional can help the couple explore other ways to accomplish this goal. Such exploration also provides the professional with an opportunity to discover how the couple's ideas about parenting were influenced by their parents.

A third challenge is to help the couple determine when they are ready to stop infertility treatment and explore other options. This is likely to be a time of great tension in the relationship, particularly if both partners do not agree that "enough is enough." Often, the infertile partner needs to pursue doggedly every opportunity to achieve a pregnancy, fueled by guilt for being the one responsible for the couple's inability to have a baby. In other cases, one partner will push to end treatment out of concern for what the treatment is doing to the mate, either emotionally or physically. One man recounts:

> Rachel has had six surgical procedures for her infertility over the past four years. Each time is

harder for both of us, because we're so steeled for
the disappointment that we've come to expect. I
admit I'm the one who has been reluctant to pursue adoption all these years. But when our doctor
proposed yet one more surgery and couldn't even
be encouraging about our chances of conceiving
afterwards, something snapped. I realized that I
couldn't keep watching Rachel undergo surgery
only to have our hopes shattered once more. When
I came straight out and told her I was ready to pursue adoption instead, her eyes just lit up, and I
knew we could face this new challenge together!

The intrusion of infertility on the couple's sexual intimacy, financial resources, careers, education, family relationships, friendships, and self-esteem should ultimately be discussed, because each partner may be unaware of the other's
experiences in many of these areas. There are several reasons
why these matters are difficult to discuss. First, infertility hurts,
and living with it is painful even without an open discussion
about the specific sources of the pain. Second, ending treatment
means "giving up" for some couples; and, because of the time
and resources already invested in trying to achieve a pregnancy,
giving up may make them feel like losers. Third, exploring what
a baby represents is likely to serve as a poignant reminder of
something that the couple desperately want but cannot have.
Finally, any discussion of ending treatment implies that the couple will have to confront the profound grief that they have been
able to avoid while they still had hope that they could have a
birth child.

The emotional work that the couple face at this juncture
is reminiscent of the stage of acceptance that other couples
reach during the process of acute grief. The couple struggling
with chronic grief may experience the stages of mourning for
many years; yet there is no closure, no acceptance of the finality that their birth child will forever be a dream and never a
reality. They are reluctant to accept this finality and move on
with their lives, especially if they have been told by medical

professionals that they deserve to cling to hope. When they finally let go of this elusive hope, some couples choose to use
birth control to emphasize the finality of their decision and to
forge ahead with other ways of building their lives together.
Ironic as the use of birth control will seem to them, many couples find that it is a welcome change from temperature charts,
ovulation kits, medications, and all the other interventions that
have consumed their energies over the years. Acceptance does
not necessarily mean giving up hope for a child, however; many
couples will now choose to explore adoption. Such couples recognize that their dream of becoming birth parents will not come
true, but they are ready to look ahead to life's opportunities,
despite the detour that infertility forced them to take on their
path to enlarging their family.

   Whether a chronic condition has strong physiological
components, as with endometriosis, or predominantly psychological dimensions, as with unexplained infertility, the need for
long-term coping mechanisms is essential. The professional's
role is to help the couple respond constructively to the feelings
of helplessness that besiege them and to encourage them to
make active decisions rather than remain in the psychological
limbo that causes such emotional pain.

   The frequency of contacts with the individual or couple
may depend on where they are in their emotional work. If they
need support in managing periodic painful episodes, short-term,
task-centered counseling approaches may be sufficient. If terminating infertility treatment and moving ahead is the decision, a
more prolonged period will be necessary to work on the final
stages of the mourning process and to explore the other options.

   The helping professional, both as an integral extension of
the couple's support network and as a therapist prepared to encourage movement in painful emotional areas, can add a crucial
psychosocial dimension to the years of medical treatment endured by the couple for whom infertility is a chronic condition.

4

Mourning the Many Losses of Infertility

Unsuccessful treatment for infertility represents a profound tragedy for the couple who invested hope, time, and money and made lifestyle adjustments so that they might one day give birth to a baby. At some point, however, the couple and their physicians must acknowledge that further treatment is unlikely to be successful and that the couple should end their medical quest for fertility. Some couples will move ahead toward adoption as a way of building their family, while others will choose to remain childfree and channel their nurturing capacities into other activities.

Couples for whom treatment is unsuccessful must come to terms with the many losses that their infertility represents. These losses will need to be mourned, and the readiness to undertake this difficult emotional work differs with each individual. The professional familiar with techniques of grief counseling (Melges and DeMaso, 1980; Worden, 1982; Simos, 1979) will find many opportunities to apply this knowledge when working with infertile individuals and couples.

Several authors (Menning, 1977; Rosenfeld and Mitchell, 1979; Shapiro, 1982) utilize the framework developed by Elisabeth Kübler-Ross (1969) to explain the mourning process that infertile individuals work through. In this framework, a person grappling with a loss first experiences the stage of denial, in which the full impact of the loss is not absorbed. During the next stage, the individual feels and expresses the anger associated with the loss. A stage of bargaining often follows; here the individual makes real or symbolic offers of good behavior, as if in an effort to delay a perceived punishment for unatoned bad deeds. When the period of bargaining passes, the individual enters a period of active grief, manifested by tears, sadness, and preoccupation with the lost object. Ultimately, most individuals emerge from the stage of active mourning and progress to a stage of acceptance, in which they are able to reorder their lives around the loss they have sustained without being preoccupied with the loss. These stages are not always experienced chronologically, nor do all individuals experience them with the same intensity. Yet an awareness of a framework in which the mourning process occurs can enable one to understand the therapeutic value of such otherwise disruptive responses to infertility as denial, anger, bargaining, and grief.

The Stages of Mourning

Denial. The threat of infertility is perceived on many levels; it is a threat to life dreams, to self-esteem, and to one's image as a sexual being. In efforts to cushion themselves against the enormity of such threats, many individuals use denial as the first method of coping with the initial impact of infertility. In fact, prior to seeking medical help and the dreaded diagnosis, many couples have alternated between denial and anticipatory mourning as they face month after month of thwarted attempts to conceive or to bear a child. For some couples, denial by one or both partners can prolong the quest for medical help, as they go from doctor to doctor hoping for a more favorable prognosis.

> As I look back, I realize that neither of us was willing to apply the term *infertile* to us, even though several doctors had. We coped by changing doctors, by trying harder to time intercourse with ovulation, and by keeping our desperation to ourselves.

The uncertainty of many diagnoses, the varied suggestions for ways to enhance the likelihood of conception, and the couple's own defense of denial often combine to prevent the couple from moving forward in the mourning process.

Anger. Anger is the second stage in Kübler-Ross's framework of mourning. For infertile people, the anger is most frequently a response to the helplessness and powerlessness they feel as they lose control over their life choices. For some, the anger is linked to instances in the past that they associate with their infertility, such as physicians who prescribed the intrauterine device or who did not diagnose pelvic inflammatory disease. Others feel angry that their private sexual lives and reproductive parts must now be accessible to physicians who probe relentlessly in order to arrive at a diagnosis. In an effort to regain control, many people become preoccupied with timing their sexual activity to coincide with the woman's fertile periods and with anxiously waiting to see whether pregnancy results. The desperation and purposefulness associated with sexual activity often are unrecognized sources of anger for couples who once enjoyed sexual spontaneity. Many couples who avoid intercourse except during the wife's fertile period are so beset by the anger and sadness of the situation that they somehow feel not entitled to sexual pleasure.

> Making love requires such an effort. I just don't feel like it anymore. We have sex on schedule, and I'm relieved when my wife finishes ovulating so we don't have to subject ourselves to one more futile effort at making a baby.

Indirect channeling of anger over infertility can cause tension not only to surface but also to become distorted in areas previously handled adequately. This tension presents special problems for the couple. Some may discharge anger over false issues instead of channeling it into coping with feelings about their shared problem of infertility. For some individuals, the anger is directed inward, against the self, resulting in depression and emotional isolation. The phenomenon of learned helplessness (Seligman, 1975), an individual's belief that no effort can result in a favorable outcome, is a frequent response to infertility. Learned helplessness is a logical outcome for couples who believe that they have lost control over their carefully laid life plans. Feeling cheated of an option they had long taken for granted, the couple struggle for control—only to find that the all-consuming effort to conceive is in itself disruptive. Vacations are postponed, employment or educational opportunities are rejected, and business trips are synchronized with doctors' appointments and ovulation schedules. The resulting depression of one or both partners is likely to have a debilitating impact on the relationship. The situation may also arouse guilt in whichever partner is thought to be responsible for the couple's inability to conceive. A useful defense against the sense of helplessness is information. People who become knowledgeable in their special areas of concern are able to feel like active participants in the process, thereby regaining some measure of intellectual mastery over previously intimidating medical procedures and baffling emotional reactions connected with infertility.

When anger is expressed directly, it can have the cathartic effect of releasing tension and clarifying feelings—clearly a goal for couples trying to work through feelings of rage and bitterness. Many individuals find, however, that in spite of efforts to be purposeful in expressing their anger, they are overwhelmed by the perceived incompetence of medical professionals, the unhelpful advice of well-meaning friends, and the intrusiveness of family. When anger is expressed to these significant others, it often can have the effect of further isolating the couple from potential sources of medical and emotional support.

Bargaining. One way of channeling feelings of anger is through symbolic bargaining. In effect, the infertile individual—unwilling to accept the finality of infertility—proposes new efforts to find successful treatments. Since many new technologies are available to infertile people, a person can spend a significant amount of time researching treatments, contacting medical personnel, and, at some level, believing that a successful treatment can be found if only enough effort is expended. The individual at this stage may make conscientious efforts to improve her physical health through diet and exercise—offering good behavior in the hope of delaying the symbolic punishment of infertility. Ultimately, however, the futility of these efforts gives rise to expressions of grief:

> I feel absolutely crazy! From the time I ovulate until my period comes, I don't take any medicine, I don't have any caffeinated drinks, and I don't even indulge in a glass of wine. Then when I get my period, I just let go—eating junk food, making up for all those lost glasses of wine, and treating myself to an aspirin if I have a headache.

Grief. Feelings of intense grief surface as infertile individuals begin to perceive the crisis of infertility as a loss of profound dimensions. It is first and most poignantly the loss of a dream, the loss of children not to be born. Also important is the loss of the potential role of genetic parent—giving birth to and raising one's own birth children.

> The other day I saw a little boy in the park pitching a baseball with his father. My eyes just filled up with tears. I want so much to have a kid I can throw a ball around with.

Grief is not felt by the infertile couple alone. When would-be grandparents learn of their children's plight, they often bear the narcissistic hurt that accompanies awareness of their child's infertility (Ilse and Leininger, 1985). Parents feel powerless to help and, in their own grief, often retreat from their child at the very time the child needs to be nurtured and reassured of his or her worth as a human being.

Erich Lindemann (1965), in his classic research on grief, cites several responses that are expected in grief reactions. These responses can be identified in the grief of infertile individuals.

One such response is somatic distress. In addition to stress-related discomfort such as tension headaches and upset stomachs, the reproductive system is also vulnerable to the stress of grief as individuals experience bouts of impotence, dysmenorrhea, and amenorrhea. Disruption of sleep and eating patterns is also common.

Another reaction to grief is a preoccupation with the image of the deceased. Infertile individuals may have fantasies about what their child might have looked like or achieved. The fantasies might include elaborate images reflecting family resemblances, special talents, and hoped-for achievements. Characteristic of the cognitive distortion experienced by the grieving person, such images may be triggered by the sight of an infant or a young child.

Another common response in grief reactions is guilt. In an effort to establish the cause of their infertility, many individuals scrutinize their past sexual behaviors and reproductive histories and later castigate themselves because they delayed childbearing, chose the wrong birth control method, contracted a sexually transmitted disease, had a pelvic inflammation, or obtained an abortion. The fertile partner also feels guilty because his or her grief may cause the other partner to bear a double load of guilt. Such guilt is often at the root of serious rifts in the relationship. The infertile partner, either directly or subtly, may encourage the fertile partner to seek a mate with whom he or she can bear children. Although infertility is often present in both partners, if a thorough medical diagnosis has not been reached, one partner may carry a disproportionate burden of guilt for what is actually a shared biological problem.

Acceptance. Acceptance of infertility and all its implications is the last stage in the mourning process. Once the hope for birth children has been relinquished, the individual is able to look ahead to alternatives. The partners may reach this stage at different times. In fact, the entire mourning process may have been unsynchronized, as one partner struggled in one stage while the other mourned at a different level.

It is perhaps most difficult to reach the stage of acceptance when no definite diagnosis of infertility can be established. These couples, the so-called "normal infertiles," constitute 10 percent of all couples unable to conceive (Menning, 1977). As these couples await the outcome of interminable tests in the infertility workup, the mourning process more accurately can be understood as anticipatory mourning. Lebow (1976) identifies two elements in anticipatory mourning that differ from other mourning processes: the element of uncertainty that is present and the increase in feelings of grief with the passage of time. Without a definite diagnosis, the couple are tempted to cling to the slender hope that they might yet conceive. Such uncertainty plays havoc with the mourning process and often leaves individuals grappling with denial, anger, or grief but unable to move ahead toward acceptance of the likelihood that they will never bear a child. As mentioned, some normal infertile couples choose to use birth control as a means of ending their chronic tension and anxiety, and to give themselves an opportunity to work through their grief. The lingering doubts about who is "responsible" for the couple's infertility may put even greater strains on the relationship than in situations where a conclusive diagnosis can be reached.

The stage of acceptance is characterized by a replenished energy level and an increased readiness to view the future with hope instead of despair. Acceptance does not imply that the painful emotions associated with infertility are forever laid to rest. Rather, acceptance suggests that one is no longer preoccupied with the earlier stages of the mourning process and is, instead, ready to move ahead with life decisions and new directions. Menning (1980, p. 318) describes behaviors in the acceptance stage of some infertile people she has counseled:

> There is a return of energy, perhaps even a surge of zest and well-being; a sense of perspective emerges which puts infertility in its proper place in life; a sense of optimism and faith returns; a sense of humor returns, and some of the past absurdities may even become grist for story telling. The concepts of sexuality, self-image, and self-esteem are reworked to become disconnected from childbearing, but nevertheless wholesome and complete. Plans for the future are begun again, building a way around the obstacle of infertility.

Unless both partners have acknowledged and worked through the loss that their infertility represents, they may find that unresolved mourning interferes with the success of other options they choose to pursue. Alternatives for the infertile couple to consider include childfree living, adoption, artificial insemination, in vitro fertilization, GIFT, a surrogate mother, or other nurturing experiences such as foster parenthood or volunteer work with children. Choices are more open once individuals have a clearer sense of the shared hopes for their relationship.

The Professional's Role

The needs of infertile people shift as they progress through the stages of the mourning process. The helping professional can be a source of emotional support, a facilitator, and a provider of concrete information in promoting a healthy resolution of the infertile person's efforts to mourn. Some individuals will appreciate having the professional suggest reading material that helps them feel justified in their grief (Times, 1977; Freese, 1977; Tatelbaum, 1980; Compassionate Friends, 1982). If both partners are involved in counseling, the professional will need to be sensitive to the different paces at which they acknowledge and work through their feelings about the impact of infertility on their lives and on their relationship.

Denial. During the initial denial stage of the mourning process, preoccupation with diagnosis is common. Some couples "shop around" among physicians as they seek a diagnosis that is compatible with their wish to bear children. Others prefer to remain in the care of familiar local physicians long past the point where more specialized medical attention should have been sought. Given the sensitive nature of an infertility workup, it is understandable that a couple would prefer to remain in the care of physicians who have performed initial diagnostic procedures. The physicians also may have an ego investment in continuing diagnosis or treatment beyond the point where they can be helpful.

In addition to the medical advantages of specialized care for infertility, there are psychological advantages as well. In a local community, the woman is usually seen by a gynecologist and the man by a urologist; medical facilities specializing in infertility, however, make a concerted effort to view infertility as a problem of the couple. Amidst open communication by the infertility team, an atmosphere is created in which both partners are helped to understand the outcomes of the tests that each undergoes. In addition, couples seeking help from a facility specializing in infertility do not face the anguishing experience of sharing the waiting room with happily pregnant women, as frequently occurs in the office of a local physician. The infertility workup performed by a team of specialists can often proceed more rapidly than a local effort involving coordination by several physicians who see the male and female on separate occasions over an extended period of time. Given the anxiety associated with waiting for the outcome of diagnostic tests and the wish to place confidence in the results, couples may find that traveling to a specialized facility is well worth the inconvenience.

Anger. When couples are trying to come to terms with anger and outrage at their inability to conceive or bear a child, the professional can help them recognize that anger is a predictable response to feeling that an important aspect of life is beyond their control. The couple need to feel entitled to the angry emotions and to find nondestructive ways of expressing them. To the extent that a partner may turn unexpressed anger inward, depression may emerge as a dysfunctional coping mechanism. Couples need help in understanding that depression can be far more debilitating in their relationship than the appropriate expression of angry feelings.

Helping the couple express their anger during counseling sessions is therapeutic, as is helping them communicate openly about their anger with one another. The provocation for angry feelings, however, does not rest exclusively with the couple. Parents, in-laws, and friends may make thoughtless remarks that may infuriate the man or woman. The couple also may feel anger toward their physicians at various stages of diagnosis and treatment. Helping professionals who are familiar with the principles of assertiveness training may find that their infertile clients can use assertive behavior (as described in Chapter Five) to communicate openly with those persons who provoke emotional responses, including anger.

The assertive person can express feelings and beliefs straightforwardly and without violating the other person's rights. To the extent that assertion involves respect—not deference—its use can enable an infertile individual to maintain dignity while communicating clearly. Since being infertile engenders a sense of lost control, infertile people have a special need to remain in control when interactions with others evoke anger.

Bargaining. The helping professional must recognize bargaining behavior as an effort to hold at bay the feelings of grief associated with infertility. An important function at this point is to help the infertile person with reality testing. One can communicate an understanding of the infertile person's wish to exhaust every possibility before "giving up," while at the same time encouraging the person to acknowledge the statistical success associated with alternative treatments or the more advanced technologies. Infertile people may need to use this time to speak of the importance of doing all they can to explore even the most remote possibilities of successful treatment. Ultimately, they may be receptive to discussing the way in which their bargaining behavior is proving frustrating, expensive, and anger producing, as chances of conception diminish. The sadness as each month passes without a pregnancy provides an opportunity for the professional to encourage active grieving for the birth child that seems increasingly elusive.

Grief. In addition to offering support as infertile individuals shed tears, the professional also will want to help identify situations that are painful reminders of the loss that infertility represents. Once individuals are aware that certain events or situations are emotionally stressful for them, they can be helped to respond appropriately. For instance, they might decide not to attend baby showers and christenings until their feelings of grief have been dealt with more fully. Families with babies or small children may serve as reminders of a yearned-for lifestyle that is too painful to encounter, and the presence of pregnant women may evoke a sense of anguish that is overwhelming when feelings of grief are close to the surface. In potentially painful circumstances, assertive statements can help infertile individuals to be honest in their responses to others while at the same time affirming that they are entitled to honor their own emotional needs.

In addition to suggestions about managing social encounters, the professional also must attend to the physical exhaustion that grieving incurs. Individuals should be encouraged to pay attention to their physical health at a time when patterns of eating and sleeping may be disrupted. In addition, since grieving takes its toll on self-esteem, the professional will need to make every effort to acknowledge verbally how hard the infertile person is working to come to terms with the many losses now acknowledged. Some people try to compensate for low self-esteem by trying to be productive in other spheres of their lives. While this is laudable in general, the professional may want to caution the infertile person against demanding too much of himself while he is engaged in the energy-depleting task of grieving. Overextending oneself can result in frustration rather than self-esteem; the professional may be most supportive in helping the individual nourish depleting reserves of energy rather than making unrelenting demands at such a stressful time.

The counselor can serve as a source of support to infertile individuals as they acknowledge and find ways to express their grief. By offering reassurance that the raw pain of sorrow will diminish, the professional can provide realistic reassurance that the stage of grief is time limited.

Acceptance. When the couple reach the stage of acceptance of their infertility, they are ready to look ahead to other life options. Acceptance is one way of coming to terms with the mourning process, although it can also become the prelude to more emotional work and decision making as couples pursue continuing dimensions of their infertility. The professional can convey to the couple that they have a right to move ahead on decisions for the future. The professional also can point out that the choices of adoption, artificial insemination by donor, GIFT, surrogate mothers, in vitro fertilization, and childfree living carry both frustrations and potential rewards.

Summary

Although this chapter has focused on the stages of mourning, it recognizes that mourning is unique for each person and may not encompass all the stages or the sequence proposed by Kübler-Ross. However, the discussion may help the professional recognize that certain behaviors belong to one or another stage in the mourning process. Infertile individuals often ask for help by proclaiming that they think they are going crazy, because their thoughts and behaviors seem irrational. When the professional can cognitively reframe their infertility experience as one involving many losses, the individual can more easily understand the need to mourn and, with the professional's help, the complexity in the grief work.

Although the primary need of many infertile people may be to work on issues of mourning, a variety of other needs accompany the struggle with infertility. The next four chapters offer specific strategies for professionals to use with infertile individuals who are grappling with the day-to-day disruptions of infertility.

5

Teaching
Assertive Coping Skills

Professionals learn that much of the anger and frustration felt
by infertile people is generated through interactions with others.
The following remarks are typical examples cited by infertile
individuals who feel thwarted in their efforts to communicate
their needs effectively.

From a co-worker: "What do you mean, you don't feel
like coming to the office baby shower for Alice? What's wrong
with you anyway?"

From a friend who is also a parent: "You're really getting
too worked up about this business of not being able to have
kids. You should relish your freedom, believe me!"

From a parent: "I fail to understand what your infertility
has to do with not wanting to be at our house for the holidays.
After all, your sisters and their families will all be there."

From a physician: "Look, just leave the medical aspects
to me. There's no need for you to get all involved in trying to
understand something that will be beyond you."

From a new acquaintance: "No kids? You'd better get
started before it's too late to turn back the clock!"

From an in-law: "I do hope you two are really working at
beginning a family. I know how much having children means to
my child. As for me, I've spent enough years waiting to become
a grandparent."

These are but a few of the comments that infertile people
encounter frequently. Sometimes they stem from ignorance; at

other times they reflect another's insensitivity. Regardless of what lies behind the comments, the effects of such remarks on an infertile person range from irritation to deep emotional hurt. Many infertile people find that the difficulty of coping with their infertility is compounded by feelings of inadequacy in responding to ignorant and insensitive remarks. At a time when a person's infertility may cause feelings of loss of control, a helping professional should do whatever possible to increase feelings of competence and control in other areas. Infertile people can work productively, for example, in responding to offensive or upsetting remarks. The strategy that is well suited to this task is assertive communication.

A variety of books have been written on the topic of assertive communication and behavior (Jakubowski-Specter, 1973; Alberti and Emmons, 1974; Smith, 1975; Lazarus and Fay, 1975; Fensterheim and Baer, 1975; Bloom, Coburn, and Pearlman, 1975; Bowers and Bowers, 1976). Although none addresses infertility specifically, all are concerned with conditions and personality characteristics that inhibit individuals from asserting their needs clearly.

What Is Assertive Communication?

Assertive communication is the honest and straightforward expression of one's personal needs in ways that do not violate another person's rights. An assertive message will communicate: "This is how I feel. This is my perception of the situation. This is what I think." Assertive communication enables individuals to stand up for their personal rights and communicate their thoughts and feelings clearly and straightforwardly.

There are a number of advantages to behaving assertively. First, assertive persons are more likely than nonassertive persons to get their needs met and their preferences respected. Second, honesty and straightforwardness can increase self-respect, because others recognize one's needs as valid and respond to them in a supportive way. Persons who use assertive communication constructively may eventually acquire greater self-confidence, which, in turn, reduces the need to win approval from others.

Third, when individuals have the courage to take stands, deal with conflict openly and fairly, and show respect for themselves and others, they often elicit admiration and respect from other people in their lives.

Assertion Versus Aggression. Aggression often is confused with assertion, but it differs in that the aggressive person makes no effort to understand the needs of the other person and, in fact, may utilize insults or humiliation to try to force the other person to meet the aggressor's needs. The usual goal in aggression is to win, thereby forcing the other person to lose. Aggression is unbalanced communication; it leaves out the rights, feelings, and needs of the other person in an effort to gain domination. This type of behavior may bring results, but in the long run the relationship is likely to suffer, because few people choose to interact with someone who disregards their needs and feelings. The message that is conveyed by someone who is communicating aggressively is: "This is what I want; what you want doesn't count. This is what I need; your needs are unimportant. This is how I feel; I don't care how you feel."

There are a number of reasons why people are aggressive in their communication. Sometimes an individual has learned aggressiveness by observing it at home or in other environments. If such a person consistently gets his own way, albeit at the expense of someone else, he may feel that this style of communication is effective. Other people may behave aggressively because that is the only response they know or because it seems the only way to get through to the other person. Sometimes an aggressive response represents an overreaction to a situation that is reminiscent of some past unresolved emotional experience. Sometimes it is the response of a usually nonassertive person who explodes after having allowed feelings of hurt and anger to build to an intolerable level. Other people, in an effort not to slip into nonassertive communication, use aggressive communication to express their needs, without realizing the destructive elements that are inherent in it.

Assertion Versus Nonassertion. In contrast to both the assertive person and the aggressive person, the nonassertive person fails to express needs and feelings and allows others to violate or disregard her rights or needs. By not expressing or by subordinating her needs, the nonassertive communicator remains open to being victimized, usually by someone who behaves aggressively. The message conveyed by the nonassertive person is: "My needs and feelings are unimportant, but yours are worth satisfying. I don't matter; you can take advantage of me." The person who communicates nonassertively presents an apologetic appearance, often concentrates inordinately on the needs of others, assumes that others are capable of guessing her unexpressed needs, and plays the role of someone who keeps the peace in situations of indecision or conflict.

People behave nonassertively for several reasons. Often they wish to avoid unpleasantness or conflict, and they behave nonassertively in order to placate the other person and perhaps gain that person's approval. Such people often confuse nonassertive behavior with politeness, just as they may tend to confuse assertive behavior with aggression. Some people resort regularly to nonassertive communication because they are afraid of the response that assertive communication might elicit. Many people who habitually are nonassertive do not believe they have the right to express their preferences, to stand up for themselves, or to take care of their needs. They not only have difficulty in expressing their needs, but they also may feel that they are not even entitled to have such needs or feelings in the first place. Some nonassertive people have submerged and denied their own needs for so long that they are no longer even aware of their preferences and feelings, except as an expression of what would please or satisfy someone else. Many nonassertive people have low self-esteem because they have allowed other people to run their lives and therefore do not feel in control. Nonassertive people who are in touch with their own feelings often express frustration, disappointment, and resentment at submerging their needs to those of other people.

Barriers to Assertive Communication

A number of barriers prevent many people from utilizing assertive communication effectively.

Fear of Rejection. The person who does not react to a hurtful remark may already have felt rejected and therefore has ceased to respond at all to such remarks, choosing instead to fume inwardly or to feel alienated from the speaker. Others, who may not have experienced rejection, are sufficiently fearful of such a response that they do not dare to risk communicating their real feelings. The need for the approval of others may be stronger in someone who is coping with infertility because that person already may be dealing with declining self-esteem. The role of the speaker in the life of the infertile person is also relevant. It is one thing to risk rejection from a new acquaintance and another altogether to threaten the ties of dependency with one's physician.

Confusion Between Assertion and Aggression. Many people shy away from learning or using assertive communication because they perceive it as synonymous with aggression. Infertile people frequently are goaded into feeling aggressive, and many fear that any effort to communicate about emotionally sensitive issues may unleash their aggressive emotions. However, by learning to communicate assertively, they can control the destructive emotions that clamor for expression and also can elicit constructive responses from others.

Belief That Assertive Communication Is Not Polite. The need to be polite may surface more in some interactions than in others. When the other person has higher status (such as a boss), when there are strong feelings of dependence on the other (as with a physician or a spouse), or when a history of polite behavior has been the norm (with parents or one's elders), it becomes more difficult to break the habitual response and declare assertively one's needs and feelings.

The person who is hesitant to be assertive might be asked how she would prefer to be treated: in a straightforward manner or in an indirect or manipulative way. By putting herself in another's shoes, she can begin to appreciate the virtues of assertive communication even though there are risks associated with it.

Fear of Provoking an Aggressive Response. The fear of an aggressive response stems from apprehensive feelings about unknown territory. Professionals can best deal with this fear by asking the individual to offer scenarios in which an assertive response might provoke an aggressive response. As cases are presented, the helping professional can help the person determine whether he made an effort to communicate assertively, whether assertive communication was used appropriately, and how to handle aggressive responses when they occur.

Goals of Assertive Communication

At the outset, those seeking to communicate assertively should be clear about their goals. The professional should ask the individual to write down two or three specific goals and, at the same time, should discuss the barriers that interfere with the accomplishment of the goals. Some examples of goals and barriers that might emerge include:

Goal: To communicate my needs more clearly to my spouse, particularly when I am feeling depressed about our infertility.

Barrier: I don't want to burden my spouse with my troubles. I tend to withdraw from others when I'm feeling depressed.

Goal: To be able to turn down invitations to family gatherings or social functions where the presence of children or pregnant women is especially painful to me.

Barrier: My (or our) family make me feel guilty for not attending, and our friends don't understand that certain kinds of social events are painful reminders of the joy I cannot have.

Goal: To be more clear with my physician about my wish to become knowledgeable about the unfolding aspects of our infertility.

Barrier: I tend to view my physician as an expert who is busy enough without being asked to explain every little thing to me (us).

Goal: To be able to have a ready response for some of the hurtful and insensitive remarks that people make.

Barrier: I know that sometimes people make those remarks
without intending to be hurtful, and I don't want to
appear hurtful in return, even though I'm crying inside. Also, for those people who really are insensitive
clods, I just want to explode at them!

In conveying information about assertive behavior, the
professional becomes an educator and the infertile person a
learner who is encouraged to take an active role in identifying
needs and goals and, ultimately, incorporating new skills into
the existing repertoire of responses in difficult situations. For
initial goals, the learner and the helping professional should identify areas that are troublesome on a regular basis, so that the
learner will have ample opportunity to try out and to refine the
newly learned assertive skills. If invitations to potentially painful social gatherings occur once every two months, and doctor
visits occur every two weeks, for example, it would make more
sense initially to emphasize skills in communicating one's needs
to the physician.

The learner should be clear in setting specific goals. The
last goal above, about responding to hurtful remarks, is a good
example of an unclear goal. No single response is appropriate for
all situations, and, as the goal setter indicated, one may need to
vary responses depending on whether the speaker's insensitivity
was intentional or unintentional. A more appropriate goal might
be: "To learn to differentiate between intentional and unintentional hurtful remarks. For unintentional hurtful remarks, to
learn to communicate about my infertility succinctly, in the
hope that it will make the person more sensitive to my needs in
the future. For intentional hurtful remarks, to communicate
assertively the impact of the remark and let the speaker know
that I hope he or she will be more sensitive to my infertility in
the future." Here the desired change in behavior is made more
specific. If necessary, the person could write minigoals to encompass the total area of desired change. The clearer the goal,
the easier it will be to identify new assertive behaviors to achieve
the goal.

Verbal and Nonverbal Cues

Assertive communication consists of both nonverbal and verbal skills. It may be less threatening to focus initially on nonverbal messages, because they are usually considered fun. At the same time, the helping professional may provide feedback about the learner's verbal responses in a variety of situations. The professional should stress that nonverbal cues have the power to render an assertive message nonassertive. Assessing how the individual communicates on a nonverbal level is, therefore, an important component in any effort to teach assertive communication. The learner may be encouraged to brainstorm about nonverbal behaviors that can distort a verbally assertive message. Callahan (1980) details a range of counterproductive nonverbal behaviors: apologizing profusely, beating around the bush, not saying what you really mean or feel, not saying anything, letting things slide by without comment, and being unclear. Nonverbal facial gestures, voice tone, eyes, and body position may support a passive, frightened, or half-hearted verbal pattern. A slouched body; downcast, tearful, or pathetic eyes; sticky, cold, or nervously clenching hands; a soft, weak, or unsteady voice; and a hopeful, pleading demeanor, a "take care of me and understand my needs" look, are typical counterproductive nonverbal behaviors.

Aggressive responses include actions such as blaming, labeling, or accusing others. Callahan suggests that an air of superiority often accompanies demonstrations of strength or sarcasm. A loud, piercingly shrill voice or a chillingly cold and detached voice is typical. Aggressive people look through others or stare blankly. The stone or grim face may be accompanied by a rigid or haughty posture, which often leans into or over the other's space intrusively. The body's rigidity is expressed by jerky, domineering motions like table pounding and finger pointing.

Assertive communication, on the other hand, is characterized by clarity, directness, and honesty. By using "I" messages (see next section), the speaker states needs, feelings, and beliefs in a straightforward way. Someone who is communicating assertively maintains good eye contact, has a well-modulated voice, and holds a relaxed, yet attentive, body stance.

The helping professional might encourage the learner to role-play, using assertive, aggressive, and nonassertive styles of communication for each phrase.

> No, we don't have any children. My partner and I are infertile.

> Dr. Jones, I would like you to take more time with me to discuss the available options for the treatment of our infertility.

> I'm feeling really out of control these days, and I need for you to be patient with me.

> No, Mother, there's nothing new to report on our infertility workup.

After rehearsing the differences among the various approaches, the professional and the learner are ready to move onto the next step of learning assertive skills, the use of "I" statements.

"I" Statements

"I" statements begin with the word *I* and enable the speaker to take responsibility for her feelings, needs, and beliefs. The advantage of "I" statements is that the speaker is discouraged from blaming another person and encouraged to be clear about what she is experiencing at the current time. "I" statements involve four specific components:

1. *When* (speaker objectively describes the other person's behavior).
2. *The effects are* (speaker specifies how the other person's behavior concretely affects her life or feelings).
3. *I feel* (speaker describes feelings, if distinct from effects already verbalized).
4. *I would prefer* (speaker indicates how she wants current or future behavior to change).

To be able to communicate "I" messages clearly to another person, the learner must be in touch with his own feelings. The professional may need to explore with the learner how much he acknowledges needs and feelings and the extent to which he feels entitled to those needs and feelings. After the helping professional has helped the learner identify needs and has offered reassurance that the learner is entitled to them, it is time to look closely at the emotions that have the power to interfere with assertive communication.

Emotions That Detract from Assertive Communication

Anxiety. Anxiety is natural to expect whenever one is undertaking a new behavior or a new experience. If the learner has been unable to act assertively in the past, then she probably will feel anxious about whether she can change old behaviors. There are risks involved whenever one tries something new, and taking risks can generate anxiety. Avoiding anxiety is not healthy either, especially if it leaves a person stuck in nonproductive behavior patterns. Trying to reduce anxiety to a manageable level by taking reasonable risks, therefore, is a goal. One way is to be clear and specific about the new behavior and the situation in which it will be practiced.

Shaping is a method that can be very helpful in reducing anxiety. It consists of breaking down the desired behavioral change into small and specific tasks, with each task being somewhat more demanding than the previous one. By using shaping, the learner can gain a gradual sense of accomplishment without being overwhelmed by the enormity of the total behavioral change. An example of shaping might look like this:

1. Identify the situation in which the learner wants to behave assertively—for example, in discussing with her physician her wish to pursue treatments beyond those that have been made available to her.
2. Identify barriers to the goal: feeling intimidated by the physician who is the "expert"; feeling a need to maintain good relations with the physician in order to get the best

possible treatment; feeling fearful that the physician will be insulted by her insinuation that not enough is being done medically to treat her infertility.

3. Write down some assertive statements that would be appropriate for the next meeting with the physician. Visualize the meeting with the physician and indicate how the learner could behave assertively, including verbal and nonverbal communication. By visualizing several different scenarios, with each handled assertively, the learner can review potential interactions and feel more confident that she has anticipated a range of possible interactions.

4. Practice the assertive communication, with the helping professional in the role of physician. The initial role plays should offer the learner feelings of success, with little resistance or defensiveness on the part of the physician. After each role play, the learner and the professional can process together the strengths and limitations demonstrated by the learner, continuing to practice until both are satisfied that appropriate assertive behavior was used. Subsequent role plays should increase in difficulty until the learner feels that she has encountered and mastered a variety of intimidating potential encounters.

5. If the learner finds herself becoming especially tense in anticipation of an assertive encounter, it may be worthwhile to teach her some relaxation techniques.

6. The learner should remind herself of the benefits of asserting herself with her physician, so that she will be sufficiently motivated to carry through in an anxiety-provoking situation.

7. The learner might be encouraged to give herself a reward after the visit with her physician, whatever the outcome. The reward is for taking the risk involved in being assertive and should not be contingent on the success of her visit.

8. The learner should process with the helping professional the actual meeting with the physician—how she felt she did and how that experience makes her feel about future use of assertive communication.

9. The next situation in which the learner plans to use assertive

skills should be slightly more challenging than the one with the physician, with new skills built on ones already used.

Guilt. Guilt is a familiar emotion to most infertile people. Much of this guilt comes from the disappointment in oneself, and some of it comes from the awareness that one's infertility has caused pain or disappointment to others. Because of this guilt, some infertile people feel that they are unworthy of asking others to accommodate to their needs. The low self-esteem that sometimes ensues fuels future guilt about asserting needs. Two areas in particular present difficulties for persons who tend to feel guilty.

Making requests: Asking for the help of others when one feels generally unworthy is a burdensome task. The infertile person tends to focus on all the barriers to making a request (rejection, inconveniencing someone else, indebting oneself to another person), rather than on emphasizing his right to have needs and to make requests.

Refusing requests: To feel needed or wanted is a comforting palliative to the low self-esteem that often accompanies infertility. For this reason, refusing requests may be particularly difficult for someone grappling with infertility. It can be even more difficult if the refusal is related to one's infertility—for instance, in situations where an infertile person does not wish to attend a baby shower or a family gathering with many young children. The guilt over refusing is further fueled by the fear that the other person will not be understanding or, worse still, may be punishing or rejecting. Typical nonassertive responses might include profuse apologizing, offering numerous excuses for why an acceptance is impossible, or berating oneself for being unable to accept. The professional needs to help the infertile person understand that such nonassertive responses are confusing to the listener, whereas an honest and straightforward refusal is far more desirable. The learner should realize that he is entitled to refuse requests that would cause emotional discomfort or pain, and at this difficult time it is most important not to add stressful situations to the infertility struggle.

Anger. Anger is an integral component of the effort to

resolve feelings about infertility. Rather than denying that anger is present, the infertile person needs to acknowledge its existence and learn to express it in appropriate ways, instead of in uncontrolled outbursts that will be hurtful to others. The professional can ask the person what messages he learned about anger when growing up, from parents, siblings, friends, and role models. Those messages are likely to have been powerful, and probably need to be reexamined in adulthood to see whether they are still valid. It may be important to distinguish between "It is bad to express anger destructively" and "It is bad to feel angry." Feeling anger is normal and healthy; learning to express it constructively is the challenge.

The learner should be encouraged to write down the barriers that he perceives in expressing anger. Typical barriers include fear of rejection, fear of losing control, fear of disapproval, and the temptation to substitute other behaviors in place of anger, such as denial, withdrawal, emotional isolation, or projection of blame onto someone else.

Once the barriers are recognized, it becomes easier to work on changing them in a conscious way. The technique of shaping, described earlier, is relevant here and may help the learner feel gradual mastery over a difficult emotion. Additional pointers include taking responsibility for angry feelings and accepting that they are normal; expressing anger when it occurs, rather than keeping it bottled up until it reaches destructive proportions; using "I" language in expressing anger; assuming an assertive body posture when communicating anger; and using a nondestructive physical outlet when the feelings of anger are intense (scrub a floor, punch a pillow, swim laps, run several blocks, write down the angry feelings) before expressing them verbally.

Handling Difficult Situations

Many people refrain from assertive communication because they fear that it will create new difficulties in a relationship—for example, with a person who cannot handle an assertive response in a mutually beneficial way. If the risks of being assertive outweigh the benefits, the learner may choose not to be assertive with that person or in a particular situation. Choosing not to be assertive, though, is very different from being unable to act assertively.

The fear of provoking a retaliatory response can be a deterrent to someone who would otherwise choose to be assertive. In general, it does not pay to respond to an aggressive reaction. Ignoring aggressive responses will prevent the situation from escalating and deprive the aggressor of the satisfaction of upsetting the assertive speaker. A reply such as "I don't want to pursue this discussion while you are so angry" enables the speaker to communicate her needs while, at the same time, acknowledging the respondent's emotions.

In helping infertile people learn assertive communication skills, the professional accomplishes a number of tasks. Goal setting helps the learner acknowledge his needs and explore barriers that interfere with reaching the identified goals. The barriers may affect the learner's life in realms other than the specified goal, so the opportunity to discuss such barriers may provide insight into areas not even associated with infertility. The helping professional plays the roles of educator, mentor, and evaluator by teaching assertive skills and by promoting the confidence that can accompany the successful application of such skills. By assuming these roles supportively and creatively, the professional provides encouragement and critical feedback as the learner masters skills that ultimately can empower him in situations that previously had proven frustrating or difficult.

6

Conducting Support Groups

Because they provide opportunities for peer support, new learning, and personal insight, groups can be especially helpful for infertile individuals and couples (Abarbanel and Bach, 1959; Menning, 1984; Goodman and Rothman, 1984; Shapiro, 1982). Many infertile individuals feel socially isolated, misunderstood, and out of step with their peers, many of whom are beginning families and unable to understand the pain of infertility. Even family members may be unable to relate to the issues that infertility raises for their children and siblings. To counteract the feeling of isolation, many infertile individuals and couples have found that support groups offer much-needed solace and encouragement, as well as access to concrete information on medical resources. Infertility groups are being offered in many communities, with leadership coming from an experienced RESOLVE counselor or mental health professional. Infertility and in vitro clinics also find that groups can offer important support when infertile individuals and couples are experiencing the unique strains of diagnosis and treatment.

For the professional interested in beginning an infertility support group, there are a number of issues that should be anticipated before the group begins.

Laying the Groundwork

Finding Potential Group Members. One of the first considerations is whether there is enough interest locally among infertile people to offer a group. The answer may depend on the sponsorship of the group—whether it is through an infertility clinic, a RESOLVE chapter, or a professional's private practice.

If the setting is an infertility clinic, it is fairly easy to gain access to potential group members and to assess their interest in a support group. Since patients at infertility clinics already have made a firm decision to acknowledge and treat their infertility, they may perceive group support as an extension of the medical attention they are already receiving. In addition, since infertility treatment involves its own special set of stressors, individuals may feel a more pronounced need for group support. In any case, since most patients at infertility clinics are seen on a some-what regular basis, the group facilitator has a number of opportunities to assess whether there are enough individuals interested to warrant the formation of a group. It makes sense first to talk with the medical professionals at the clinic about the purpose of the support group, the kinds of patients who might be most appropriate for the group, and the potential benefits for those who participate in the group. The medical professionals then could be asked to suggest which clinic patients might be interested, and the facilitator could follow up by contacting and meeting these individuals to discuss the support group in more detail.

If a RESOLVE chapter is the sponsor of the support group, gaining access to potential members will require outreach efforts. Although membership of the group may come exclusively from RESOLVE members, newspaper publicity may also be desirable. Ideally, it should be accompanied by a feature story on infertility, so that readers can determine whether their needs and the purpose of the support group are compatible. Notifying local gynecologists and obstetricians of plans for the group is another option; some physicians may be willing to display fliers about the group in their waiting room, and some may be willing to mention the group to selected patients, who may then contact the facilitator directly. Local Planned Parenthood chapters that offer infertility services also may be willing to inform new and continuing patients about the group. The facilitator will need to decide whether fees will be charged to members of RESOLVE and whether a different fee scale will be used for individuals who are not RESOLVE members.

If a mental health professional in a community is interested in forming an infertility support group, that person will want to contact the local RESOLVE chapter, if one exists, as well as local gynecologists, obstetricians, Planned Parenthood, and other health professionals.

From the beginning, the group facilitator should distinguish between a support group and a therapy group. Potential group members should understand that the group will offer information, support, and referrals, but not psychotherapy for issues that may be more appropriate to work on in a long-term and in-depth context.

Leadership. Before a group begins, the leadership should be determined. Some support groups have cofacilitators, ideally a male and a female, to lend a gender-balanced perspective to the range of feelings and topics that the group explores. Since male membership in infertility groups tends to be sparse, having a male cofacilitator may encourage males to join a group. Even if there is little or no male attendance in the group, a male cofacilitator may offer crucial perspectives to females in the group, who will, of necessity, be preoccupied with their own issues.

Some groups have a rotating leadership function, with a different member taking responsibility for facilitating the group at each meeting. Group members who are impatient with the approaches of the many professionals whom they have consulted about their infertility may choose this route. A rotating leadership also enables members to contribute and be productive in the group at the very time in their lives that infertility threatens to damage their fragile self-esteem. A rotating leadership has the potential of backfiring, however, if group members feel awkward about assuming the leadership role, if members get "stuck" on some issues, or if the group sessions tend to focus on griping and commiserating, rather than working toward constructive solutions. If the members of a support group cannot find a professional who has worked on infertility issues, leadership can be provided by a professional who is skilled in working with groups; that professional can be asked to read some key books and articles on infertility as a way of providing concrete knowledge to complement the therapeutic skills that the person already possesses. If a group cannot afford to have a professional facilitator for all its meetings, it might consider inviting the professional to facilitate the first few sessions and then to return at regular intervals to keep pace with the group and provide feedback on the group's own facilitation skills. This "consultant" could also be called in if the group members need support on especially difficult issues, either interpersonal or related to infertility struggles.

A group may decide that one of its own members can serve as the desired facilitator. Although likely to feel flattered at the invitation, the potential facilitator should be aware of certain risks inherent in the position. First, a facilitator who is also a group member must be clear with herself and with the group about her role. If she accepts the invitation to facilitate the group, she must be careful to respect the needs of the group, even when they do not coincide with her own. She must be aware that the needs of group members may require a response, such as confrontation, that is not consistent with the response the facilitator would have given as a friend. And, finally, since the role of facilitator implies attendance at every support group meeting, the member/facilitator—more than other group members—will feel a responsibility to give priority to the group's schedule over other commitments in her life.

Group Structure. Aside from leadership, the structure of the group itself needs to be determined. Will the group be open or closed? How many members are desirable to ensure the stability and vitality of the group? Will pregnant women be welcome? How frequently should meetings be held? How long should each meeting be?

In considering whether to have a time-limited (closed) or ongoing (open) group, the facilitator needs to consider the reason for initiating the group in the first place. A closed group, one that meets for a specified duration and admits no new members after it has begun, may be most appropriate for new groups in a community. Its members need to gain a sense of what it is like to be involved in a support group and to consolidate their relationships in that group. There is always the possibility that the closed group will choose to "terminate" and then continue as an open group, welcoming new members as they wish to join, bidding goodbye to old members whose needs have been met, and evolving as the membership of the group changes. An open group is likely to be the initial choice for infertile people in a community where there have been opportunities to gather for information and programs. The existing feelings of identity around the problem of infertility will enable the group membership to fluctuate without posing a threat to their group cohesion. Hartford (1971) asserts that instability—resulting from loss of leadership, turnover, and loss of group identity—is the basic shortcoming of the open group. These factors may be minimized by an adequate size so that the group is not threatened by member loss.

The size of the group should be related to the purpose of the group. Since the facilitator hopes to encourage trust and intimacy, the group must not be too large. On the other hand, since infertility evokes powerful emotions that individuals may need to examine privately before sharing them publicly, the group should be large enough so that members do not feel obligated to participate when they need occasionally to withdraw. Experts on verbally oriented groups, including support groups, have recommended that such groups have about seven members (Berelson and Steiner, 1964; Hare, 1962; Shepherd, 1964). Given the inevitability of absences in a support group, a closed group may want to begin with eight members. In an open group, where members come into the group at different times, feelings of trust and intimacy will evolve more slowly than in a closed group, where everyone began at the same time. For this reason, the size of an open group should be slightly larger in order to maximize the likelihood that new members can identify with a group member who has similar needs and problems (Ziller, 1965).

The group may decide how frequently to meet. Many support groups find that meetings on alternate weeks allow them to recall the last session easily and still to have enough time between meetings to think about issues discussed as well as ones they want to introduce. Although some members may feel that alternate weeks are too frequent, because they are simultaneously juggling medical treatments and other infertility-related concerns, those pressures may, in fact, be assuaged by the availability of meetings. These questions can be discussed during the first meeting. If group members are uncertain or divided on how often to meet, the facilitator can suggest meeting at specified intervals for the first four or five times and then polling the group members again to see how that arrangement is working for them.

Group facilitators usually find that one and a half hours is an appropriate length of time for a support group to raise and explore issues of importance without emotionally exhausting group members. Some infertility support groups try to allow some informal time prior to each session, so that members can browse through any literature or resource materials that may be available, either from the local RESOLVE library or from group members. Having refreshments available at group meetings can promote a comfortable atmosphere; the responsibility for bringing refreshments can either be assumed by the facilitator or rotated among group members.

The duration of the group is probably not an issue for open groups, which will meet as long as there are enough members to keep the group active and vital. For closed groups, however, an initial plan to meet for eight to twelve sessions is feasible. As the last sessions approach, members may determine whether to end, to continue, or to end for some members while continuing as an open group, thereby enabling participation of both old and new members.

Support group facilitators need to consider the sensitive issue of whether to have pregnant women as members. When recruiting members, the facilitator might want to explore each potential member's feelings on the subject. Strong negative feelings are likely to sound something like: "I want to view the support group as a place where I can verbalize my anger at women who can become pregnant when I can't." "A support group should be a refuge from all the pressures of the fertile world—and that doesn't include having pregnant women!" "The mere sight of a pregnant woman makes me break into tears these days." "My wife had a miscarriage last year, and now it's just too painful to be around pregnant women and the joy that they feel." Others may view the presence of pregnant women very differently, as shown by the following remarks: "Sure, let her be in the group. Anyone who has had to battle infertility must be having an anxious pregnancy." "Of course pregnant women would be welcome. I miscarried six months ago, and if I ever become pregnant again, I know I'll need a support group!" "Pregnant women don't bother me as much as little babies." "Seeing a pregnant woman in our group would give me a sense of hope that maybe I, too, could get pregnant!"

Clearly, the facilitator must take these strong feelings into account before deciding whether pregnant women should be included in the group. In particular, those opposed to their inclusion should be made aware that any pregnant woman coming to the group has a history of infertility or pregnancy loss. That shared pain of infertility may enable initially hostile members to revise their objections to including pregnant women in the group. If not, then the facilitator will probably decide not to include pregnant women, both to protect them from undeserved hostility in the group and to help group members work on their anger, which they might not be able to express as comfortably in the presence of pregnant women. Groups should probably not be asked to decide on this issue; the discussion might be too divisive, or members with strong negative feelings might feel intimidated from sharing them openly so soon. In some communities, there are enough pregnant women with a history of infertility to form a separate group for them and their partners.

The location for the support group meetings will vary with the needs of the group and the availability of meeting places in the community. Accessibility is a major consideration. Some communities will require a safe location where individuals can meet comfortably at night; others may require a central location, either near public transportation or with parking facilities nearby. Some members may offer their homes for meetings, but this is not an ideal solution, because they may live in areas that are inconvenient for other group members. Members wishing to offer hospitality can best do so when the need for providing refreshments arises. Ideally, the group should meet in the same room each week, to promote a sense of stability as membership changes or as different issues are discussed (Hartford, 1971). The room should be as aesthetically pleasing as possible and should have comfortable furniture that can be moved into a circle for group meetings. If the room is too large, a section of the room can be used and the furniture arranged within that imaginary boundary for each session. The facilitator should avoid a room that is too small; in addition to being physically cramped, members may also feel that the tight quarters force a sense of intimacy before it has evolved naturally within the group (Sommer, 1969).

Just as the building location should be accessible to group members, the accessibility of the room in the building is also important. If meetings are held in a building where there is a receptionist, this person should know about the group and its meeting place and be able to direct members easily to the correct room. If there is no receptionist, each entrance of the building should be marked with signs indicating how to find the appropriate room. The facilitator should arrive early at the first meeting, since some members also may arrive earlier than the actual beginning time of the group.

The First Meeting

At the beginning of a group, feelings of uncertainty, hopefulness, and initial awkwardness are common among group facilitators (Garvin, 1981). Rather than deny these feelings by being overcontrolling or by putting on a façade of confidence, the facilitator should be truthful with the group, thereby eliciting and validating the members' rights to have similar feelings about the beginning of the group. After eliciting common feelings about the group, the facilitator can then emphasize the readiness of the group to move ahead on these and other issues together.

The first meeting provides opportunities for getting acquainted, finding common purposes, establishing norms, and beginning to negotiate relationships with the facilitator and other group members (Hartford, 1971; Levine, 1979). Some groups find that name tags help to promote interactions.

Once it is time for the group to start, the facilitator needs to determine how many members have not yet arrived. The beginning of the group can be delayed a short time, but not longer than ten minutes, out of respect for those members who have made an effort to be prompt. The facilitator may want to leave the door of the room slightly ajar, with a note welcoming latecomers. When beginning the group, the facilitator may welcome group members and explain that there are a few people who had difficulty arriving on time but who may be joining the group later. The facilitator will want to review how the group evolved, offer some information about himself, and explain that confidentiality will be respected in the group. The explanation about confidentiality might go something like this:

> Many of us are at different points in our struggles with infertility. We have also made different kinds of decisions about how public or private to be in sharing information about our infertility with others. It is my hope that we can foster a spirit of openness in this group, since we all share the common bond of infertility and have a great deal to offer one another. However, no matter how open we will be in this group, it is important to keep the information shared here confidential. That means that, although we may choose to share information about our participation in this group with friends, we must never violate the confidentiality of others by revealing that they are members of this group, or by revealing anything they share with the group. Do any of you have any questions or comments on the group's respect for the confidentiality of its members?

The facilitator may also ask whether the meeting time and place are agreeable to all members, remind closed groups of the time limits set for the group, and invite members to introduce themselves and share information about themselves. The facilitator should probably not do any probing at this time but, rather, allow members to present their situations as they choose.

If any member seems to be monopolizing a great deal of time, the facilitator may say something like "Thank you for speaking in so much detail about your situation. Since we want to be sure that everyone has a chance to speak today, perhaps you could save some of your experiences for future sessions when there will be more time to elaborate."

When all members have had an opportunity to share something about themselves (and the facilitator should be certain that everyone has said something, although shy or reluctant participants may give only their first names), the facilitator may make some remarks about what the group has in common and ask group members to help in this process. Differences among members should also be identified:

> Although all of you are grappling with issues of infertility, some of you are at different places in the process. While some of you are just beginning the treatment process, others of you are trying to decide between continuing treatment or pursuing adoption. These are all difficult issues, but they are bound together by the common thread of infertility and the emotional sadness that we feel, no matter at what stage of the process we may be.

So, even in delineating differences, the facilitator still has the opportunity to emphasize commonalities.

If any of the group members are pregnant, this is likely to be the right time to acknowledge the issue. The facilitator might approach the topic this way:

> One difference that is more visually apparent than others is the pregnancy of some of our group members. Both Anna and Colleen have shared with us their history of infertility, and yet their being with us is a reminder that feelings of infertility do not go away when a pregnancy is achieved. In fact, someone who becomes pregnant after a period of infertility may have anxieties that only other infertile couples can relate to.

The facilitator might then ask Anna and Colleen what they hope to gain by being in the group. After they have shared their feelings, other group members can be encouraged to state their purposes in coming to the group. Once again, the facilitator will want to recognize both differences and similarities among members. Undoubtedly, by this time the group will need to end, perhaps with the facilitator saying that at the next session the group will continue to explore what members hope to get from the group.

Initial Stages of Group Development

Norms. Group norms evolve throughout a group and can be assisted by the modeling of the facilitator (Garvin, 1981; Yalom, 1975; Levine, 1979; Hartford, 1971). In some circumstances, the facilitator will state hopes for expected group behavior—for instance, regarding confidentiality or perhaps: "It is my hope that we can foster a spirit of openness in this group." In other circumstances, norms will be unspoken but accepted, such as when, without prior discussion, the facilitator and members call one another by their first names. One group norm that may be verbalized by the facilitator and subsequently emphasized in group interaction is that all members have responsibility for the group. Although the facilitator may have taken the initial responsibility for forming the group, he must enable members to assume leadership functions and to utilize behaviors that contribute to the group's functioning.

Relationship with the Facilitator. Group members often assume that the facilitator will take responsibility for solving the problems of group members (Yalom, 1975). Members often address their remarks to the facilitator rather than to one another, they ask for concrete pieces of information, and they look to the facilitator for help when there are uncomfortable interactions or when the group gets "stuck" and is not sure how to proceed. Initially, as group members become acquainted with one another and with the group norms, the facilitator needs to be a strong role model who can communicate by behavior the ways in which comfortable group interactions can occur. For example, the facilitator may redirect a question to other group members, ask members whether they have any comment on a particular issue, or single out individual members for a comment, a question, or a supportive remark. As the facilitator continues to communicate her confidence that group members can find their own solutions, the participants will gradually assume responsibility for the well-being of the group. The facilitator will continue, however, to take responsibility for beginning each group meeting, helping members work through difficult issues, and ending each session, thereby carrying responsibility in areas where her expertise in group facilitation can best be utilized by the group.

Ambivalence. In the beginning stages of any group, members view the group with mixed emotions (Garland, Jones, and Kolodny, 1965). On the one hand, members come to the group with certain expectations and needs that could be met through rewarding interactions with the facilitator or group members. On the other hand, most group members feel an initial reluctance about group membership. They anticipate that they may be uncomfortable in the group or that the group itself may not meet their needs. If the early group sessions enable members to feel positive about the group, members will invest themselves in the work of the group and find the strength and confidence to deal with the periodic discomforts of group membership. If the early experiences of group members tend to confirm their negative apprehensions, however, some members may drop out, thereby putting the future of the group in jeopardy. During this initial period, Garvin (1981) suggests that the facilitator comment on these ambivalent feelings to help sustain the members through difficulties that are usually present in group beginnings. This action should have an empathic quality, which can also enhance member-facilitator relationships. In addition, an empathic response invites members to work on their feelings about group beginnings and to cope with fears about the group.

Relationships Among Members. Early meetings may be characterized by feelings of interpersonal awkwardness as group members learn about one another's infertility experiences and decide how much of their own private infertility struggles they wish to reveal. Sometimes members will defend against feelings of social awkwardness by focusing on superficial topics or by allying with the facilitator to gain that person's approval or support (Garland, Jones, and Kolodny, 1965; Hartford, 1971). The facilitator should be sensitive to the group's need to move slowly into the emotions associated with infertility; nevertheless, the facilitator can remind members of their purpose in coming to the group and of the things they have in common, so that they need not feel overdependent on the facilitator. The facilitator may find it useful to mention pointedly that members can help one another, thereby encouraging them to assume responsibility for the group's well-being.

Emerging Themes

Some members come to an infertility support group with clear ideas of what they hope to gain. Others come with feelings of discomfort that they hope will be relieved through discussion with others in similar circumstances. Still others have denied some of the painful feelings associated with infertility and hope that the group will provide validation for their outlook. When members are asked in the first sessions to indicate what their purposes are in coming to the group, the facilitator will need to find enough areas of commonality to help the group establish shared goals that are consistent with individual needs. Some authors refer to this shared understanding by the facilitator and group members as a contract (Schwartz, 1971; Garvin and Glasser, 1974; Rose, 1977). From time to time, the facilitator will need to remind the group members of their purpose; and, as the last sessions of the group approach, the facilitator should review the members' feelings about achieving their initial goals.

The kinds of themes that are likely to surface in an infertility support group include decision making; the mourning process; difficulties in social relationships; problems in the workplace generated by infertility; challenges in relating to medical professionals; feelings of anger and how to discharge them; interactions with parents, in-laws, and siblings; feelings that one's career is suffering during the infertility struggle; financial hardships associated with infertility; other options for parenting; feelings of emotional vulnerability and lack of control; relationship difficulties with one's partner, stemming from or exacerbated by infertility; and the readiness to ask for and expect support.

Approaching Termination

During the course of the support group meetings, many issues will be raised. Ideally, the facilitator will help members engage in discussion, encourage one another, empathize with the feelings being expressed, and identify areas of hopefulness in lives that revolve constantly around issues of infertility. If the members have developed a sense of group identity, the challenge of the ending of the group will need special sensitivity.

Endings in American society often are ignored or are ritualized in ways that hide true feelings. Farewells, such as retirements, graduations, or geographical moves, are celebrated with parties and ceremonies. Although some endings imply new beginnings to look forward to, the unrecognized element in many endings is the letting go of the good times and warm relationships that have been important. The literature available to people in the helping professions is replete with information on how to begin relationships with clients, but considerably less attention is given to ending relationships in a way that enables clients to consolidate their gains and move ahead in life with new perspectives (Fox, Nelson, and Bolman, 1969). For that reason, it becomes easy for facilitators to believe that their major goal has been accomplished once the group has been established and its members are working toward specified goals. Yet, just as challenges to the integrity of the group can occur as members work toward their goals, threats to the group are posed at the time of termination.

In ending an infertility support group, the facilitator must be especially sensitive to the meanings that group members may attach to its dissolution. Some members will regret that they will never again be surrounded by a group of people who readily empathize with their struggle over infertility. Others may feel that they have just begun to acknowledge their emotions of loss and anger, only to be left to continue this work without the group. Some members may be facing difficult decisions in the months ahead and may regret that the group will not be there to offer information and support. And, finally, since infertility is itself a series of losses, the loss of the group can feel to some members like a final blow.

Several authors (Shapiro, 1980; Garvin, 1981) speak of the parallels between termination of a helping relationship and the stages of mourning set forth by Elisabeth Kübler-Ross (1969). Since many group members come to support groups for help in mourning the losses associated with infertility, emotions during termination may be powerful. Emotions that have been troublesome during the infertility struggle may present a special challenge as the facilitator encourages the group to come to terms with denial, anger, bargaining, grief, and, ultimately, acceptance. Denial is a common response as termination issues are raised with the group (Bennis and Shepherd, 1956). Anger may be expressed by some members in the form of protest that the group has not been helpful enough, that the facilitator could have done more, or that they did not utilize the group as fully as they might have. Members who have difficulty expressing anger will need the facilitator's support to do so, and may need to be reassured that angry feelings are appropriate at a time of loss (Levine, 1979). The facilitator should avoid being provoked into a defensive position if members directly or indirectly criticize the group or the facilitator. Instead, the facilitator can acknowledge that these feelings exist, that they are frustrating and anger producing, and that the group members must decide how to come to terms with their anger. The facilitator may want to assess whether members are falling into old patterns of reacting to anger or whether they are using new skills that they learned in the group. The facilitator will want to discourage members from becoming "stuck" around their anger and, instead, guide them to process and channel it into action that more closely meets the members' needs.

Bargaining, as described by Kübler-Ross, is used to delay an ending. This phenomenon is frequently seen in groups facing termination as they try to extend the number of sessions. Since literature on time-limited counseling (Reid and Epstein, 1972) indicates that time limits can actually help mobilize a group to do important work as the end approaches, the facilitator should recognize any request for delaying termination as an effort by the group to cope with its anger at the prospect of ending. Unless extraordinary and unforeseen circumstances (such as repeated cancellations due to inclement weather) have prevented the group from doing its work in a timely manner, the facilitator may empathize with the members' wish to continue but, at the same time, must remain firm about plans for ending. Some members may try to demonstrate their continuing need for the group by regressing to earlier issues or ways of relating that have already been resolved in the group. The facilitator also should be prepared for members to bring up new crises as a way to express their continuing dependence on the group. The facilitator should avoid becoming sidetracked from the termination issues and, instead, will want to focus on how new learning from the group may have prepared the member to deal with the crisis that he is facing. As the group members shift from being critical of group shortcomings to renewing their appeals for group input and support, they are likely to focus on missed opportunities. Since the concept of missed opportunities is at the very heart of the struggle with infertility, the facilitator may want to discuss why it may be especially hard for members to "let go" at the same time that they face letting go in their medical treatments, and in their hopes and dreams for a birth child.

Connecting the bargaining efforts of the group with the missed opportunities of their infertility is likely to precipitate some feelings of grief in members (Mann, 1967). Individuals may speak of the futility they feel as one door after another closes in their quest for fertility, or they may speak of the importance of their attachments to members at a time in their lives when relationships assume a special significance. The sadness over letting go of these relationships will elicit, for some members, the feeling that they should be moving on to other relationships. When the one relationship they covet, that of themselves and a baby, seems elusive, the sadness of losing the group relationship is even more poignant. This expression of grief by group members may be fleeting or intense, depending on the group and how comfortable the facilitator is with the expression of painful feelings.

At this stage in the termination process, a member may appear less committed to the needs of others in the group because she is anticipating how to cope with infertility without the group's support. Sometimes a member will choose this time to drop out of the group—either to avoid dealing with the pain of ending or to take control over the ending date rather than allowing the facilitator to have this power. In any case, the facilitator should contact any member who leaves the group prematurely, to explore the reasons for the precipitous ending. Often the facilitator's expression of concern is sufficient to bring the absent member back to the group, but if the member persists in terminating prematurely, the facilitator must be prepared to ask group members how they feel about the void this person's leaving creates in the group. If at all possible, the member should be encouraged to attend one last session to say goodbye and to allow the other members to express their farewells.

Occasionally, a group will begin to lose its membership even before termination issues have been introduced. When the facilitator sees that members are dropping out and that the group appears to be ending on its own accord, she should assemble the members for one last meeting. The purpose is to bring the group to a formal end and to elicit from members both their satisfactions and dissatisfactions with the group experience. Members who need more help with their infertility problems can be referred to alternate resources.

In groups that explore the issues of termination, members who have had a successful experience in the group will become aware of the many positive feelings associated with their group participation. These positive feelings may stimulate a surge of energy to deal with the emotional demands of termination, as members have an increasing sense of leaving the group feeling somewhat replenished. Members can be encouraged to reflect on the hard work they have done and the feeling of accomplishment that has resulted. While members may wish that the group could continue, they may also feel some relief about the termination, in that a considerable amount of time, energy, and, perhaps, money was committed to the group experience. As they explore their ambivalence about ending, members often become willing to look at other endings with energy and courage, knowing that they have done all that they can and there comes a time when one must move forward.

Several authors (Garvin, 1981; Fox, Nelson, and Bolman, 1969; Shapiro, 1980) assert that clients who experience termination successfully will be more likely to transfer the learning from the helping relationship to other life situations, to enter into other helping relationships when the need arises, and to remember the helping experience with positive feelings rather than with guilt and anger. Facilitators, who themselves will have feelings about the ending of the group, need to be aware of the importance of helping the group deal with issues that the facilitator may find painful or awkward.

When the group experience is generally a positive one and all members terminate simultaneously, the facilitator's tasks include helping the group evaluate itself in relation to its goals, exploring feelings about termination, encouraging members to use the gains from the group experience in different circumstances, and referring clients to new services if they need them (Garvin, 1981). Clearly, several sessions will be necessary to enable members to work on their own issues and the group's experience of drawing to a close. The facilitator should prepare the group for termination issues by mentioning periodically during the life of the group the amount of time remaining before the last session. As the last four sessions approach, the facilitator might ask members what it feels like to anticipate the ending of the group. The facilitator should not be surprised if the group members fail to pick up on this invitation, for they are likely to resist ending, preferring instead to remain absorbed in the issues they bring to the group. The facilitator will need to ask members about their reluctance to discuss the inevitable ending of the group, perhaps volunteering some personal feelings about the meaning of the ending for the facilitator. Such modeling may encourage members to share their thoughts.

The facilitator now has an ideal opportunity to ask the group members to discuss what they have gained from the group, particularly as it relates to the initial goals of the group (Mann, 1967). Although the facilitator may have some fairly clear ideas of the gains the group has made, it is important to "start where the client is" and to ask group members about the gains that have been important to them. In some cases, the group members may reveal what they especially valued or found irritating about the facilitator. During this period, group members also can give and receive feedback about their own roles and behaviors that contributed to the group's success in reaching its goals. Most members probably had some latent goals, separate from the goals of the group, and they may choose this time to share their satisfaction in meeting such goals. For example, a group member may have used discussion with the group to gain enough confidence to assert herself with her physician and, as a result, may feel that her medical needs are being attended to more satisfactorily. Another member may have come to the group, as many infertile people do, feeling that there was something "wrong" with her for feeling so intensely angry about the loss of control that infertility causes. Hearing her feelings validated by other group members may have enabled her to feel less alone in her feelings of being out of control and, further, may have helped her find new ways of channeling her anger in constructive directions. The sharing of gains helps members feel that their time in the group has been productive.

The facilitator will want to challenge the group members to think ahead to when they will no longer be meeting as a group, to anticipate ways to consolidate the gains they have made, and to meet any new difficulties that their infertility may present. In addition, the facilitator may want to remind group members that new behaviors will need to be practiced to prevent the temptation to regress to familiar, less productive behaviors under stress. The facilitator also may want to warn the group members that it will not be easy for them to use their new knowledge and skills in other environments. Doctors may be uncomfortable with assertive patients; partners may resist new patterns of interaction; co-workers may continue to be insensitive, in spite of efforts to modify their behavior. Some members of the group may decide to remain in contact with other group members in order to have someone to turn to for a fresh perspective when pressures about infertility mount. Although each group member will have unique issues as the infertility struggle continues, the facilitator can encourage members to share with the group their forthcoming challenges and the ways that the support group may have prepared them to respond to potential concerns.

The facilitator will recognize the need for some members to work on infertility issues after the group ends. Some members may want to begin therapy to examine personal issues that perpetuate their difficulties in grappling with infertility. Some may find that continuing contact with a local RESOLVE chapter is sufficient for their needs. Others may decide to pursue medical treatment and may need a referral to an appropriate facility. Still others may decide to investigate or pursue adoption; the facilitator can help them in making initial contacts and can suggest helpful reading material. Many communities have support groups of adoptive parents, which prospective adoptive parents are welcome to join. The facilitator should be sensitive to the reluctance that many group members will have in following through on referrals. They can be helped by the group to verbalize their expectations and apprehensions about referral services. If members anticipate barriers in gaining the desired service (such as waiting lists, age, financial pressures, or travel), the group can help the member decide how to deal with such barriers. Members of the group who already have used similar services may be able to suggest helpful coping strategies.

Although not all members will need aid in connecting with referral services, they all can be helped to anticipate future months without the group's ongoing support. The facilitator may want to space out the last three or four group meetings, so that group members have ample opportunity to try out new ways of coping and time to report back to the group their successes and frustrations.

Many groups have a special ritual or ceremony at their last group meeting. This idea may come from the group itself;

if not, it can be suggested by the facilitator. When members have acknowledged the many emotions surrounding termination and have worked hard, investing much of their energy into the group, the ritual offers an opportunity for lightheartedness and sociability. It also enables the group to end with warm memories of its last time together. The group may choose to meet in a member's home or in a restaurant, a group picture may be taken, and there may be a short speech by the facilitator or final remarks by group members. The planning of the ending ritual should be shared to ensure that it represents the needs of the group.

Termination sometimes is complicated by negative feelings about the group. Members may look forward with relief to the termination of the group and may express their dissatisfaction with the group's lack of progress toward its goals. The work of the facilitator under these circumstances is challenging. First of all, he will want to ask for specific reasons for the group's failure. These reasons may be administrative, interpersonal, or process related. Both the facilitator and the group may be able to learn how to avoid similar difficult group experiences in the future. The facilitator also will want to be sure that all the reasons for the group's difficulties are explored, since members may try to scapegoat one person or seize on only one cause. Even difficult experiences have valuable elements, though, and members should be encouraged to identify some positive aspects of the group experience—a particularly meaningful discussion, a helpful relationship, or new and useful information.

The above discussion focuses on termination in closed groups with fixed memberships and clear time limits. In open groups—those meeting indefinitely and with fluctuating memberships—people join and leave in accordance with their needs. Yet all members have gained from and contributed to the life and learning of the group, and each member's departure therefore should be attended to by the group. When termination goes unrecognized, the departing members wonder whether their presence has been important to others and whether they will be missed. A member's impending departure provides an opportunity for the remaining members to express their feelings of gratitude and loss. The departing member can be encouraged to express the meaning of the group experience in his life, thereby bringing closure to that person's experience while offering hope to continuing members about what the group could come to represent for them.

Termination in an infertility support group is a crucial process for the consolidation of gains by group members. Struggling with the ongoing challenges of infertility, members may find the ending of the group both symbolically and realistically painful. Since one of the greatest challenges in infertility, however, is to move on and look ahead, the sensitive termination of a support group can contribute dramatically to its members' readiness to see in endings the promise of new beginnings.

7

Helping Clients Cope
with Ongoing Sources of Stress

Infertile individuals must spend much of their time and energy
undergoing medical workups and treatments, engaging in anticipatory mourning, becoming familiar with the literature on infertility, and deciding how much or what to communicate to others
about their infertility. Some people handle the stress of infertility more smoothly than others, but particular issues seem especially troublesome for almost all infertile couples. Although
many infertile individuals will not spontaneously raise these
issues, new opportunities for relief from the stress of the infertility experience arise when the professional addresses them.

Self-Nurturing

The emotional drain that occurs in infertile people is, in
part, a result of a tremendous output of energy without a cor-
responding input of new stimulation, nurturing, and pampering. In some cases, the unwillingness to indulge oneself stems
from the feeling of unworthiness that plagues some infertile
people. They tell themselves that they will take care of their
own needs once they achieve a pregnancy or a healthy birth,
not realizing that months and perhaps years of striving for this
goal without replenishing vital energy will take a terrible toll.

I went for a whole year without buying any new
clothes because I was convinced that the next arti-

cle of clothing I bought would be a maternity outfit. All the money I saved by not buying clothes I
tucked away so that I could use it to buy a really
spiffy maternity wardrobe when I became pregnant. To dip into that money now would be an ac-
knowledgment that our infertility is going to be a
long struggle, and I'm just not able to handle that
yet.

The helping professional must encourage the infertile individual to structure the infertility experience so that it does
not take total control. The individual can balance the anticipated stress by consciously nurturing herself. For example, she
can make a wish list of activities that she enjoys (or would like
to try) regardless of whether they seem reasonable to assimilate
into her current lifestyle. Next, she can be asked to indicate
how often she engages in that activity and how often she would
like to do so. Then she should list the barriers that prohibit her
from enjoying the activity to the desired extent. Many individuals are reluctant even to think about enjoying themselves for fear
of undermining their efforts to resolve their infertility. The helping professional needs to explore with them the assumption that
they will become fertile more quickly if they deny themselves
pleasure. They can also be reminded that self-nurturing can provide more energy for facing life and for pursuing the battle with
infertility. When asked directly whether they actually want infertility to consume so much of their time and energy, most
individuals gratefully acknowledge that they would welcome a
respite from its unrelenting grip. It is at this point that the
wish list becomes a meaningful task.

The wish list not only helps individuals infuse new energy
into their personal lives; it also can instill new vigor into the
couple's relationship. Some couples find that they are tempted
to talk incessantly about their infertility when they are together. Even when they are not discussing it, the presence of literature, basal body thermometers, ovulation kits, medications, and
other reminders make them feel that they cannot escape from
their infertility to enjoy life as a couple. The helping profession-

al can encourage them to include some items on the wish list that represent individual activities and some that focus on the enjoyment of the couple together.

In order for these pleasurable activities actually to accomplish their intended purpose, the helping professional may want to put clear limits on the ways that the couple allow infertility to intrude on their lives. One way is to ask the couple to designate a certain part of the house as the only place where they may talk about infertility issues. They may not choose their bedroom or any other place that is specifically associated with pleasurable activities (such as the kitchen). Keeping their infertility discussions physically limited will have several payoffs for the couple. First, these discussions will no longer consume their leisure time and monopolize their relationship. Second, they will be forced to focus on their discussion and will be aware that this discussion will be time limited, since they are unlikely to want to remain in that room endlessly. Third, they can have fun and develop other aspects of their relationship when they are not in their "infertility room." Last, and perhaps more abstractly, using a specific room represents the establishment of some control over their lives and forces the intrusive issue of infertility to be put into a perspective that allows the couple to move forward with life.

If it is an individual, rather than a couple, who needs to set limits on being preoccupied with infertility, the professional may suggest time constraints as well. Once an individual knows that he can count on time in a given day to deal with infertility issues, he is usually able to postpone thinking or talking about infertility until there is access to the specified environment. Of course, thoughts about infertility still will occur from time to time, but detailed thoughts can usually be held off until later. There will always be some exceptions, however, that the individual and the helping professional need to anticipate; these include visits to the physician and the feelings that ensue, lunch with a sympathetic friend, trips to the library to gather literature on infertility, and unpredictable stressors such as the announcement of a friend's pregnancy or the birth of a baby. The purpose here is to help couples and individuals develop strategies to manage the impact of infertility on their lives while, at the same time, giving strong encouragement to ways to emotionally replenish their spirits, scarred by the infertility battle, and muster the energy necessary to forge ahead with whatever opportunities life holds.

Vacations

Vacations need not be in the Caribbean or on the ski slopes. The kind of vacation that the helping professional needs to encourage the infertile couple to take is a vacation from their infertility. Despite the reminders in the home environment (many of which can be put out of sight), the couple may need to be urged to take time off from their quest for fertility in order to regain perspective and to renew their energy for future decisions or treatments. During this time off, they are to stay away from doctors, medications, temperature charts, counselors, discussions or books on infertility, and, in general, all efforts expended on infertility-related concerns.

Most couples have never considered that they can choose to take a vacation from their infertility; and when such a vacation is suggested by the helping professional, they may want to take a few weeks or months to consider just how they would arrange it. They might choose to time it so that it corresponds with an actual vacation, or they might find it a welcome respite in the midst of an existence that seems to be controlled by doctors' appointments, temperature charts, scheduled sex, and test results. In any case, the professional and the couple together can weigh the potential risks and benefits of such a vacation before deciding how or whether such relief would enable the couple to gain a new perspective on their life.

Actually, our doctor ordered us to take our first vacation. I had a low-grade infection that was affecting my sperm production, and Janet was being treated for the infection as well. The doctor said she didn't want to see us for two months, and we used that time to distance ourselves from our infertility. We actually learned to relax and have fun again, once there wasn't anything we could do to improve our fertility over those two months. The two months are history now, but we've been careful to remember that having fun can be possible in the midst of the infertility struggle. We've even resolved to take a one-month vacation from our infertility treatments later this year, as a way of guarding against letting infertility take over our lives altogether.

Holidays

Holidays assume a bittersweet poignance for the infertile person. On the one hand, they are times for setting aside the usual day-to-day concerns in favor of special celebration, often with family or loved ones. On the other hand, celebration is often difficult for the individual who feels that the one thing worth celebrating has been denied and who encounters young children, infants, and pregnant women at holiday celebrations—visual reminders of what the individual wants but cannot have.

Holidays also serve as the markers of a year passing by. Many couples and individuals say quietly to themselves, "By this holiday next year, maybe we'll have a baby to love," and then, as the holiday passes without a pregnancy or a healthy birth, the feelings of defeat flood in, ruining any hopes for a happy holiday. Some individuals remember earlier, happier holidays before their infertility was diagnosed, and the contrast reminds them poignantly of the depth of their sadness.

Some holidays have symbolic significance for childbearing: the symbol of Madonna and child at Christmas, not to mention the attention that children receive at this time of the year; the focus during Hanukkah on rededicating ideals; the family gatherings on Mother's Day and Father's Day, with attention and cards showered on the parent of the day; the holiday of Passover, with its story of the Angel of Death passing over the homes of Jewish children; and the Passover Seder, which has special rituals for the children. Other holidays are painful for other reasons: Halloween, with its hordes of cavorting children ringing doorbells; Valentine's Day, where somehow even the expressions of love are not enough to take away the heartache of infertility; and Thanksgiving, when families gather to express gratitude for life's blessings.

The infertile person is likely to experience a variety of reactions to holidays, with some eliciting stronger emotional responses than others. In discussing holidays with infertile people, the helping professional initially wants to determine whether infertility causes a particular holiday to be perceived differently than in the days before infertility. Discussions about the sources of pain, whether symbolic, familial, or otherwise, will enable the infertile person to understand issues that must be confronted and dealt with. Several suggestions offered by Jody Earle, past president of RESOLVE of Central New York, may be appropriate once the underlying issues have been elicited.

1. Have the infertile person do something very special just for herself, just for the delight of it. Indulge in a favorite hobby, a good book, a visit with a special person, a yearned-for purchase. The emphasis here is on pampering oneself without needing to think about the needs or expectations of others.

2. In the midst of pampering, the couple should remember to take time out for themselves as a couple. Too often infertility has the capacity to drive a wedge between partners—a wedge that takes time and effort to pry out. During a holiday period, when memories of happier days come to mind, the couple may find that they are more amenable to sharing both the pain and the joy of their lives together, rather than suffering in emotional isolation.

3. Recognize that holidays are for relatives too. Gatherings necessitate "good performances," and no one enjoys bad times. So the couple should be encouraged to make holiday visits at the times that are least difficult. It may be important to forewarn relatives, in advance or early in a visit, in order to eliminate hurtful comments. During visits, the couple should

feel entitled to assert themselves and establish ground rules to avoid continuing annoyances.

4. Individuals and couples might be encouraged to do something for others, rather than wallowing in self-indulgent misery. Perhaps giving holidays gifts to people who would least expect them can bring feelings of reciprocal happiness into relationships that have not been cultivated recently.

5. Since the holidays can be a source of emotional pain, individuals should acknowledge that pain without becoming overwhelmed by it. Having a good cry, discharging angry energy, or just taking time to sort out the source of the pain can be productive, as long as those efforts are time limited and not a perpetual preoccupation.

6. Individuals should be encouraged to initiate and perpetuate holiday traditions that evoke pleasure. It is the familiarity with tradition that comforts and consoles. Clinging to little customs can offer reassurance that, in the midst of uncertainty, some things are certain.

7. Setting some goals for the new year can be invigorating for individuals who cling to feelings of helplessness and loss of control. The new resolutions should involve a willingness to find a new perspective and relinquish some dreams. Resolutions should be small, manageable, and rewarding to work toward; otherwise, the familiar feelings of defeat will return.

8. Individuals can be helped to recognize that no one experiences our romanticized idea of the holidays. Holidays are too loaded to be perfect, and even fertile people experience tremendous feelings of letdown as they realize that holidays are often far more fulfilling in anticipation than in reality.

9. Sometimes a couple will benefit from the encouragement to make a dramatic change of pace at holiday time. Perhaps they would like to have the holiday meal at their home this year, rather than being the guests; or maybe the anticipation of getting away to a balmy beach or a ski lodge appeals more than the prospect of a holiday stifling in its traditions. In any case, couples need to feel entitled to do those things that will bring them pleasure, rather than doing what others expect of them.

Sexual Relations

The strain that infertility introduces into the sexual relationship is common among infertile couples. Some will feel able to raise this issue with a helping professional; others will be more comfortable being asked the extent to which it is a problem for them. All couples are likely to feel reassured that this is not a unique problem for them but, rather, that most infertile couples experience sexual stress from several sources. One source of stress is the gradual recognition that procreation rather than sexual pleasure is the goal of most efforts at lovemaking. Therefore, the couple may abandon sexual relations except when the woman is ovulating; the male may feel such pressure to perform that he becomes temporarily impotent; and any events that threaten to separate the couple when the woman will be ovulating may have to be canceled. It is understandable that resentment begins to build in subtle ways as sexual spontaneity is abandoned in favor of maximizing the possibility of conception.

A second source of stress is the imagined presence of others in the bedroom. Since many couples keep charts that include basal body temperature, cervical mucus viscosity, and occasions on which intercourse is performed, they begin to feel as though their gynecologist is peering over the bedpost to make sure that they are attending to babymaking on schedule. Conscious of the judgmental eye of their physician, couples may even chart occasions of intercourse when, in fact, no sex has occurred. During medical visits, the questions about body positions, frequency of intercourse, and female body posture after intercourse can cause the couple to feel that their capacity to make love is being examined under a microscope—hardly a stimulus to passion!

A third source of stress for some couples is the demise of their sexual self-esteem as their infertility persists. This association of sexuality with fertility is rooted in earlier experiences—often memories carried over from adolescence, when sexual myths were taken seriously and never quite discarded, even though the individual knows better intellectually. Discussing sexual self-esteem openly can be a helpful experience for the couple, since it is likely that these feelings have been carefully guarded during the tension of their infertility.

One couple, Jennifer and Dan, were encouraged by their counselor to discuss their mutual dissatisfactions with their sexual relationship.

Dan: Jennifer seems to get so moody and depressed at the end of the day that I try to hug her to comfort her, but I don't initiate sex because I don't want to put any demands on her while she's so sad.

Jennifer: When Dan treats me platonically night after night, I can't help thinking how unattractive I must have become in his eyes. Not only has infertility robbed me of a baby, but it's robbed me of good sex as well! Sure I'm sad, but I'm not asexual! If he would only be open to a sexual relationship, we might get some vitality back into our lives again.

Clearly, the counselor would want to help Dan and Jennifer sort out more carefully the messages they intend to communicate, as opposed to the mistaken meanings each attaches to the other's behaviors. At the outset, the counselor should ask them to speak directly to each other, rather than to the counselor. In addition, each partner should be encouraged to use "I" messages, as described in Chapter Five, rather than second-guessing one another. The counselor also can encourage them to state their needs clearly instead of assigning blame. When these new "rules" of couple communication are observed, a revised view of the earlier scenario might look like this:

Dan: Jennifer, I hold and comfort you, but I don't initiate sex any more because I'm not sure whether you're interested in more than hugs. Are you?

Jennifer: I know I'm often sad, Dan, but part of my sadness is feeling that you think of me as sexually undesirable. It would really make me feel more alive if we could have some good lovemaking again. I've assumed

>   you've been avoiding me because you're not attracted
>   to me anymore. Have you felt that way?
>
> *Dan:*   Hell, no! I adore you, but I've felt so confused about
>   what I could do to comfort you. If making love
>   would feel good to you, I'm all for it too!

The helping professional cannot banish all the threats that infertility presents to a fulfilling sexual relationship, but a number of efforts can be made to help the couple come to terms with their bedroom demons. First, simply the act of bringing sexual issues into the open can be immensely freeing for the couple. They need the professional's reassurance that they are not sexually maladjusted but, rather, are responding as many infertile couples do to the strains that infertility puts on sex. The professional may want to encourage the couple to acknowledge the very real pressure they feel when the woman is ovulating and to examine why they have difficulty giving and experiencing sexual pleasure at other times of the month. Perhaps they do not feel entitled to such pleasure as long as they are unsuccessful in conceiving a baby, or perhaps guilt over sexual enjoyment causes them to view procreation as the only valid purpose of lovemaking; sometimes the very act of making love is emotionally painful because it reminds the couple of their repeated failure to achieve a pregnancy. In any case, when these issues are explored, individuals can begin to understand their behavior more clearly and may be able to continue such discussions between themselves if sexual fulfillment becomes difficult.

The helping professional also may want to encourage the couple to be innovative about their sexual practices as a way to offset the sexual monotony that can arise from purposeful lovemaking. In addition to encouraging the couple to introduce fun, humor, renewed passion, and experimentation into their lovemaking, the professional should also remind the couple that orgasm and intercourse are not necessary components of lovemaking. Clearly, at the time of the woman's ovulation, the couple will feel compelled to have intercourse to maximize the possibilities of conceiving, but this pressure need not characterize

every sexual encounter. The intimacy that comes from caress-
ing, cuddling, manual stimulation, and physical closeness can be
viewed by the couple as an extended dimension of their lovemaking, and a valid end in itself, rather than as a prelude to
more active sex.

Depression in one or both partners may interfere signifi-
cantly with libido. While the helping professional will need to
be certain that the couple or individual is dealing with that depression through therapy, it is also useful to recognize that the
depression may represent repressed anger or feelings of helplessness. Encouraging the individual to recognize the anger and
to express it can be very therapeutic—particularly since the anger may otherwise be expressed over matters that have little or
nothing to do with infertility, the real source of the anger. Tensions in the relationship, at work, and in other social roles may
signify an inability or an unwillingness to face the pain of the
infertility and the anger that is associated with such pain. The
helping professional may be able to help the individual actively deal with depression once the anger is correctly identified
as stemming from the infertility.

The feelings of helplessness that underlie depression can
be handled in a variety of ways. If the helplessness is associated
with feelings of being overwhelmed, the professional can help
the individual sort out the many problems that are present and
deal with them on a task-by-task basis. The professional also can
provide resources, such as reading material or access to a support group. If the helplessness is associated with a feeling that
the individual can do nothing to affect the course of the infertility, this feeling should be carefully explored. The individual
may need to learn some assertiveness skills to communicate his
needs more clearly to medical staff.

If, in fact, the individual can do nothing beyond being
dependent on medical staff for treatment, the helping professional can encourage the individual to participate actively in all
decision making. Also, the professional can assess whether the
couple want to consider other ways of starting a family. If the
couple choose to pursue their infertility treatment, the professional will want to be sensitive to viewing their infertility as a

chronic condition, as discussed in Chapter Three. If they are ready to consider other options, material on decision making, such as that found in Chapter Eight, may be useful as a guide for discussions.

Emotional Isolation

Most individuals who cope with infertility express their sense of emotional isolation at various times. This aloneness may be felt in relationship to one's partner, family, friends, or other infertile people.

> I'm so sick of being infertile! It's not enough that my infertility occupies all my waking hours, but even when I try to go out to have fun my friends are forever asking me how the treatments are going, whether we've considered adoption, and how I'm feeling. I guess I should be glad to have friends who care, but these days it just reminds me that everyone relates to me as an infertile person.

Involvement with a helping professional can reduce such isolation because it encourages the individual to communicate openly about feelings that she cannot otherwise easily express and because the professional may be able to suggest ways to reduce or eliminate the emotional barriers that separate the individual from others.

Isolation from one's partner can be minimized if one learns to be clear and assertive about communicating needs, as presented in Chapter Five. Two areas of difficulty, however, are commonly faced by infertile couples. One partner (usually the female) often tries to protect her partner from the magnitude of her emotional pain because in the past he has retreated, either physically or emotionally, from her presence whenever she expressed that pain. This pattern needs to be explored for the messages behind the actions. Ideally, the partners should tell each other what messages they attached to the other's behavior and why they reacted as they did. If only one partner (for instance, the woman) is seeing the helping professional, then she can be encouraged to begin such discussions at home or, if the absent partner is willing, to have him come to some meetings with the professional, to discuss the emotional isolation in their relationship. The professional could begin such a discussion as follows:

Professional: Lorraine, could you discuss with Jim why you are so reluctant to let him see your tears and your desperation?

Lorraine: I guess I'm afraid to.
(silence)

Professional: Jim, maybe you could find out from Lorraine more about her fear.

Jim: Why are you afraid to let me know that you've been crying? I know I may not be much good at cheering you up, but I don't want you to go into hiding each time you need to cry.

(silence)

Professional: Lorraine, I hear Jim saying that he is willing for you to share your tears with him, even though he feels helpless to comfort you.

Lorraine: But, Jim, I keep remembering what you said before we were married about hoping I didn't turn into a loony like my mother.

Jim: Look, your mother's a different situation altogether. Her alcoholism has made her impossible for the whole family to be around. There's a big difference in my book between someone who drowns her sorrow in a bottle and someone who has a good cry when things get to be too much.

Lorraine: You mean I can cry and you won't start comparing me to my mother?

Jim: Absolutely! You mean that's what has been keeping you from crying in front of me? I just figured I was such a lousy comforter that you decided to tough it out alone. To tell the truth, it would be easier for me to see you crying than

to see you putting on a happy face even though
your eyes are bloodshot and puffy.

Professional: You've each made good progress at getting to
the heart of an issue that was troubling to both
of you. If you're able to continue this open communication at home, I suspect that Lorraine may
even be able to tell you, Jim, more clearly what
you could do to offer comfort during sad mo-
ments. Could both of you work on that when
you're at home over the next week? We can begin next session by having you tell me what
progress you're making on the issue of comforting.

In these discussions, the unresponsive partner may retreat emotionally because he is unable to relieve his partner's pain. What
he does not realize is that his partner does not expect him to ex-
tinguish the pain. Rather, she hopes that he can offer comfort
in soothing ways, such as by hugging, staying in the room, offering a back rub, or being willing to acknowledge her anguish and
to share any of his own. Too often the emotionally distant partner tries to cheer up his mate, denies that there is any cause for
emotional distress, or ignores her tears altogether as a plea for
togetherness and, instead, responds with feelings of inadequacy
and subsequently retreats. Once the emotionally demonstrative
partner can communicate clearly the meaning of her tears and
indicate how she would like her partner to respond, the couple
can begin to come together emotionally.

Emotional isolation also can occur when one partner has
a strong desire to conceive a baby and the other does not. This
pattern is common when one partner has had a child or children in a previous relationship and does not have the same need
to build a family; it occurs in relationships where one of the
pair is hesitant to undertake the responsibility that raising a
child entails or when one partner feels fulfilled in life without
children, whereas the other perceives a void and wants to fill it
with a child.

There is more at stake here than emotional isolation.

When this discrepancy in life hopes emerges, there is a profound threat to the security of the relationship itself. Since only the partner who wants a family is likely to seek the help of a professional at this time, the whole task of couple communication becomes very difficult. If possible, the absent partner should be encouraged to come in, so that the couple can be helped in communicating needs and goals, both individually and as a pair. If one partner is firmly opposed to beginning a family, the other partner will ultimately need to evaluate which is more important: the relationship or the need to have children. If the relationship is important enough to preserve at the expense of building a family, the partner who wants children will need to be encouraged to mourn the loss that has been endured, to be careful that anger over the loss does not emerge in disruptive ways in the relationship, and to find other ways to fill the void created by the lack of children. This is complex emotional work and is likely to take months of careful exploration and expression of emotions.

If, on the other hand, the decision is to leave the partner who is unwilling to build a family, in the hope of finding a more satisfying relationship with someone who wants children, different complexities surface. Here the mourning process will encompass not only the deferred dreams of trying to have a child but also the loss of a partner and all the hopes that had been invested in that relationship. Clearly, there are no guarantees that the person will be able to find a new relationship in which building a family is a shared and realistic goal. In addition, if infertility is a problem for the partner who leaves the relationship, there is the additional burden of worrying whether that will interfere with family-building efforts with another partner. There is also the concern that infertility may make one less desirable as a mate, especially if the prospective partner is someone who has a strong need for birth children.

When emotional isolation occurs because of one partner's lack of enthusiasm for childrearing, the more child-oriented partner needs to determine whether this lack of enthusiasm will block the couple's efforts to pursue a workup and treatment for their infertility and, if pregnancy does occur, whether the responsibilities of childrearing will fall inordinately on one partner, while the other continues to pursue those activities that currently provide fulfillment. It is usually difficult for a couple to anticipate the many ways in which having a child could change their lives; therefore, the professional should help the couple examine their attitudes about family building and the stability of their relationship.

Social and Work Relationships

Since infertility often is not openly discussed, and since many friends and co-workers who learn about a couple's infertility are either awkward or insensitive in their comments, the couple may begin to feel socially isolated from fertile people. This social isolation may extend to complete strangers, as the couple find themselves avoiding any contact with pregnant women, families with infants and small children, maternity shops, toy stores, and other reminders of the joys that they want but cannot have (Lalos and others, 1985a). They also find sources of friction in their extended families, where adult siblings may be easily achieving pregnancies and drawing familial attention to new babies and away from the sadness of the infertile couple (Mazor, 1984). Parents and in-laws may give well-meaning but inappropriate advice, which the couple construe as a message to "try harder," when they believe that they have exhausted all available forms of medical help. Families are sometimes unable to understand the infertile couple's wish to avoid painful events, such as christenings, baby showers, children's birthdays, and celebrations over the announcement of a relative's pregnancy. The isolation and misunderstanding of family and friends increase the couple's sense of defectiveness at a time when they most need support and acceptance (Mahlstedt, 1985).

Among fertile friends, the couple's feelings of isolation are perpetuated when social talk turns to topics related to pregnancy and childrearing or when social gatherings inevitably include pregnant women, infants, and small children. These reminders of their shattered hopes and dreams are extremely painful for many infertile people; and, although they may choose to avoid their fertile friends altogether, what they receive in exchange is a feeling of being different and alone in their grief. Conversely, some infertile individuals make efforts to increase their level of contact with children and young people, in part as a way of satisfying their wish to nurture and in part to make up for the disappointment they feel in their personal lives.

Work relationships, too, are affected by a couple's infertility. Many individuals complain that they are unable to concentrate on their work because their sadness threatens to overwhelm them in the workplace. In interviews with thirteen infertile couples, Leitko and Greil (1985) report that involuntary childlessness increases worry about work, especially for men. Male respondents claimed that they were distracted from their work by conflicts and pressures at home revolving around childlessness, infertility treatment, and adoption. Others complained about the expense of treatment and adoption. Still others noted that having to take time off for treatment for themselves or their wives would hurt their job performance or bring to the attention of their co-workers a physical problem that they would prefer to keep to themselves.

Listening to co-workers exchanging complaints about everyday problems can be irritating to the infertile person, who views these complaints as petty in comparison to the emotional pain of infertility.

> It kills me to hear my friends complain about their babies' colic, millions of diapers, constant fatigue, and trying to get their figures back. I'd give anything to have those problems. They're manageable, but my emptiness isn't.

There are concrete irritants as well, since—as already noted—many individuals must take time away from work for doctors' appointments, sometimes traveling considerable distances and undergoing procedures that may last for days or weeks (Mahlstedt, 1985). For couples who are trying to conceive, there remains the pressure to have intercourse at the time the woman is ovulating, which may conflict with business activities (for example, a scheduled business trip). Women being treated for infertility also must consider whether to postpone making career advances, because they may need to slow down to guard a long-awaited pregnancy (Andrews, 1984). After a period of time grappling with their infertility, many individuals reorganize their priorities so that work and professional concerns no longer are paramount and do not consume the time or attention they once did. On the other hand, some infertile individuals find that their work serves as a cushion against the pain of their infertility and that, even if they cannot be productive in the sense of bearing a child, they are capable of being productive in other spheres of their work lives. However, Leitko and Greil (1985) report that employment is not likely to reduce the emotional distress produced by involuntary childlessness. In some cases, individuals who are working in occupations with pregnant women, infants, or children may find that they need to change their employment to avoid reminders of their pain on a day-to-day basis.

Summary

In both personal and workplace relationships, the infertile individual is likely to encounter a range of pressures and supports and must learn to draw on appropriate resources without being overwhelmed by the pressures. One source of comfort for some infertile couples is the opportunity to meet and share information with other infertile couples. Sometimes these meetings occur informally, sometimes through the availability of a nearby chapter of RESOLVE. Couples find that contact with other infertile people allows them to be open about their emotional pain and to feel accepted and valued by others who, like them, are struggling with the impact of their infertility. The helping professional must be sensitive to the various sources of stress for infertile couples: emotional drain, vacations, holidays, sexual relations, emotional isolation, and problems in the workplace. Infertile couples and individuals are often reluctant to mention these problems because they might reflect poorly on them at a time when their self-esteem is already threatened. The reassurance of the professional that these are common concerns of infertile people will help set the stage for a counseling relationship in which the issues can be explored in more detail. Although infertility may not be the focus nearly as much as the couple's relationship or an individual's coping skills, the professional must keep in mind that the frustration and anger from the inability to have a baby is an ever present dimension of the emotional work that lies ahead.

8

⟫⟩⟫⟩⟫⟩⟫⟩⟫⟩⟫⟩⟫⟩⟫⟩⟫⟩⟫⟩⟫⟩⟫⟩

Helping Clients Handle
Infertility Decisions

Professionals who work with infertile people must guide these individuals and couples through a decision-making process involving highly emotional issues. The professional who is familiar with research on decision making and who appreciates the range of infertility issues requiring decisions can provide strong support as individuals strive to move forward in the infertility struggle.

From the moment that they learn of their infertility until the moment that some resolution to their infertility is reached, infertile couples are constantly forced to make decisions. The decision-making process is complicated by a variety of factors. Thomas (1977, p. 143) cautions that "marital decision making should be undertaken when you are reasonably calm, rested, and clear-headed. Under no circumstances should you try to make decisions when one of you is highly fatigued, sick, in pain, . . . or emotionally upset." Yet, by its very nature, infertility makes it difficult for many couples to feel "calm, rested, and clear-headed." In addition, fatigue and emotional upset are frequent concomitants of the stress that infertility generates. The mourning process that many infertile individuals experience causes a dearth of emotional energy necessary for decision making, thereby placing them at a disadvantage when decisions are required. Couples just learning about the seriousness of their infertility may undergo a crisis period when it is extremely difficult to make decisions. The professional working with infertile individuals must be sensitive to these unique issues when trying to offer support in decision making.

The Professional's Role

A professional attempting to help an individual or a couple reach a decision should be nonjudgmental, just as in psychotherapy. The professional's goal is to elicit the individuals' reasons for their decisions and to help them examine these reasons in the light of their particular circumstances. The professional may need to state at the outset that she has no intention of criticizing or admonishing the individual, no matter what information is disclosed in the process of working toward a decision. Likewise, the professional may need to explain that she will not offer advice or recommendations but will provide information and access to resources that the infertile individual may use in the process of making a decision. In addition, the professional will serve as a guide in the decision-making process, helping the individual or couple process information and feelings in an orderly way.

Janis and Mann (1977, p. 371) suggest a series of questions that the professional must answer to help a person move ahead in the decision-making process.

1. Has the individual thoroughly canvassed a wide range of alternative courses of action?
2. Has the individual surveyed the full range of objectives to be fulfilled by the choice and the values implicated by it?
3. Has the individual carefully weighed whatever he knows about the costs or drawbacks of each alternative, the risks of negative consequences, and the potential for positive consequences?
4. Has the individual intensively searched for new information relevant to further evaluation of the consequences?
5. Has the individual correctly assimilated and

taken account of any new information or expert judgment he has received, even when the information or judgment does not support the course of action he prefers?

6. Has the individual reexamined the positive and negative consequences of all known alternatives, including those originally regarded as unacceptable, before making a final choice?

7. Has the individual made detailed provisions for implementing or executing the chosen course of action, with special attention to contingencies that might be required if various known risks were to materialize?

The purpose of determining the individual's (or couple's) response to the above diagnostic questions is to identify gaps in the existing decision-making effort, to discuss these gaps objectively with the individual, and to stimulate more vigorous efforts to search and appraise. When Hackman and Morris (1975) reviewed a number of experimental studies in which people were asked to engage in problem-solving tasks related to decision making, they found that people seldom took the time to obtain, assimilate, and apply the information available to them but, instead, tended to weigh the pros and cons of the first solution that occurred to them. By encouraging the individual to do a thorough job of information gathering and appraisal, the professional can help the person understand both his personal needs and the available resources.

Janis and Mann (1977, p. 373) have developed an additional set of questions to help determine the specific defects in the individual's search and appraisal activities. These questions enable the professional to explore the risks and consequences anticipated by the individual.

1. Does the individual believe that the risks are serious if he does not change his present course of action?

2. Does the individual believe that the risks are

serious if he does change his present course of
action?
3. Does the individual believe that it is realistic to
hope to find a satisfactory alternative?
4. Does the individual believe that there is sufficient time to search for and evaluate a satisfactory alternative?

These questions help the professional assess the individual's motivation for change. If the individual seems immobilized,
the professional should determine whether intervention in other
ways may be necessary before the individual is ready to tackle
the decisions ahead. For example, if the individual is assessed as
being in crisis, the professional will want first to employ crisis
intervention techniques designed to improve cognitive clarity,
coping capacities, and feelings of self-esteem. If the individual
is mourning one or more of the major losses that infertility presents, the professional will want to be supportive, recognizing
that the individual has little energy left for decision making
prior to the resolution stage.

At some point, the individual probably will feel motivated to move ahead toward a decision. At that time, Janis and
Mann (1977, p. 373) suggest the use of a decisional balance
sheet. The questions that each individual must complete on the
balance sheet pertain to the consequences that the individual
anticipates in the following areas:

1. Gains and losses for self
2. Gains and losses for significant others
3. Self-approval or self-disapproval
4. Social approval or disapproval from significant others

Once the individual has explored these consequences, he becomes aware that the decision is influenced not only by his own
needs and feelings but also by the perceived needs and feelings
of others. Before making a decision, he may first want to discuss with significant others in his life how they are affecting his
efforts to arrive at a satisfactory decision. Open dialogue may

eliminate some concerns, raise others, and ultimately clarify the ways in which a potential decision will affect both the individual and significant others.

Once the infertile individual has completed the balance sheet, the professional should probe further to ascertain whether any considerations have been neglected. The professional should encourage the individual to fill in the balance sheet in all areas and should focus discussion on the categories where there are few or no entries. Often the categories of approval or disapproval from the self and from significant others prove especially challenging. Janis and Mann (1977, p. 379) conducted three field experiments on the effects of using this procedure to induce people to fill out their balance sheets as completely as possible. In all instances, those who completed the balance sheets tended to approve of the decision that they made and to adhere to that decision. Thus, both the decisional balance sheet and the attention by the professional to neglected considerations may hold special promise for infertile people in the process of making decisions that are crucial to their future well-being.

Common Infertility Decisions

Throughout the infertility struggle, numerous decisions must be made. Many are influenced by access to information, resources, and available support. The following are some of the considerations that infertile people face at different stages of their infertility.

Whom to Tell

Most people regard their sexual lives as private and tend not to discuss sexual concerns with others, except possibly a therapist or a physician. When an assessment of infertility has been made, even if a specific diagnosis has not been reached, the individual is forced to rethink the social taboo on disclosure of sexual information. Since there is rarely an association between sexual performance and infertility, the professional might wonder why a person is reluctant to discuss infertility, a medical condition. The individual, however, has suffered a severe blow to self-esteem and, by refusing to discuss the infertility, may be trying to prevent exposure of this damaged self-esteem and also to avoid a nonsympathetic response. If the partners know or suspect who is responsible for the infertility, they may be tempted to assign or assume blame, and they may expect that others would do the same if informed about the infertility.

Also, if the news of infertility is perceived as a crisis, the couple's initial reaction may be denial; discussing it with others might make the pain more real. Even when individuals can say logically that they are facing a medical problem, few can discuss their infertility as easily as their gall bladder condition. As mentioned, some may be reluctant to discuss it for fear that it will be greeted with an insensitive remark, whether based on lack of information or on sheer rudeness. People who are infertile rarely are willing or able to educate uninformed friends; they are too busy attending to their own feelings of emotional isolation, wishing desperately that someone could understand their pain. In this era of preoccupation with physical health, some infertile individuals think that others may view them as damaged and will treat them differently, either by being oversolicitous or by avoiding contact altogether. Some fear being cross-examined about what has been done to correct the infertility and then offered a variety of well-meaning, but thoroughly unwelcome, suggestions. Infertile people constantly worry about whether the course of action they are taking is the best one, and additional suggestions can produce feelings of intense resentment.

The motivation to tell about one's infertility usually can be traced to the person's need for support. The professional can help the person identify friends, family members, or clergy who would be attentive to the individual's emotional needs. In some cases, the individual feels pressured to offer an explanation—for example, to give an employer a specific reason for numerous absences because of medical appointments. The professional can help the person rehearse an explanation and anticipate potential responses from the employer. Similar dilemmas may occur when the individual wants to decline an invitation to a baby shower, or to answer the question "And how many children do you have?" from a new acquaintance, or to change the subject when a friend persists in sharing details of her pregnancy. The individual would prefer not to raise the issue but feels that her behavior requires an explanation, however brief.

Those wishing to avoid disclosure of their infertility will be able to do so for an interminable time if they are determined to keep this information secret. However, the professional may want to help them examine the benefits and disadvantages of this secretive stance. If the couple rely totally on each other to meet the emotional needs generated by their infertility, they may be placing a tremendous burden on their relationship. Unless the social and familial support network is completely devoid of empathic individuals, the infertile person is being cheated of the opportunity to receive support and encouragement during a difficult time. In addition, countless infertile people who do decide to mention their infertility are surprised to learn that friends and relatives have the same problem. In some situations, an infertile person may gain initial comfort from attending a RESOLVE meeting, where one can choose to be an observer rather than a participant. Exposure to other infertile people who share many of the same challenges may enable the person to disclose information gradually in a setting where infertility is well understood.

What to Tell

Once the person has decided to disclose information about his infertility, the next decision is what to tell. Infertile people are afraid that their infertility may turn other people off, bore them, or cause them to feel pity. So, even when comfortable with sharing information, individuals may be cautious about what to disclose. For example, one couple pursuing artificial insemination by donor (AID) feared that any child they conceived would be viewed differently if it were known that the sperm had come from a donor. In this case, the couple decided to discuss the emotional pain of their infertility with friends and relatives but did not share the diagnosis or information about the treatment being pursued. In other situations, the details of the treatment may seem too personal for an individual to want to disclose, but he may still feel able to ask for emotional support. The professional needs to be alert to individuals who feel pressure from friends to share more than they are ready to discuss. Some rehearsal of past discussions with assertive responses may prove helpful. The professional may also need to elicit from some individuals their concern that they are "wearing out" their support network of friends and relatives. It may be highly appropriate for the infertile person to ask friends directly about their continuing tolerance for the ups and downs of the infertility struggle; in addition, the infertile person may benefit from being reminded that friendship is reciprocal and that he may feel more ready to lean on friends if he is able to extend himself in helpful ways as friends' needs become apparent.

Whether to Pursue Treatment

An infertility workup may end with a diagnosis that requires one or both members of the couple to enter medical treatment. Since their infertility is now confirmed by medical professionals as a serious barrier to their being able to conceive, the couple may experience this time as a crisis for which past coping mechanisms have not prepared them. Denial, confusion, and emotional stress may be among their reactions, and they may feel especially unable to make decisions at this time. Unless the diagnosis includes some life-threatening factors, or unless age is a pressing consideration, the couple can be reassured that there is no immediate need to rush into a decision, and the professional can concentrate instead on helping both members sort out their feelings and reactions to the diagnosis and treatment recommendations. After they have had a chance to process their reactions and develop some informal support systems in addition to the professional, they can then explore the risks and potential consequences of the recommended treatment. Some couples may seek a second opinion to be more certain that the recommended treatment is indeed considered the best course of action. Other couples may go to the library, to RESOLVE meetings, or back to their physician, for answers to the following questions:

1. What are the potential side effects of any recommended medication? For how long would this medication be continued before another form of treatment is considered? How costly is the medication? How is it administered? What is its success rate in people with conditions like mine?

2. If surgery is recommended, what are the risks? How frequently does the physician perform this surgery? What are his or her rates of success with this procedure? Are there other physicians who specialize in this procedure? If so, what are their names and the clinics where they do their work? After surgery, what is the anticipated postoperative course of recovery? How much of this time will be spent in the hospital? At home? When can one expect to resume normal activities again? What costs are associated with the surgical procedure? To what extent will any of these costs be covered by insurance? Is this surgical procedure the last hope, or are there other medical interventions if a pregnancy is not conceived? Could any adhesions from the operation further contribute to the individual's infertility?

3. If both members of the couple need medical treatment, what sequence of treatment is advised? Is an effort being made to do the least intrusive treatments first? How much time should elapse between recommended treatments?

The couple also should ask their physician to outline an anticipated schedule for the next twelve to eighteen months, so that they are aware of the treatment plan and time frame involved.

The helping professional will want to be especially attentive to the previous medical experiences of both partners. Negative medical experiences—fears associated with anesthesia, hospitals, surgery, drug dependency, and pain—should be explored carefully. The apprehensive individual should be helped to gather information to learn what to expect as each form of treatment is undertaken. Part of the decision-making process may need to focus on the differing feelings each partner has about the direction that treatment should take. Reaching resolution of differences can be time consuming, but unless effort is directed to this challenge, the couple may ultimately discontinue treatment because of their own differences and subsequent inability to reach a resolution.

Which Treatment Should Be Pursued?

Artificial Insemination by Husband (AIH). Although artificial insemination with the husband's sperm is a clinical rather than a coital way of achieving a pregnancy, the couple will probably feel both regret and resentment as the medical profession intrudes into the most intimate area of their lives. They may feel that they have failed in the area of sexuality and consequently are not sufficiently virile or feminine, and they probably will react negatively to the mechanical act of the insemination because it is far removed from the more familiar and preferred act of lovemaking. The couple should be informed about the specific insemination procedure and their roles in it. Since there will be tremendous pressure on the male to perform, he should be encouraged to determine in advance what can be done to minimize this pressure. Some males benefit by taking sexually arousing pictures or reading material with them when they must masturbate to produce a semen specimen. In many clinics, the woman can accompany her partner and help him if he so requests.

In some clinics, the male can participate in the insemination; when this is not possible or preferred, the couple may want to reduce the tension with a toast of wine or champagne. The woman will want to know what precautions she should take following the insemination to maximize its chances of success. The professional should be especially sensitive to the couple's tension while waiting to learn whether or not they have conceived.

Artificial Insemination by Donor (AID). Artificial insemination by donor (AID) is used when the male is infertile. Currently, about 10,000 to 20,000 AID children are born in the United States each year. The process has a national success rate of 57 percent (Andrews, 1984, p. 160). Although many of the same feelings of AIH patients are felt by individuals undergoing AID, there are additional dimensions that the professional needs to consider as a couple contemplate this choice (Snowden and Mitchell, 1981; Notman, 1984). A prime concern will be the health of the donor, particularly the reassurance that the sperm bank has carefully tested for sexually transmitted diseases, especially acquired immune deficiency syndrome (AIDS). Another concern will be the extent of the effort to match the physical characteristics of the donor with those of the male partner. Couples can request that the sperm of a particular donor be frozen, so that any future children conceived through AID will have the same genetic heritage and some of the same physical characteristics. It is relevant to ask the physician how many pregnancies any one donor is allowed to create. The concern here is that widespread use of a single donor in a limited geographical area could lead to unwitting incest if children of the same donor grow up and marry one another.

Couples may also have some concerns about how prepared the male is to love this child who is not genetically his. If necessary, the professional can explore this issue when concern about physical characteristics arises. Along similar lines, the male may be encouraged to share his feelings about his mate's being pregnant by another man. Catholic or Orthodox Jewish couples will need to come to terms with their religion's prohibition against AID in order to feel less conflicted about the procedure.

Couples will want to ask about the use of frozen sperm. Frozen sperm has both advantages and disadvantages. Unlike fresh sperm, which loses its ability to fertilize after about half an hour, frozen sperm can be tested. Moreover, the use of frozen sperm permits a greater choice of donors or, as mentioned earlier, the option to use the same donor's sperm for future inseminations. There are some uncertainties associated with frozen sperm, however, mostly having to do with the quality of the sperm after freezing. Speculation that the current freezing system will do genetic damage does not seem to have been borne out. Andrews (1984, p. 177) cites an international report that 5,000 children who had been conceived with frozen sperm were just as healthy as children conceived naturally. Currently, the major problem with frozen sperm is that its success rate at achieving pregnancies is about 25 percent less than that of fresh sperm (Andrews, 1984, p. 178). Frozen sperm also has a shorter life span in a woman's reproductive tract than fresh sperm, and doctors who use it must be very accurate in identifying the woman's time of ovulation. To improve accuracy, many clinics now utilize blood tests to measure hormones or ultrasound to measure ovarian follicle size.

In Vitro Fertilization and GIFT. Because of the immense amount of publicity surrounding in vitro fertilization (IVF) and gamete intrafallopian transfer (GIFT) and the growing number of clinics offering these procedures, many couples may consider these options before they have thoroughly researched their suitability. It is best for couples to write various infertility clinics in their geographical area, asking such questions as suggested by Andrews (1984)—for example, "How long has the clinic been offering IVF or GIFT?" "How many couples has the clinic treated?" and "How many successes has the clinic had so far?" Reports in medical journals and at meetings of the American Fertility Society indicate that IVF pregnancies occur 10 to 20 percent of the time—one or two chances in ten. The GIFT procedure has only been in use since 1984, so statistics for most clinics are sparse. In asking about "successes," with both IVF and GIFT, one should specify healthy births, because some clinics report their successes in terms of chemical pregnancies.

It is also important to make sure that the physician does not sterilize the woman by closing her tubes before the IVF procedure. Some doctors advocate this approach, partly because they do not want their patients to suffer through an ectopic pregnancy. But, as Andrews points out, a selfish motivation also is present; if the woman's tubes are surgically closed, she will not be able to conceive naturally. Thus, the doctor can take full credit for any subsequent pregnancy.

The financial costs of IVF and GIFT also must be considered. Most American programs estimate that the couple's medical expenses will be about $5,000 per attempt at IVF. The expenses associated with GIFT vary by clinic; in many cases, they are comparable to the expenses for IVF. Some programs require the couple to agree to make at least four attempts, which increases the financial commitment. Since insurance coverage varies with the carrier, couples will want to do some careful exploration in this area. In addition to the medical costs, there are expenses associated with travel, hotel, food, and lost time from work.

The chances of disappointment are high for the couple using IVF or GIFT (Clapp and Bombardieri, 1984). According to research on fertilization occurring within the body, there is only a 32 percent chance that a baby will result when egg and sperm meet. Of 100 instances when egg meets sperm, in 16 the egg will fail to fertilize, in 15 a fertilized egg will fail to implant, in 27 the embryo will abort before the woman even notices she is pregnant, and, in an additional 10, spontaneous abortion (miscarriage) will occur later. Yet, in viewing IVF or GIFT as their last chance at a birth child, most couples cling to the hope that the procedure will result in conception, and their feelings of emotional letdown can be powerful.

Some couples will want to consider whether—in view of the costliness and the low success rates of IVF or GIFT—adoption might be preferable. The couple with a strong investment in a genetic child or a pregnancy are likely to favor IVF or GIFT over adoption as long as their money holds out and the experience of repeated failures to conceive or carry a pregnancy to term does not prove too stressful. Other couples who favor IVF or GIFT over adoption may be those whom society labels as high achievers; they believe that if they try hard enough, they will succeed. These couples may need help to identify their fear of failure when and if they decide to terminate treatment. They need to examine whether it is a baby they want or proof of their fertility after so many disappointments. Some couples lose sight of their ultimate goal—to become parents—and, instead, become caught up in the importance of conception. The professional will want to explore with these couples at what point they will decide to discontinue IVF or GIFT and what their next step will be. The individuals may need to mourn the loss of the birth child they will never have before being able to move ahead in the decision-making process.

When to Discontinue Treatment

The decision to discontinue treatment can be a wrenching one for couples who had hoped that medical procedures would prove successful. Most couples will carry the fantasy that "one more procedure" might have resulted in a precious pregnancy. The decision to discontinue treatment, therefore, often represents a giving up and, for some couples, a profound sense of failure to persevere long enough to beat the odds stacked against them.

In his book *Quitting: Knowing When to Leave,* Dauten (1980) offers some interesting ideas for people contemplating an end to their infertility treatments. Dauten conceptualizes four elements of success in quitting or predicting the likelihood of termination:

1. Realization of failure: a definitive recognition that events cannot change or be changed
2. Awareness of the future: an understanding that the future will not bring change and increasing openness to new alternatives
3. Selfishness: increasing self-interest in altering one's situation
4. The clean decision: taking control of the above three elements and acting on alternatives with some certainty

Now that they are finally contemplating an end to their quest for a birth child, the couple are likely to feel grief and emotional exhaustion after months of having their hopes raised and then dashed. Mixed with their anger about all the time and money they devoted to their infertility struggle will be confusion about what steps to take next. For couples involved in medical treatment, physicians often provided the guidance regarding procedures and treatments. Now that the couple contemplate ending treatment, they are likely to need guidance as they continue to confront their desire for a baby. If possible, the professional should be available as a source of support during this difficult time. Initially, the partners will need to grieve the loss of the birth child they will never have, and this process will drain them of the energy needed for subsequent decision making. The professional can assure the couple that their grief work is every bit as important for their future as is the decision making that they will ultimately feel ready to undertake. The professional needs to validate the couple's right to grieve, and even to say that decision making will be clearer later if they have been able to put to rest their dreams for a birth child.

In addition to grief, other emotions will emerge with the decision to end treatment. Anger and frustration are common, especially among couples who believe that if one tries hard enough and "does everything right," one can expect to achieve life goals. The individuals often feel somehow defective and suspect that they would be able to have a baby if only they were more dedicated to their infertility treatment. They also may fear that perhaps there is something so terrible about them that they are really unfit to be parents.

There are practical matters to consider as well. During infertility treatments, work schedules are disrupted by medical appointments, financial resources are drained, physical well-being is threatened as medications and surgical procedures take their toll, and life revolves totally around the quest for fertility, forcing other pleasures far into the background. Eventually, couples begin to question whether the quest for a birth child is worth the many sacrifices involved. After months or years of turning themselves over to medical science, they begin to need to reclaim their lives again. The professional can be supportive at this juncture by reminding the couple that they have shown strength in reaching such a decision. This affirmation of their capabilities can help to boost their depleted self-esteem.

What Other Options Should Be Considered?

Surrogate Mothers. With the publicity surrounding Baby M, the infant girl whose surrogate mother decided not to surrender the child after her birth to her genetic father and his wife, many infertile couples are highly sensitive to the risks of using a surrogate mother. Yet, when a woman's uterus and ovaries have been removed or damaged, or when a woman cannot carry a baby to term, surrogate mothering offers the only hope of procreation of a child genetically related to the couple. Surrogate mothering has the advantage over adoption of requiring only a nine-month wait from the time of conception; it also allows the couple some choice over who will carry their child. Couples have the additional advantage of being able to ignore their own biological clock or the age limitations imposed by adoption agencies.

The initial difficulty is finding a surrogate. In some instances, family members or close friends are willing to be inseminated with the husband's sperm and carry the pregnancy to term. Other couples contact former classmates, distant friends, and co-workers, asking whether they know someone who might be willing to serve as a surrogate. Still other couples put advertisements in the classified section of city or campus newspapers. Doctors or lawyers can sometimes be helpful in locating a potential surrogate, and, of course, a growing number of surrogate mother agencies are springing up as the demand for this service increases. No matter what method the couple use to select a surrogate, there are risks. A close friend or a family member may agree to the arrangement without thoroughly examining how she will feel about being pregnant by another man, what it will mean to have the infertile couple vitally involved in and concerned with the pregnancy, and whether she will be ready to surrender the baby to the couple after it is born. Since friends and family are likely to be in touch with the couple after the baby's birth, the capacity of the surrogate and her husband (and children) to see the baby as belonging to the couple must be assessed and discussed.

If the surrogate is not known to the couple, but responds to a classified ad or to an inquiry from someone known to the couple, then there are additional risks: What is her motivation in undertaking a pregnancy for a stranger? How scrupulously will she attend to good prenatal health care? Will she surrender the baby after its birth? Will she intrude in the couple's life as they raise the child she bore?

Salzer (1986, p. 231) suggests several questions that a

couple may want to ask in order to decrease the possibility that the surrogate will refuse to relinquish the baby:

1. What is the surrogate trying to get out of the experience? It is important to explore her motivation and evaluate how sincere she appears in expressing her reasons for becoming a surrogate.
2. How stable is her personal life and how fulfilling is her support system? The more stable her life is and the more supports she has, the greater the likelihood of the contract being upheld.
3. What is the attitude of the surrogate's husband? Her parents and in-laws? If close and influential family members are not supportive of the surrogate arrangement, the surrogate herself may have great difficulty carrying through on her commitment.
4. How reliable does the surrogate appear to be? Is there anything in her history to suggest erratic or irresponsible behavior? It is difficult to predict the future, but a woman with a fairly stable history and a responsible character offers a better gamble.
5. Does the surrogate have children of her own? Some professionals involved with surrogate parenting feel that there are advantages when the surrogate has previously had children. Not only does it ensure that she is aware of what is in store for her regarding the pregnancy and delivery, but it may also make it easier for her to release the baby for adoption if she has a family of her own.

If the couple decide to consult an agency that specializes in matching potential surrogates with infertile couples, they must be aware of the wide range of professionalism and procedures at individual centers. Agency costs can amount to over

$30,000. Rather than choosing a center based on geographical proximity, couples should select a center that has personnel whom they trust. Although professionals should be bound by ethical values and beliefs, some may care more about making money than looking after the best interests of the infertile couple. Couples should feel comfortable in asking questions, in suggesting alternative procedures, and in describing their reactions to the process. They should ask how the surrogates are screened, how matches between the surrogate and a couple are made, how much and what kind of contact with the surrogate is considered beneficial, what psychological and medical screening is done, whether the couple will have access to screening results, what type of counseling is available to the surrogate and couple during the pregnancy, what counseling and support are provided to the surrogate following the birth, and what legal rights and responsibilities the couple and the surrogate (and her spouse) have at each stage of the process.

The couple must also decide how much contact they want with the surrogate. Some agencies believe that there is less stress for everyone involved if there is no contact between couples and their surrogate; other agencies believe that one visit allows the couple and the surrogate to "bond" without the negative stresses that might accompany more prolonged contact. Still other agencies leave the choice up to the parties involved. In some cases, the surrogate has moved in with the couple during the last months of her pregnancy. Although the temptation to become close to the surrogate may be pressing during her pregnancy, the couple should also consider the feelings of obligation that may arise for contact with the surrogate after the baby's birth. While grateful to the surrogate, many couples want the baby to grow up with a strong sense of the couple as its parents. Although some couples are comfortable with continued contact with the surrogate, particularly if she is a close friend or a family member, most prefer not to be reminded of the extraordinary means they had to use to bring this precious baby into their family. The couple will undoubtedly be aware of the surrogate's own need to come to terms with the loss of the baby she carried for nine months, and they should encourage the agency to offer her support during the difficult postpartum weeks. Once the couple know that the surrogate's emotional needs are being acknowledged and validated, they will feel freer to rejoice in their new parenthood.

Couples who use a surrogate must also decide how open to be and with whom. This decision will undoubtedly be closely related to what the couple decide to tell their child later. Many professionals encourage parents to be honest with the child from the beginning and to promote open discussion on the subject of the child's conception and birth. Some parents prefer to say that the child was adopted. Certainly, adoption is a more familiar and less controversial way of bringing a child into the family than is the use of a surrogate, and in this sense it may be easier for everyone to accept. It does, however, ignore the fact that the child is genetically related to the father and his heritage.

Adoption. The decision to adopt is influenced by many factors. As the professional helps the couple assess whether adoption will satisfy their needs to become parents, it is important to ascertain why the couple want a child. They may need to consider carefully whether the loss of such experiences as genetic heritage, pregnancy, childbirth, and breastfeeding will affect their feelings toward adopting a child. Likewise, couples who have viewed the quest for a birth child as some measure of their worth need to explore whether they see adoption as a viable alternative or as "second best." Some couples may have been through years of infertility treatments, assuming that their goal was to have children when, in actuality, it was to become fertile. When asked why they want children or how their lives would be changed by children, some couples may express ambivalence about children, whether adopted or born to them. A former infertility patient who became pregnant several years after treatment, for example, wrote her doctor that she had had an abortion because she and her husband realized that they did not want to be parents after all. She felt better knowing, however, that she had the choice of whether to become a parent or not. This situation, though extreme, is an indication that the quest for fertility can sometimes overshadow other important issues connected with the quest for parenthood.

The decision to adopt a child is far more complex today than it was a generation ago. Today's adoptive parents are likely to have invested a considerable amount of time, money, and emotional energy in infertility workups and treatments, only to decide at some point that they must relinquish their quest for a birth child. For these couples, the possibility of adoption sustains the hope for a baby and, at the same time, presents the reality of long waits, agency evaluations, and the possibility that the baby they adopt will be a child with health problems, an older child, or a child of a different ethnic background from their own. The initial feeling that they are starting over again may cause a couple to feel depressed and angry, especially when confronted with the uncertainties involved in the adoption outcome. After they have made the decision to adopt, most couples want to plunge ahead and often have little patience for the various adoption procedures. In some ways, adoption will remind the couple of the least palatable aspects of their infertility treatments: periodic waits between procedures, the intrusiveness of professionals into personal and private areas of their lives, the haunting feeling that maybe they were not meant to be parents, and, always, the eternal wait for the telephone call with good news.

One decision that couples need to make early in their quest for an adoptive child is how to locate a child. Only the most traditional of clients can limit themselves to agency adoptions. International sources should be investigated as well as independent sources unless they are completely forbidden in the couple's state of residence.

Independent adoption entails locating a birth mother (often accomplished through advertisements in newspapers or contacts with physicians, lawyers, teachers, and sympathetic friends), working with a lawyer to draw up adoption papers, and covering the medical and legal expenses of the baby's birth and adoption. In agency adoption, the agency locates an infant; matches the infant with the couple, after making a home study of the couple; and, often, gathers information about the couple from reference checks. The agency serves several important functions for the couple: it becomes an important source of information and orientation as the couple learn about the special joys and challenges of adoptive parenthood, and it serves as a continuing source of support to adoptive parents.

Before deciding to plunge ahead on their own into the unfamiliar territory of orchestrating an independent adoption, couples should consider whether they need some of the services that adoption agencies provide. Many couples are able to handle the arrangements of an independent adoption, while others find themselves mired in uncertainties as they contemplate the birth mother's prenatal care, her ambivalence about surrendering the baby, and the legal procedures involved. Couples should be clear in their own minds about their reason for choosing agency, independent, or international adoption, since their priorities in pursuing these routes should come from a realistic perspective that includes an awareness of both advantages and limitations.

Speed is one of the most appealing advantages of international adoption. Many couples are unaware of this option, or they fear that it is too expensive, too complicated, or too time consuming for them to contemplate. They also may be hesitant to adopt a child of a different race, either because of latent feelings of prejudice or because they are concerned that in their community the child would bear the brunt of other people's prejudice. While matters of cost and complexity can usually be dealt with, racial prejudice deserves serious exploration and may, in fact, be an appropriate reason for eliminating international adoption as a possibility. A number of books on adoption offer details about the process and the issues that couples will want to be sensitive to. The *Penguin Adoption Handbook* (Bolles, 1984) and the *Adoption Resource Book* (Gilman, 1984) are comprehensive books intended for prospective adoptive parents. *Infertility and Adoption* (Valentine, 1988) is intended for professionals who work with prospective adoptive parents.

Couples contemplating adoption will need to have accepted their infertility in order to appreciate their adopted child for what it is—not a replacement for the child the couple could not have by birth but, rather, a unique child welcomed into the family for its own worth. In addition, prospective adoptive parents must accept the fact that adoption is different from biological parenthood. Couples who continue to fantasize about a birth child or who have difficulty with the many emotional issues of adoption (telling others, answering questions, accepting the reality of the child's birth parents and heritage, eventually discussing adoption with the child) will need additional time and help to examine their feelings and attitudes about adoption. An excellent resource is *The Adopter's Advocate* (Johnston, 1984).

Childfree Living. The decision to be childfree is distinct from being childless. "Childfree" implies an open approach to life that is positive and can lead to fulfillment, whereas "childless" suggests an emptiness or a void. Many couples who are pursuing infertility treatment would characterize themselves as childless; indeed, they feel the emptiness and strive to complete their families by having a child. Once couples have terminated their treatment and face the alternatives, some will seriously consider childfree living as the best of the existing alternatives.

One might ask why, after so much effort to have a baby, a couple would decide to live a life without a child. Just as the decision to end treatment involves some careful insight into one's needs and motivations, so does the decision about alternatives. Couples who have doggedly pursued infertility treatments may, in fact, have fulfilled other needs even if they did not bear a child. Menning (1977) asserts that some infertile couples search more for an answer than a pregnancy. They want to know why they cannot have children or what their chances would be with medical intervention. Once they have this information, they will need to reassess how strongly they feel about wanting a child, a separate question from the earlier one, "Why can't we have a child?"

Bombardieri (1981) offers some helpful perspectives for couples in the throes of trying to decide how best to meet their needs. She reminds readers of the many pressures in today's society to have children, only some of which are actually related to the couple's desire to become parents. As mentioned earlier, some couples are more intent on achieving fertility than parenthood; such couples want to be able to make the choice rather than having infertility imposed upon them. Other couples, now well acquainted with the disruptions that medical treatment has caused in their lives, may yearn for an orderly existence once again and may decide that having a child would in many ways precipitate more juggling of time, money, career, education, and family relationships. Such couples are understandably exhausted after the tensions of infertility treatment. As they resume their lives without the intrusiveness of medical regimens, they may find pleasures in one another and in other neglected relationships and may discover that life can be fulfilling even without children. Many couples are so drained by the waiting and the uncertainty of past medical treatment that they do not want to face more waits and uncertainties associated with adoption. These couples often will make a conscious decision to view themselves as a family, to enjoy one another, and to move ahead with plans that have been unrealized or on hold during the lengthy period of infertility treatment.

Couples who do not want to parent another person's birth child, or who doubt that they could commit their energies to the special issues inherent in adoption, should seriously explore childfree living as an alternative. Salzer (1986) suggests that couples who decide to live childfree must also mourn the fantasized adopted child. In doing so, they are less likely to be plagued later with thoughts of "what if?" or with doubts about whether the choice they made was explored carefully enough.

In the process of discussing childfree living, partners may disagree on their needs and the impact of a potential choice on their lives together. As with any decision, both partners deserve time to contemplate new ideas fully and to anticipate the consequences of a decision on their lives together. In many ways, the earlier decisions allowed a certain amount of disagreement and give and take because the couple felt that they were together in the quest for a child. The decision of childfree living has a feeling of finality to it, and if one partner is committed to it while the other is still adamant about parenting, their relationship will be in jeopardy. Essentially, each would be asking the other to sacrifice a whole vision of the future. The professional will need to use many skills as she helps the couple explore the history of their quest for a child; their opposition to other possible choices; their present irreconcilable position (whether it developed suddenly, in which case more time may be needed to allow for discussion, or whether it evolved gradually during their infertility struggle); and, finally, their ability to reconcile their differences without lasting bitterness and resentment.

Summary

Whatever decisions couples make together, the professional can be a helpful third party, encouraging the couples to consider alternatives and other perspectives and to anticipate how their needs and motivations may change over time. Options that earlier would not have been contemplated by a couple may look far more plausible as time passes and rigidities diminish. The professional also serves a valuable function by asking the couple to take their time to explore all the issues before pressing for a decision; many couples feel an urgency about decision making that is self-imposed and, in fact, may be detrimental to the quality of the final decision. In the long run, the skills that the professional models and practices with the couple in their infertility decisions have the potential to be incorporated by the couple in the years ahead, whether with or without children.

9

Pregnancy After Infertility:
A Dubious Joy?

The diagnosis of pregnancy for most women and their partners calls forth many emotional responses, ranging from panic to ecstasy. For the infertile couple who have been trying desperately to achieve a pregnancy, there is the universal expectation that a positive pregnancy test will be met with immense relief and joyous anticipation of the remaining months of the pregnancy. Once a pregnancy has been achieved and the initial feelings of joy and hopefulness have subsided, however, many previously infertile couples experience an unanticipated series of concerns in addition to the expected adjustments of pregnancy.

First Trimester

Implications for the Couple. After months or years of fervently hoping that the next menstrual cycle will signal a pregnancy, many couples cannot believe that the actual diagnosis of pregnancy is correct (Salzer, 1986). They have long been accustomed to disappointments and to their role as infertile people. Denial or disbelief allows them to protect themselves from further disappointment while gradually absorbing the impact of the diagnosis. One woman relates this response to a positive pregnancy test:

> I had been asked to telephone the doctor's office to learn the results of my pregnancy test. I must

133

have called three times that afternoon, each time
to learn that the results should be back from the
lab "any time now." Finally the nurse told me that
the pregnancy test was positive. My heart stopped,
and I felt myself gasping for breath and asking if
there were any possibility the results could be a
mistake. The nurse assured me my results were positive, and I just dissolved in tears! She, knowing
nothing of my infertility, tried to be comforting,
and as I calmed down I heard her say, "You know,
dear, if this pregnancy is so upsetting, you needn't
go through with it." I wasted no time in telling her
that these were tears of absolute joy and that I
couldn't wait to "go through with it."

A husband tells of his incredulity:

When Jan told me the news of her positive pregnancy test after four years of our infertility, I was
totally skeptical. I was sure they had confused her
results with someone else's, and I wasn't about to
get excited over a lab mixup. It was only after I insisted that she have a second test, which also came
back positive, that I was able to believe the pregnancy was real.

For couples who have experienced an earlier pregnancy
loss, the initial response is tied less to doubts about the reality
of the pregnancy than to their fears that the fetus may not be
viable. Since the greatest risk for miscarriage occurs during the
first trimester, these couples figuratively hold their breaths during the first twelve weeks. This symbolic breath holding often
extends to keeping the pregnancy a secret in case a miscarriage
does occur. These couples deprive themselves of much-needed
support from others during an emotionally difficult time and, in
the event of an actual miscarriage, become isolated in their silent grief. Couples with pregnancies that progress in an uncomplicated way, despite fears to the contrary, may be reluctant to

feel joyful for fear that such emotions will tempt fate. Many couples find that they are unable to enjoy their pregnancies until they have passed the week when their earlier pregnancy loss occurred (Friedman and Gradstein, 1982).

In fact, the memory of their earlier loss is but one factor that prevents the couple from taking full pleasure in their newly pregnant state. Couples who have experienced a previous miscarriage often are advised by their obstetrician to abstain from intercourse during the first trimester. At a time when they are feeling the emotional strain of a pregnancy and strive for closeness to allay their apprehensions, it can be doubly frustrating to be denied the intimacy that intercourse can bring. Previously infertile couples are likely to have a long history of "programmed sex," in which intercourse was strictly scheduled during the woman's fertile period. For these couples to be again denied the spontaneity of intercourse serves as one more reminder that the threat of infertility still lurks despite their success in achieving a pregnancy.

The nausea, vomiting, and exhaustion that can occur during the first trimester elicit a variety of responses from the previously infertile woman. As Salzer (1986) observes, some feel a profound discouragement that the experience of the idealized pregnancy begins in such an unpleasant way. Others, with the anxiety of recent infertility fresh in their minds, fear that the difficulties encountered during the first trimester may presage additional complications as the pregnancy progresses. Still others revel in their predictable symptoms of pregnancy as a confirmation that they are in fact pregnant. A common feeling experienced during this time is the need to be stoic about the less comfortable aspects of the pregnancy (Menning, 1977). The stoicism is in part a carryover from behavior learned during infertility and in part evidence that these women do not feel entitled to complain about any aspect of their much-coveted pregnancy.

A dilemma for couples who have experienced an earlier pregnancy loss is how much to invest emotionally in the current pregnancy and in hopes for a healthy birth. Couples sometimes are unable to become attached to the fetus, because they have vivid memories of emotional pain from the earlier loss and they fear the grief of a subsequent loss. When pregnancy fails, the parents lose both the developing baby that they have begun to know and love and also the baby that they imagined it would one day become. To sustain such a loss once more is an unspoken fear. The couple may believe that the less attached they allow themselves to become, the less traumatic a repeated loss would be.

Sometimes one spouse will become attached while the other remains resolutely detached. For example, Sally, who became pregnant after three years of trying to conceive, was absorbed in all the details of her pregnancy. She read voraciously on pregnancy and childbirth, was conscientious about nutrition and exercise, knitted and sewed clothing for the baby in her leisure time, and glowed with happiness at being pregnant. Despite repeated efforts, Sally was unable to involve her husband in either her emotional enthusiasm or in concrete preparations for the baby's arrival. When she eventually insisted that he talk about the reasons for his aloofness, he confided that he was equally joyful about the pregnancy itself but terrified that something might happen to prevent the birth of a healthy baby:

> You're so attached to the baby already that you would need me to be strong for you if it didn't survive. The easiest way for me to help you is not to get too attached until we're sure everything will turn out all right.

The male often is the emotionally aloof partner. His body is not reminding him on a daily basis of the developing fetus, and American males often are socialized to be circumspect about experiencing or displaying their emotions.

Many previously infertile couples must undergo prenatal diagnostic procedures during the first and second trimesters. Amniocentesis and chorionic villi sampling are available for those couples considered at special risk of producing a baby with genetic defects. These include previously infertile women whose pregnancy losses were attributed to genetic abnormalities and women thirty-five years and older who are considered at special risk for producing children with genetic defects, particularly Down's syndrome. Couples who already have undergone many invasive and painful treatments for their infertility may question the "worthwhileness" of a test that involves one more period of waiting anxiously for results and wondering whether they can ever succeed in their efforts to have a baby. In addition, the risk of the procedure must be considered. Statistics show that there is less than a 1 percent chance of a miscarriage following an amniocentesis (Borg and Lasker, 1981, p. 43), but women with a history of miscarriages may have a higher percentage of risk. So couples find themselves in the position of weighing the "need to know" against the fear that the pregnancy could be interrupted.

Despite specific concerns, most couples consider the end of the first trimester a very special milestone: the threat of miscarriage is statistically less, the feelings of nausea and exhaustion begin to abate, and the woman's blossoming shape and wearing of maternity clothes signal to the public the news that the couple has waited so long to share.

Implications for the Professional. Given the high level of anxiety experienced by many couples during the first trimester, professional intervention can help the couple gain some of the control that had been lacking during their period of infertility. Several specific skills that the professional can encourage during this time are anxiety reduction, information seeking, open communication, and decision making.

Anxiety reduction is a major task for the infertile individual during the first trimester. It is often useful for the professional to ask the couple how they managed stress during their infertility. Becoming familiar with their coping mechanisms will help the professional reinforce productive ones, discourage dysfunctional ones, and suggest additional means of managing stress effectively. Relaxation exercises can be helpful at this time. Such exercises have a later payoff in labor and delivery.

Information seeking is also important for infertile individuals at this time. The couple should be encouraged to make lists of questions for their obstetrician or midwife, so that they can acquire accurate information and have a chance to process it with a knowledgeable medical professional. Although it is tempting for the professional to become involved in the medical details of the pregnancy, it is far more appropriate to focus on helping the couple obtain and use the information needed. The couple also should be encouraged to read the extensive literature available for expectant parents. Such literature emphasizes the normalcy of some of the more uncomfortable aspects of the first trimester and can help the couple feel more connected to the pregnancy rather than alienated from it or unentitled to complain about the very real discomforts, despite the joy of being pregnant.

Communication skills can reduce the anxiety that many previously infertile people feel. Couples need to be able to identify their feelings and discuss them openly with one another. To the extent that partners can support one another through their anxiety, new channels of communication can be explored. Assertive communication skills can prove extremely effective, especially with medical professionals and family members who may not understand the couple's feelings of anxiety and who may not know how to be helpful to them. Couples who have been advised to abstain from intercourse during the first trimester can explore alternate means of sexual pleasuring and can be encouraged to find a variety of ways of achieving closeness.

Decision-making skills are often most needed when amniocentesis and chorionic villi sampling are being considered. Since there is a slight risk of miscarriage or damage to the fetus, most couples weigh the decision carefully. The professional can be helpful in this decision-making process by encouraging the couple to seek genetic counseling. In addition to helping the couple ascertain the extent of risk of genetic problems for the fetus, a genetics counselor can also discuss the risks, benefits, and limitations of the procedure. Once the couple have the necessary information, the professional may ask whether both partners usually are willing to take risks, how satisfied they have been with risk-related decisions in the past, and whether they can tolerate the uncertainty of the fetus's genetic health for the remaining months of the pregnancy. Couples also should be asked to consider whether they are able to raise a child with special needs. In part, decisions about a prenatal diagnostic procedure may be difficult because, as mentioned, the couple are reluctant to submit to one more test to assess their reproductive capacities. By venting anger about earlier procedures, they may be able to work through some of the negative emotions that impede progress on the decision about prenatal diagnostic procedures.

Second Trimester

Implications for the Couple. The baby's existence becomes more tangible during the second trimester. The baby's heartbeat is clearly audible on a fetal stethoscope during visits to the obstetrician or midwife, the baby's movements become increasingly pronounced, and the woman's blossoming figure evokes questions and comments from friends and strangers alike. The couple may begin to talk about the changes that the baby's arrival will bring: the joys and responsibilities of becoming parents, the need to balance career and family, the financial demands, the desire to remain close as spouses despite the baby's need for attention, and the lack of experience in the parental roles.

As the couple discuss the prospect of parenthood, it is normal for them to feel some ambivalence about the changes the baby will bring into their lives. Infertile couples often have focused so resolutely on the joys of parenthood during their efforts to conceive that they have not given much attention to the sacrifices of time, energy, and finances that parenthood will bring. As the baby becomes increasingly real to them, some previously infertile couples refuse to acknowledge the ambivalent feelings that the pregnancy evokes; somehow they feel unentitled to anything but joyful emotions. It is almost as though acknowledging some of the mixed or negative feelings would take away the importance of their accomplishment and the validity of their desire for parenthood. Some couples are openly superstitious in voicing only good thoughts for fear that any doubts could threaten the success of the pregnancy. The stoicism that the couple learned to demonstrate during their period of infertility may discourage them from exploring emotions with negative overtones; as a result, many infertile couples avoid discussing some of the concerns and adjustments that all prospective parents face and instead focus with singularly positive thoughts on the preparations for the baby's arrival.

The visibility of the pregnancy during the second trimester may bring new challenges to the couple. Whether or not people were aware of the couple's infertility, everyone assumes that the second trimester is a carefree and joy-filled time. The couple may perceive others as insensitive to the anxieties they feel, particularly if these anxieties are not tied to concrete medical problems in the current pregnancy. This sense of being misunderstood may contribute to feelings of social isolation just when the couple might otherwise have begun to resume relationships with friends who had grown distant during the period of infertility.

Couples who have developed close emotional ties to other infertile people may need to discuss with these friends the impact of the pregnancy on the friendship (Salzer, 1986). Although it is natural for infertile friends to be envious of the newly pregnant couple, these feelings can be discussed and worked on. In most friendships, the infertile friends will, at some level, be happy for the couple who are no longer infertile and encouraged to believe that they too may enjoy a pregnancy some day. In turn, the previously infertile couple may feel guilty or apologetic about their pregnancy when in the company of infertile friends. One woman tells of her experience with a friend:

> Sarah and I had been commiserating about our infertility for two years before I became pregnant. We comforted one another when mutual friends easily conceived, we psyched ourselves up for going to baby showers, and we shared a lot of tears over baby announcements, medical treatments, and monthly periods. How could I tell her that I was pregnant? I felt like the enemy! I didn't know if our friendship was strong enough to survive during my pregnancy, let alone during my life as a new mother.

Such awkwardness and the wish not to cause emotional stress may tempt a pregnant woman and her mate to avoid infertile friends. These complex emotions can place a strain on friendships, and the couple may have a strong need for support as they renegotiate old friendships with both fertile and infertile friends.

Although most previously infertile couples are fortunate in having uncomplicated pregnancies, the risk of problems in pregnancy is statistically higher for couples who have had previous miscarriages, ectopic pregnancies, or stillbirths. For these couples, the anxiety of the first trimester may continue throughout the pregnancy. Complications can include spotting, cramping, contractions, and premature dilation of the cervix. Medical responses to such symptoms usually include instructions for bed rest and the curtailing of normal activity until the symptoms disappear. Women with such complications face tremendous strains, since they must interrupt their employment, depend on partner, friends, and family for help with daily routines, and spend hours in bed. For the woman who already has felt inadequate in her ability to conceive or to carry a pregnancy to term, the complications of pregnancy are an intrusive reminder of previous insecurities. The frequent visits to her obstetrician remind her of the past infertility investigation and treatments, and the couple's feelings of loss of control return as they are once more dependent on the medical establishment to help them with the pregnancy. If the couple have experienced an earlier pregnancy loss, the feelings of desperation and panic are even more pronounced as they relive the past trauma and its accompanying grief while hoping that this pregnancy will have a more positive outcome. The hours in bed or carrying out restricted activities provide ample leisure time for frightening fantasies to assail the woman; the male, on the other hand, is often so absorbed in efforts to balance employment, housework, and worries about the pregnancy that he has little energy to assuage his partner's fears.

Implications for the Professional. During the second trimester, the couple need to anticipate lifestyle changes that the baby's birth will bring. During their infertility, when the desire to conceive a baby was all-consuming, they may not have considered these changes. Therefore, the professional should encourage them to discuss finances, problems in balancing employment and family, household and childrearing responsibilities, and expectations of themselves as parents and partners.

Many couples will have lost touch with their fertile friends, who became preoccupied with having and raising their children and could not understand the pain experienced by an infertile couple in a fertile world. If the infertile couple want to revitalize old relationships once they achieve a pregnancy, they will probably need to initiate efforts. The professional can help couples assess the most appropriate ways of reestablishing contact with old friends. They may want to begin by sharing the news of their pregnancy. Subsequent discussions about pregnancy, childbirth, and childrearing can forge common bonds quite quickly. The sense of social support during the pregnancy is often vital for the couple, who may have felt socially isolated during their period of infertility.

If medical complications require that the expectant mother spend a great deal of time in bed or in restricted activity, the professional will want to acknowledge the couple's continued sense of powerlessness and helplessness and, at the same time, help them gain some sense of productivity and control. Specifically, the professional can discuss with them the areas of their lives that are especially stressful. Sources of support, whether for housework or at-home socializing, should be explored with the couple, who may be tempted to bear the burden of prenatal tension in isolation. If the professional can help the couple improve the anxious weeks of waiting, the prospective parents may once again begin to feel in control of certain aspects of their lives.

Third Trimester

Implications for the Couple. For couples whose pregnancies are without significant complications, the last three months are a time of eager anticipation. The couple will discuss names, visit the obstetrician or midwife more frequently, make purchases, attend childbirth classes and La Leche League meetings, and make final plans for the trip to the hospital and help at home after the baby's arrival. In some ways, the couple's effort to exert control over every detail is a defense against their anxieties about labor and delivery. Knowing how precious this baby is, the previously infertile couple feel more than the normal anxiety about the outcome of the pregnancy. For many, the fears that surfaced during the first trimester recur: concerns about the baby's normalcy and good health, excitement tempered by fear, excessive attentiveness to body signals, and an eagerness to move toward the end of the trimester, since each week of pregnancy confirms the baby's continuing growth and development.

Keeping in control becomes paramount for most couples in the last trimester of pregnancy. Because the couple did not have control over their lives during their years of infertility, they now attempt to structure the most ideal situation possible (Menning, 1977). In this spirit, most couples seize the opportunity to become informed about the childbirth process through classes and discussions with the obstetrician or midwife. Couples who become fully informed about the birth process, however, also become aware of threats to their idealized scenario of childbirth. One such threat is presented by their awareness that first pregnancies are often accompanied by a longer and harder labor than subsequent pregnancies. Another threat arises from their awareness that this is an especially precious pregnancy. At the slightest hint of problems during labor, the doctor may whisk the woman away for a Cesarean section. Menning (1977, p. 139) contends that the Cesarean section rate among formerly infertile women is, by some estimates, almost twice that for the general population. For the previously infertile couple, the knowledge of potential problems is a genuine source of apprehension as they try to anticipate every potential scenario in the delivery room. The defense and coping mechanisms that enabled the couple to deal with anxieties during the first trimester may be helpful again as they prepare for the unknown outcome of the pregnancy.

For those couples who have experienced complications during the pregnancy, the last trimester brings both hope and fear. Having sustained the pregnancy until the last trimester, they feel a certain triumph, even though they are still sensitive to the risks that the final months hold. Because premature labor is the greatest concern at this time, some women must curtail their activity moderately or drastically, depending on the obstetricians' assessment of risk. A woman may be hospitalized, usually on the maternity ward, during a portion of the last trimester. In the hospital setting, the woman faces constant reminders of her body's vulnerability and unpredictability and, at the same time, observes with envy the parents on the ward who are learning to care for their newborn infants. Her partner may feel particularly isolated from the emotional closeness that many couples develop during the last trimester. Such a couple often deny themselves the opportunity to anticipate the joyful outcome of a healthy delivery. They live on a day-to-day basis, hoping for the best but not daring to assume that all will continue to go well as the last trimester progresses.

Implications for the Professional. The helping professional represents a special source of support for the couple who must cope with ongoing medical problems during the last trimester. They are now emotionally and physically exhausted and in need of new ideas for coping and for shoring up their flagging spirits. The professional will need to deal with their feelings of disillusionment regarding the much-hoped-for pregnancy while at the same time continuing to support their hopes for a healthy outcome.

Specifically, the professional can help the couple decide how to relieve the woman's boredom if her activities are restricted; alleviate the man's feelings of pressure as more roles and responsibilities shift in his direction; deal with the man's stoicism, a common response when a partner is ill and needs emotional support; develop spontaneity in the relationship in spite of all the restrictions; and cope with the periodic desperation and panic that assail them. Since the couple may not be ready to think very far into the future, the professional must keep pace with their readiness to prepare for the baby. Many couples believe that they will be tempting fate if they furnish the nursery, make purchases for the baby, or allow their family or friends to have a shower. If these feelings are present, the professional can, instead, help the couple focus on the joys and satisfaction in their lives on a day-to-day basis, so that the on-going fear of loss does not preoccupy their thoughts exclusively.

If the pregnancy is progressing uneventfully in the last tri-mester, the professional may want to discuss the couple's readi-ness to terminate the therapeutic relationship. Since the couple are now preparing for childbirth and anticipating life with their new baby, they may have less need for the support that was im-portant during the early months of the pregnancy. On the other hand, some couples may have an even greater need for the pro-fessional's support as they explore their anxieties, anticipate shifts in family roles, and try to achieve a sense of control over an event that holds many unknowns. While taking their con-cerns seriously, the professional can encourage the couple to ac-cept the reality that they will never have as much control as they might like and that life after delivery will have its ups and downs, just as it did in the recent past. However, because the couple have been able to utilize their sessions with the profes-sional to develop new coping strategies, new insights, and better interpersonal communication, the professional can now help them learn how to use their new learning in their responses to inevitable life changes. Thus, the professional helps the couple focus on their beginning feelings of competence, instead of their feelings of helplessness.

After Delivery

Many previously infertile couples are both euphoric and disbelieving when a healthy baby is placed in their arms, putting to rest the tensions surrounding their infertility and pregnancy. For those individuals who allowed themselves to enjoy the preg-nancy, to relish fantasies about life with the baby, and to bond with the fetus in utero, the transition from pregnancy to parent-hood is a joyful one. These individuals usually have assumed a sense of mastery after the early disappointments that accom-panied infertility, and this attitude is likely to continue during the early weeks of adjustment to parenthood.

Individuals who have been more hesitant to become emotionally invested in the pregnancy—either because of profound discouragement during the infertility period or because of frightening complications during the pregnancy—may regard the arrival of a healthy baby with wonder and, often, some apprehension. The coping mechanisms that allowed emotional distancing from the fetus during the pregnancy must be discarded, and the parents must become emotionally open to loving their squalling, wrinkled newcomer. Some individuals embrace this challenge with joyful relief and enthusiasm. Others need time to accept the fact that the baby is really theirs to love and cherish at last (Menning, 1977). A new mother relates:

> When the doctor placed the baby in my arms, I looked at this little stranger and thought, "Who are you?" I had dreamed of this moment for nine months and had expected to feel a warm glow and a surge of love. Instead, I felt physically empty inside, exhausted, and confused. We'd waited so long for a baby, and now I found myself feeling scared at the prospect of motherhood to this little red and wrinkled fellow.

Previously infertile couples often feel especially anxious about providing the "right" kind of care for their newborn, since they are aware that this baby is especially precious and, depending on the nature of their infertility, may be their only birth child.

In a very small percentage of births to infertile couples, there are serious complications at delivery or congenital defects diagnosed at birth. The needs of parents and family members are detailed in the literature on stillbirth (Stringham, Riley, and Ross, 1982; DeFrain, 1986; Borg and Lasker, 1981; Friedman and Gradstein, 1982), birth defects (Trout, 1983; Kennedy, 1970; Solnit and Stark, 1961), and prematurity (Hotchner, 1984; Nance, 1982). All these couples, in one form or another, must experience the process of mourning the loss of a healthy infant, although the specificity of their grief will depend on the outcome of the pregnancy.

Summary

It is important for helping professionals to be aware of the unique needs of couples who achieve a pregnancy after a period of infertility. Whereas many previously infertile couples will have few problems and will cope well with the routine discomforts and difficulties of their pregnancies, others may experience a range of difficulties, as detailed in this chapter. Professionals who are aware of the potential stress that pregnancy may cause for this population can offer outreach, education, support, and therapeutic intervention, depending on the need. Survivors of infertility can benefit greatly from sensitive efforts to help them understand how their past experiences affect their reactions to their current pregnancy.

10

Ectopic Pregnancy
and Miscarriage

Couples who have experienced an ectopic pregnancy or a miscarriage speak with regret about the preoccupation with medical details that surrounds the experience. Since either event is likely to be unexpected, and since medical intervention may occur in a crisis atmosphere made more frightening by its unfamiliarity, the couple's emotional needs are every bit as pressing as the woman's medical needs. Yet, even during the recovery, friends and family are most likely to focus on the medical details of the experience, often ignoring or avoiding the couple's need to mourn the lost pregnancy as part of the healing process. Once the immediate crisis is past, the professional can validate the couple's need to mourn their loss, ultimately helping them assess its effect on possible future efforts to conceive a baby.

Ectopic Pregnancy

An ectopic, or tubal, pregnancy is difficult on many levels for the woman and her partner. It is both a physical assault and an emotional shock. Such a pregnancy not only damages the woman's sense of bodily health and well-being but also leaves her feeling emotionally vulnerable as she contemplates the life-threatening nature of the pregnancy and the increased risk of a future ectopic pregnancy. If she has lost both of her tubes to ectopic pregnancies, or if the second tube is known to be damaged, the loss of her fertility will be an added source of pain and bodily betrayal. The woman mourns both her loss of future fertility and her body wholeness. Her mate experiences fears about his partner's close brush with death and also mourns the lost pregnancy and what that baby would have represented in their lives. If one or both of his partner's tubes were damaged or removed, then he also must come to terms with his diminished chances of becoming a birth parent.

The Medical Experience. An ectopic pregnancy occurs when a fertilized egg is lodged in an abnormal location, usually one of the two Fallopian tubes. The pregnancy cannot progress in such a restrictive environment, and if surgery to remove the embryo is not performed in time, the tube may rupture. Diagnosis of an ectopic pregnancy can be difficult, however, because the woman may not even know that she is pregnant. The symptoms—vaginal bleeding, pain in the lower abdomen (often on one side), and sometimes weakness and fainting—may be confused with other medical conditions. The tube usually bursts between the eighth and twelfth weeks of pregnancy, early enough so that an early pregnancy test may have been negative. In an ectopic pregnancy, surgery must be performed even if the tube has not ruptured. If the tube must be removed, it sometimes can be rebuilt, but adhesions or scar tissue may form subsequently and obstruct the tube.

Women who have experienced an ectopic pregnancy have a 7 to 12 percent chance of having another ectopic pregnancy (Friedman and Gradstein, 1982, p. 115). When a Fallopian tube has ruptured and cannot be reconstructed, it is removed. There also is an increased chance that something may be wrong with the remaining tube, for whatever conditions caused the ectopic pregnancy may also have impaired the other Fallopian tube.

The causes of an ectopic pregnancy are not always clear. In about half the cases, no cause is found. The most common cause of interference with the progress of the fertilized ovum is damage to the tube from pelvic inflammatory disease, previous pelvic surgery, endometriosis, a previous ectopic pregnancy, or tubal reconstructive surgery. Also, women who have had chlamydia may be at a higher than normal risk for ectopic pregnancy, because of the disease's damage to reproductive organs.

The sense of being helpless and out of control is one of the most common elements that a woman and her partner experience during an ectopic pregnancy. The physical symptoms, often difficult to diagnose, may have caused the woman to make several trips to her physician or to more than one physician to determine the cause of her symptoms. There are several diagnostic procedures that the woman may undergo prior to her surgery. They are described here so that the helping professional can understand the procedures and the couple's experience with medical professionals.

Culdocentesis is a procedure in which a needle is inserted through the vagina into the space behind the uterus to determine whether there is blood in the abdominal cavity. The presence of blood would indicate that the tube has already ruptured.

Posterior colpotomy is a surgical incision made in the vaginal wall to investigate whether blood has accumulated behind the uterus. If it has, then a tube probably has ruptured and there is internal bleeding.

Culdoscopy involves the insertion of an instrument through an incision in the vagina to view the abdominal cavity.

Laparoscopy is a procedure in which an instrument called a laparoscope is inserted through a small incision in the abdominal wall. Looking through the laparoscope, the physician can view the Fallopian tubes and other pelvic organs.

Ultrasonography uses high-frequency, shortwave, sound-wave reflections to determine whether the uterus is enlarged, whether a fetus is in the uterus, or whether an ectopic fetal mass can be distinguished outside the uterus.

A *blood test* for the beta unit of human chorionic gonadotropin (hCG) may be used to diagnose an ectopic pregnancy. This test, which is able to measure lower levels of pregnancy hormones than ordinary pregnancy tests, can aid greatly in determining whether the woman is pregnant. (This test is used because a routine pregnancy test probably will not be sensitive enough to detect the small amounts of pregnancy hormones being produced.)

Surgery will always be performed when an ectopic pregnancy is discovered. The woman will be administered a general anesthetic and will awaken in the recovery room feeling groggy, nauseated, and in pain. She also may feel disoriented, in part because of the anesthetic and in part because there may have been little time prior to the surgery for her physician to explain the details of her condition. In the recovery room, the physician will probably focus discussions on the surgery itself and the procedures that were undertaken to preserve the woman's life. Only later is the physician likely to discuss the implications of the surgery for future pregnancies.

It is common for the woman to be hospitalized from four to six days. Whether she is placed on the obstetrics ward will undoubtedly influence how she feels about her hospital stay and her ability to integrate the loss of her pregnancy. Most women prefer not to be exposed to happy parents and newborns, and the helping professional can play an important role by advocating that the woman be placed on the surgical floor during her recovery period. If possible, the helping professional should encourage the woman and her partner to begin sharing the feelings that have been accumulating since the onset of the woman's symptoms. By exploring these issues and events, the couple can sort out their feelings and ask questions that may best be answered in a medical setting.

Professional Support During the Recovery Period. A pregnancy ending so abruptly leaves the couple confused. They are relieved that it is over and that the woman is alive; at the same time, they are grieving over the loss of the baby they had hoped to have. Couples who had not planned the pregnancy will need to discuss whether it was a wanted pregnancy, so that they can come to terms with their mixed feelings of relief and sadness. Couples who had planned the pregnancy, and who have a history of infertility, will regard the loss of future fertility as a devastating blow. The couple will need support as they mourn the loss of their wished-for baby and their impaired fertility. In addition to talking with the couple in the hospital, the helping professional may want to offer them some literature on ectopic pregnancy and on infertility. Many couples welcome such reading material at a time when it is hard to put emotions into words. Literature on the emotional aspects of their loss may help them feel less alone and may prod them to talk openly with one another and the helping professional about feelings that are connected with their losses. Reading about the physiological aspects of ectopic pregnancy also may enable them to feel that they are gaining some understanding of an event that took them by surprise. Being somewhat knowledgeable about the pregnancy will in turn enable them to talk in an informed way with the woman's physician, both in the hospital and during a follow-up visit approximately two or three weeks after surgery.

If the woman is healing well at the time of this visit, her physician will probably give permission for the couple to resume sexual intercourse. They probably will be cautioned against attempting another pregnancy until the woman has had three normal menstrual cycles. A mechanical form of birth control (diaphragm, foam, condom) will be advised during this time. Couples who are eager to conceive again will find this enforced waiting period very frustrating. If they have a history of infertility, the use of birth control will seem sadly ironic.

Once the woman returns home, friends and relatives may be unable to give the couple the support that they need. These friends and relatives probably will not know what an ectopic pregnancy represents and will focus on the physiological aspects of the surgery and recovery without recognizing the emotional aftermath for the couple. Friends may encourage the couple to emphasize the hopefulness of whatever remaining fertility they have, rather than allowing them to vent their fears about their reduced fertility and their apprehensions about the increased likelihood that the woman will have another ectopic pregnancy.

If there are other children at home, they will be needing their parents' attention and reassurance at the very time the couple are trying to integrate the experience of the past weeks. Children who were frightened bystanders when their mother was in pain and whisked away to the hospital for what seemed an interminable stay are likely to demand the attention they feel they have been deprived of. They may misbehave, regress to earlier behaviors, or resist being separated from their mother. Some children express their anger at being left by ignoring their mother's return home and distancing themselves emotionally. The professional may want to warn the parents when the mother prepares to leave the hospital, so that they can understand that the children's behavior is an expression of their dependence on the mother rather than a deliberate tactic to disrupt her early days at home.

Some common problems that individuals deal with once they are at home again are tied to the grieving process. Because the ectopic pregnancy occurred so quickly and with very little warning, the couple are likely to feel bewildered by the events they have experienced. They may need to talk about the details of what happened as a way of integrating and making sense of them.

The hope of achieving a future pregnancy will be clouded by the fear of another ectopic pregnancy, which not only would result in the loss of a hoped-for baby but also would seriously risk the mother's life and future fertility. The male may feel that he cannot face the possibility of causing his wife a potentially life-threatening pregnancy. These feelings will interfere with the couple's efforts to communicate and with their sexual relationship. Therefore, both the male and the female must be encouraged to discuss their fears about pregnancy and attempt to overcome them.

Anger is a common element in the mourning process, but couples who have just coped with an ectopic pregnancy are unlikely to appreciate the normalcy of their anger unless the professional helps them understand its significance. In particular, they should be encouraged to express their anger that the ectopic pregnancy happened to them when they have done nothing to "deserve" it. Irrational as these feelings are, direct expression of them will keep the anger focused on the ectopic pregnancy. Otherwise, the couple may direct their anger at each other. For example, each partner may begin to blame the other for failing to obtain medical help more promptly; or they may become irritable about little things that would not ordinarily trigger angry outbursts at home. The professional can help them understand that the ectopic pregnancy is the real source of their short tempers.

Exhaustion may also precipitate anger. Now that the

woman is ready to take control of her life and move forward, she still finds herself tired, distracted, and unable to undertake projects that earlier would have represented no great effort. The helping professional may need to encourage the woman to pace herself carefully. Her wish to get back to normal is understandable, but the events of the past weeks have not been normal, and their toll on her body should not be underestimated. The woman may have some feelings about her physical scar, in addition to the emotional scars she carries. She may feel anger over bodily mutilation and cannot believe that the scar will ever fade and become less unsightly. More likely, the scar represents a daily reminder to her of all the difficult feelings associated with the ectopic pregnancy: her vulnerability, her impaired fertility, her loss of one baby, and the potential loss of future babies.

Sometimes, in the aftermath of an ectopic pregnancy, the couple will direct their anger at the physician, who "should have made an earlier diagnosis" or "should have been able to save the tube." Mistakes certainly do occur, and it is possible that the woman was a victim of inadequate medical care. It is also possible, though, that no physician could have arrived at an accurate diagnosis more quickly or saved the tube once it ruptured. The woman needs to consider carefully whether her own feelings of helplessness are at the source of her anger or whether, in fact, the physician acted improperly.

Women also commonly blame themselves for ectopic pregnancies. A woman may feel guilty about previous damage to her tubes as she contemplates her carelessness at contracting a sexually transmitted disease or her acquiescence to reconstructive tubal surgery in the hopes of achieving a normal pregnancy. Although an earlier abortion in no way contributed to the ectopic pregnancy, it may emerge now as a source of guilt. The woman recollects that she made a conscious choice to terminate an unintended pregnancy, never realizing how difficult it could ultimately be to have a healthy and wanted pregnancy.

The couple recovering from an ectopic pregnancy will face a variety of problems. In addition to being an available source of support for the couple, the professional can help the partners communicate between themselves about the impact that the ectopic pregnancy has had on each of them. The ectopic pregnancy initially will be experienced as a crisis and may ultimately lead at least one partner to mourn some losses associated with the pregnancy. If the ectopic pregnancy turns out to be the beginning of a series of infertility concerns, as is sometimes the case, it will be appropriate for the helping professional to explore the chronic aspects of infertility with one or both partners.

Miscarriage

A miscarriage—or spontaneous abortion, as it is called by medical professionals—is the unintended ending of a pregnancy before the fetus can survive outside the mother (that is, usually before the twentieth week of pregnancy). Early spontaneous abortions occur between the seventh and fourteenth week, but study after study has confirmed that most miscarriages occur before the sixteenth week of pregnancy (Pizer and Palinski, 1980, p. 17). A missed abortion occurs when the fetus dies in utero but there are no symptoms such as cramping, spotting, or bleeding. A pregnancy that aborts after the twenty-sixth week is called a late abortion or a premature birth, depending on the weight of the fetus.

The timing of a miscarriage gives the first clue to possible cause. Seventy-five percent occur within the first twelve weeks, and about half of these early miscarriages are caused by an abnormality in the embryo or in the process of its implantation in the uterus. The fetus may be deformed because of genetic problems inherited from the parents, but more often a chance mutation has occurred during fertilization or the early growth of the embryo (Borg and Lasker, 1981, p. 28).

Late spontaneous abortions occur between the seventeenth and twenty-eighth week of pregnancy. In late miscarriages, the fetus is usually normal, but there are problems in its attachment to the placenta or to the uterus. There may also be abnormalities in the structure of the uterus itself. Sometimes the cervix is too weak ("incompetent" is the medical term) and dilated too early.

Since the current rates of maternal and infant death in the

United States are low, a couple often interpret a positive pregnancy test as a virtual guarantee that they will have a baby in nine months. Thus, when the woman begins to have cramps and to bleed, the experience is terrifying on several levels: first, she is frightened about the implications for the remainder of her pregnancy; second, she is afraid for herself—for her body that may be experiencing pain along with the unpredictable symptoms of an impending miscarriage.

What a miscarriage means for a particular couple may depend on whether the couple had planned and hoped for the pregnancy, had experienced previous pregnancy losses, had any difficulty in conceiving the baby, have negative feelings about hospitals and emergency medical care, and are familiar with what occurs during a miscarriage. These questions are relevant for the professional to explore at least briefly, because they will suggest to what extent the miscarriage represents a disruption and loss.

Unplanned Pregnancy. In some situations, the couple may not be aware that the woman is pregnant, so her symptoms of bleeding and cramping will be frightening and bewildering. Moreover, the realization that they have lost the pregnancy before they were even aware of it can precipitate a variety of responses in the partners, ranging from lingering regret to wrenching grief.

If the pregnancy was unplanned yet wanted, the professional will want to be sensitive to several issues. First, although the couple may not have had an opportunity to form an attachment to the fetus, they may express feelings of loss in retrospect, since the idea of parenthood is something they would have welcomed. This couple, in considering the loss that the miscarriage represents, may begin to think more concretely about the meaning of beginning a family and may express the wish to try actively to achieve a pregnancy in the near future. The helping professional, realizing that the couple are heavily influenced by the emotions of loss, can be most helpful by empathizing with these feelings and also by encouraging the couple to consider what, beyond emotional fulfillment, a baby would represent in their lives.

If the couple already have at least one birth child, the miscarriage will undoubtedly be associated with earlier pregnancies, whether planned or unplanned. They are clearly aware of the meanings that they have attached to past healthy pregnancies, and knowing that this pregnancy was not a healthy one may make them feel reproductively vulnerable.

Some individuals and couples may feel guilty about having contributed in some way to the miscarriage because of past behaviors (such as abortions, drug use, or sexually transmitted diseases) or current behaviors (such as smoking, drinking, use of drugs, inattention to nutrition, or strenuous exercise). The couple should discuss these factors with a knowledgeable medical professional, so that they can sort out which factors are known to be associated with problems in pregnancy. Particularly important is the opportunity to help the couple understand which factors in their lifestyle or health care could place future pregnancies at risk.

Planned Pregnancy. If this pregnancy represented the wish to have a baby, the couple will view the miscarriage as an interruption in their life plans and feel sadness as well as anger. If the miscarriage occurred so early in the pregnancy that they were unaware the woman was pregnant, confusion will be coupled with the feeling of loss. The couple may express sadness that they did not even have the opportunity to rejoice in the pregnancy before it was taken from them. Others may view the early miscarriage as a mixed blessing because they did not have the opportunity to form any attachment to the fetus. Even though the couple did not know they had achieved a pregnancy, the professional must be sensitive to the couple's feelings of attachment to the fantasy child they had hoped to conceive.

For the couple who knew of the pregnancy, rejoiced in the news, and perhaps shared it with some friends and relatives, the miscarriage represents an unanticipated emotional and physical jolt. Fantasies of the baby and prospective parenthood may already have been shaped and shared, involvement of others in the couple's life assumed a new dimension, and the remaining months of the pregnancy were anticipated with hope and joy. Now the couple are faced with dashed hopes, an end to their attachment to their developing baby, and the need to tell others of their loss at a time when they have not fully comprehended what this loss represents. In addition to helping them attain medical information about the miscarriage, the professional should be certain that the couple have access to emotional support as well, particularly in the weeks immediately following the miscarriage, as time allows them to appreciate the dimensions of the loss they have sustained. The emotional pain may continue for months, with its intensity related to poignant memories or anticipated events.

> Our baby would have been born in the spring, and before I miscarried I had looked forward to pushing the baby carriage in the park, feeding the ducks, gathering bouquets of flowers, dressing the baby in cute sunsuits and being a mother on Mother's Day! Now that it's April I almost can't bear to go outdoors because nothing has turned out the way I dreamed it would.

> We announced our pregnancy to our families at the Thanksgiving table last year. Three days later I miscarried. I thought I had gotten over my feelings pretty well until Thanksgiving came around again. I don't know how I ever got through the meal this year, but, worse still, I can't believe that no one else appreciated how difficult it would be for me.

> My sister and I became pregnant within a week of each other. Since she lives several hundred miles away, we followed each other's pregnancies by telephone conversations—until I had a miscarriage at four months. Our telephone conversations after that were pretty strained, and when she had her baby I shed some tears for the baby I couldn't have, but what really caught me by surprise was my reaction when I held my new niece for the first time when she was several months old. I was overwhelmed

with my feelings of loss as I realized that my own baby would have been just this size, and that I wouldn't have had to put her back into my sister's arms.

For couples with a history of infertility, including pregnancy loss, the miscarriage will be a devastating blow. Many of these couples have tried for months or years to achieve a pregnancy, and all of them have had ample experience with mourning their reproductive unpredictability; therefore, the miscarriage represents many losses and a major setback. It not only means the loss of a cherished dream child, but it also threatens the couple's future roles as parents. They may regard the miscarriage as a final judgment that they will never have children, and this notion may precipitate significant depression in one or both partners. The need for ongoing emotional support after the miscarriage is especially crucial for the infertile couple, as they grapple with this latest blow to their hopes for a birth child.

The Medical and Emotional Experience of Miscarriage. After spending between a few hours to a few days at home with cramps or intermittent bleeding, the woman is advised by her physician to come to the hospital emergency room to be examined. If the miscarriage has occurred at home and the woman has collected the material expelled, this tissue will be examined. The woman's reaction to collecting the matter passed from her uterus can range from fear and revulsion to the feeling that to be able to gather together what remains of the pregnancy is a special experience, as if its very presence confirms that she once was pregnant.

Upon arriving in the emergency room, both partners experience some confusion, terror, and denial, often believing that the threatened miscarriage represents a bad scare but that everything will be fine again. But when the physician explains that the woman is miscarrying and will lose the baby, or when a dilation and curettage (D & C) or a dilation and evacuation (D & E, used for second-trimester pregnancies) is performed, the finality of the pregnancy becomes more and more apparent. Some physicians recommend that the couple be allowed to see whatever has been expelled or removed from the uterus, so that they realize the pregnancy is really over.

The physical pain involved lends its own terror to the experience. The male usually feels powerless to help his partner, while the female has little awareness of what to expect. The fear of the unknown probably adds to her physical tension and perception of pain. Most couples experiencing a miscarriage have no familiarity with the relaxation techniques associated with controlling pain in labor and, in fact, may not conceptualize the woman's experience as that of being in labor.

Another unsettling aspect to the miscarriage experience involves the couple's feelings and previous experiences with hospitals and medical care. If neither partner has had any experience as a patient in a hospital, the miscarriage will assume even more of an aura of crisis than if one of them has some awareness of what to expect. If they can simply express their needs and obtain information from medical personnel, their feelings of alienation in the hospital environment can be allayed.

Some women are sent home directly from the emergency room; others, usually those with late spontaneous abortions, may be hospitalized for a brief recovery period. Many hospitals will assign the woman to a room on the maternity floor. Although administratively and medically convenient, this practice totally ignores the feelings of the couple as they are subjected to crying babies, beaming parents, and a noisy nursery down the corridor. Women placed on maternity wards tell of confusion by hospital staff, who, assuming that presence on the maternity ward means that a baby has been born, wish the couple well, inquire about the baby, and, in the worst possible scenario, place someone else's baby into the woman's arms for feeding. A woman who has had a late spontaneous abortion may find that her breasts fill with milk on the second or third day postpartum, and if she is still in the hospital and on the maternity floor, the sound of a baby crying may stimulate her lactation.

Although the miscarriage is a loss for both partners, the male's emotions are often lost in the events that focus primarily on the female. The male is likely to feel helpless as he watches his partner in physical and emotional pain, and, very possibly, he will feel that he cannot indulge his own emotions but must be strong for his partner's sake. Many males, culturally accustomed to keeping their feelings inside, have difficulty recognizing that the miscarriage is an event that evokes strong feelings of loss; instead of acknowledging sadness, they may display other emotions, such as anger and resentment. Some males, in part because of their own inability to recognize their sorrow and in part because of the difficulty they experience in seeing their partners grieve, act cheerful and try to cheer up their emotionally bereft partner. Other males will feel responsible for causing the pain, because of their role in making the woman pregnant, and may vow never to put their partners through this again.

Another response by the male may be relief that the miscarriage is over and that his partner is all right and no longer in physical pain. The woman may experience similar emotions, including relief that she has survived an awful ordeal. These emotions are common to survivors of accidents and disasters, and usually also include feelings of guilt that they survived while others did not. In an attempt to make sense out of their emotional confusion, the couple may feel compelled to review their behavior during the pregnancy and to absolve themselves of whatever guilt they feel.

It is entirely likely that the two partners will have different, and conflicting, methods of coming to terms with their loss.

> Alan and I coped so differently! My energy was totally depleted for months, and Alan somehow needed or wanted to take on one major project after another—perhaps to gain some mastery or perhaps because my grief was too painful for him to hang in with.

Some couples, as a way of sharing their loss with others, will hold a "remembrance" service, with poems, prayers, and personal comments from the couple and from loved ones who shared the sadness of their loss. In a society that has no rituals for the often invisible loss of a pregnancy, a remembrance service can comfort the couple and validate their feelings of attachment to the baby who will never be born.

In order to counsel individuals and couples who have experienced a miscarriage, the professional not only must understand the meaning of that experience for them but also must be familiar with facts about miscarriages, especially the likelihood of recurrence, the possible causes, and the common myths that many people associate with the event of a miscarriage.

Frequency of Miscarriages. It is estimated that between 15 and 20 percent of all pregnancies end in miscarriages (Pizer and Palinski, 1980, p. 27). In fact, the real incidence of miscarriage is even higher, because statistics do not record those recognized miscarriages that do not come to a physician's attention or those that go unrecognized and are noted only as delayed or unusually heavy menstrual periods (Friedman and Gradstein, 1982, p. 30).

Age as a Contributing Factor. Age does not cause miscarriage, but the chances of having a miscarriage are associated with increasing maternal age, as the following figures (cited by Pizer and Palinski, 1980, p. 15) indicate:

Age	Spontaneous Abortions (%)
20	12
25	15
30	17
36	22
40	31
42	41

It is important to note that, until recently, most research on older women who have children has been limited by small population size.

Occupation as a Contributing Factor. The following industries have been linked to an increased frequency of spontaneous abortions:

Metallurgy plants: exposure to copper, lead, arsenic, cadmium

Radio and television manufacturing: exposure to solder
fumes
Chemical laboratories: exposure to solvents and other
chemicals
Plastics factories: exposure to polyvinyl chloride and other chemicals

Health as a Contributing Factor. A serious disease or mal-
nutrition may result in either an early or a late spontaneous
abortion. Smoking, alcohol consumption, and ingestion of medications contribute to problems in some pregnancies.

Myths Concerning Causes of Miscarriage. Misconceptions
regarding the causes of miscarriage still abound. Medical research
has now disproved some of these myths. The following factors,
cited by Pizer and Palinski (1980, p. 12), are not known to be
causes of miscarriage:

Use of an oral contraceptive prior to pregnancy
Prior use of an intrauterine device
Previous gonorrhea or other venereal disease, or pelvic in-
flammatory disease
A previous elective abortion (except for the rare case of
an incompetent cervix)
In general, horseback riding, working, or exercising
Sexual intercourse, in any position, during pregnancy

Most miscarriages have no discernible cause. The failure to
find a cause usually is a positive sign, because it indicates that
random factors were probably responsible and that a recurrent
difficulty is not present.

Likelihood of Recurrence. Most studies indicate that a
couple who have had a miscarriage have essentially the same
chance as any other couple of producing a normal baby. Some
studies reveal, in fact, that they are more likely than the average
couple to have a normal baby, possibly because the woman's
body has a proven mechanism (the spontaneous abortion) for
rejecting genetic abnormalities.

Statistics cited by Pizer and Palinski (1980, p. 19) indicate that, after the loss of a single pregnancy, the chance of another loss is only 20 percent. Women who have given birth to one child and miscarry their second pregnancy have an even better chance of successful future childbearing. After two losses, however, the chance increases to about 33 percent; after three spontaneous abortions, the chance increases to about 50 percent. Reliable studies of women who have had more than three spontaneous abortions do not exist.

Offering Professional Support. The support needed by the couple is similar to that needed after the experience of an ectopic pregnancy. Many elements of the mourning process will emerge; individuals will need support as they reach out for help from their partners and other family members. Couples experiencing a miscarriage will perceive the event uniquely, depending on their backgrounds and the experience that their miscarriage represents for them. The helping professional must understand the meaning that both the man and the woman attach to the miscarriage, in order to be most responsive to their immediate needs and to help them communicate with one another about the impact of the experience. Because the miscarriage usually has not been anticipated, it may represent a crisis for the couple as they struggle to find coping mechanisms appropriate for coming to terms with the loss of their developing baby. Although the greatest concentration of professional help at the time of a miscarriage will be from hospital personnel, all helping professionals in contact with the couple must be highly sensitive to their emotional needs, both at the time of the actual miscarriage and for whatever subsequent period of time it takes each partner to assimilate the experience in a functional way. Professionals should also keep in mind that unresolved feelings of loss around a miscarriage will be likely to surface on the anniversary date of the miscarriage and when any subsequent loss occurs; conversely, the individual who has been helped to mourn the loss of a pregnancy may be able to use those coping skills in coming to terms with any future losses.

11

Stillbirth

Stillbirth, defined as the death of the fetus between the twentieth week of pregnancy and birth, is always a devastating blow to prospective parents. Whether the baby dies prior to the onset of labor, during labor, or at delivery, the parents feel completely unprepared for this tragic outcome of the pregnancy. In the United States, one stillbirth occurs for every eighty live births (Friedman and Gradstein, 1982, p. xvi).

Before the Delivery

The interruption of an otherwise uneventful pregnancy by complications is frightening and bewildering for most prospective parents. Sometimes the woman does not feel the baby move for a day or so, and further investigation by her obstetrician reveals the lack of a fetal heartbeat. In other situations, the physician fails to detect a fetal heartbeat on a prenatal visit. Bleeding may be an indication of problems with the pregnancy. Often a sonogram will be used as a final confirmation of the news that is devastating to the parents: their baby has died. The finality of that pronouncement is usually too shocking for the couple to grasp as they try to reconcile their earlier happy anticipation with the realization that the baby they have not even met will not be theirs to cherish (DeFrain, 1986; Berezin, 1982).

In the midst of their emerging grief, the couple may be told that the pregnancy cannot be terminated until labor begins spontaneously or until labor can be induced closer to the due date. In the meantime, the couple must consider how to handle the well-intentioned questions about the pregnancy, the baby, and the due date, as well as their own ambivalence about wanting to postpone the heartache of delivery while, at the same time, wanting to get it over with. The waiting period before the delivery will be painful in many ways, and the professional will want to help the couple think through how they can gain some sense of control over their lives. Practically speaking, the couple need to add some comfort to their lives during the painful waiting period; they need to talk about their pain as a way of working through their sadness; and they may need encouragement to be open about their emotions, both with each other and with concerned friends and relatives.

Friends and relatives can be especially helpful at this time: acting as good listeners, bringing in food, running errands, and helping with child care if there are other children in the family. The couple must consider how to inform these people of their sad news and how to respond to the question "What can I do to help?" The couple also may need help in anticipating how they will respond to questions from those who do not know of their baby's death, since the external appearance of pregnancy remains the same. The woman may be tempted to seclude herself, retreat from the empathic smiles of others, avoid infants and pregnant women, and withdraw from a world that expects her to be joyful in the anticipation of parenthood.

Her mate also must respond to painful questions and comments from friends and colleagues and must decide how and with whom to share his emotions. If he is employed, he may feel that he should not take time off until after the delivery, even though he and his partner need time together during the period of mourning while they wait for labor to begin. Whether in the workplace or at home, he will inevitably be faced with questions about his mate's well-being. These inquiries may make him feel as if he is a mere bystander in the sorrow of the lost pregnancy, rather than someone who has undergone a devastating loss and who needs as much comfort and support as his partner. One husband described his experience this way:

> Since Mary Lou was too broken up to talk to anyone, I became the go-between. Friends and rela-

tives would ask me to tell Mary Lou of their love and concern, but in the process of being the family messenger I felt as if my own grief were being discounted and ignored.

The professional can help in a number of ways. The couple must be encouraged to talk and cry together about their loss and to specify the particular losses represented by their baby's death. In addition, the professional can encourage the couple to make their needs known to others, especially before the delivery and after the stillbirth. The couple must be aware enough of their needs to be able to express them to others. They may want to consider which friends and relatives offer the most comfort and support. If religion is an important force in the life of the man or woman, a member of the clergy may be able to offer important solace at a time when faith is difficult to sustain.

If the couple have not attended childbirth education classes to prepare them for the delivery, they may want to contact a childbirth education leader to learn what techniques will minimize the woman's physical pain during the delivery. Knowing what to expect during labor and delivery, and having some feelings of control under otherwise dreaded circumstances, may be important as the couple face the fresh pain of the stillbirth. The couple should be encouraged to ask the obstetrician any questions they have and to make their needs known.

Although the tragedy of carrying a dead child is inestimable, the time before delivery may allow the couple to make some important decisions in the process of mourning: whether to hold their baby after it is born; whether to keep a lock of the baby's hair, the hospital wristband, the blanket the baby was wrapped in, or a record of weight and length; and whether to have a photograph taken of the baby or of them holding the baby. They also can make decisions about having a baptism or a service, naming the baby, and sending out announcements of the baby's birth and death. They must also decide whether to have an autopsy performed. They can find out whether the woman will be placed on the maternity floor or in another section of the hospital and whether unrestricted visiting hours will be allowed for her mate. Finally, they can make plans for the difficult time when the woman leaves the hospital and returns home with empty arms. These decisions will be discussed in more detail later in the chapter.

In the Hospital

Although some couples must wait several days or weeks for labor to begin once they know the baby is dead, many couples have very little forewarning of one of the most tragic experiences they will ever have to face. The onset of labor may occur soon after the fetal heartbeat is undetected, or fetal distress during delivery may be the prelude to the delivery of their stillborn child. For these couples, the tension of childbirth gives way to shock and disbelief as they try to comprehend the death of their baby and the loss it represents in their world. The newness of the unanticipated decisions that the parents must make in the midst of their shock and grief lends an unreality to the entire experience. In this context, the involvement of a helping professional can be particularly crucial.

The professional's efforts can focus in several directions. Practically speaking, the couple need time to grieve and to be comforted. The professional can be an advocate for them in the hospital, so that they can be together as much as possible to make the difficult decisions ahead. The first question that often arises is whether the woman should be placed on the maternity floor with other obstetrical patients. If the woman prefers to be placed on another floor, away from squalling newborns and joyful parents, every effort should be made to accommodate her wishes. A single room, if available and feasible, would allow the couple the privacy to grieve without interruptions from unwanted visitors or other patients. If the couple wish, the man should be allowed unlimited visiting hours, including overnight stays. In deciding how long she should remain in the hospital, the woman and her physician should take into account her physical well-being and her psychological readiness to go home.

In the midst of the couple's raw grief, the helping professional may present some options that they will later find comforting. Memories associated with the baby will help the couple ultimately come to terms with the loss. But memories must be consciously created, because the overwhelming recollection will be the horror of the stillbirth experience and the hushed sounds after the delivery. The helping professional may want to help the couple think of ways that they can create both memories and mementoes, not of the shock of the stillbirth but of the baby itself. If the parents did not see their baby after the delivery, they may benefit from having this option offered to them again. Any resistances they feel about seeing the baby should be explored, so that misperceptions about the baby's appearance can be clarified. The helping professional might ask the couple whether someone present at the delivery should tell them what the baby looked like or whether the helping professional should view the baby's body. The professional who does so may tell the parents that, although it is sad to see a baby who has died, there is also a beauty and uniqueness in their baby.

The parents should not be pressured to see or hold their baby if they find it too difficult, but as many options as possible should be offered, so that they will have some memory of their baby to aid them in the mourning process. If one or both of the parents choose to see or hold their baby, they may wish privacy during this experience or they may prefer to have a few loved ones present. The helping professional should do everything possible to enable the parents' wishes to be respected during this time of grief. The parents should be encouraged to unwrap the baby and to look at it. Holding and looking at the baby will help the parents realize that they can cherish the memory of its uniqueness for many years.

The professional can help the couple consider whether they would like a photograph of the baby, taken by themselves or by the hospital, if provided. They may want a photograph of themselves holding the baby. If the couple do not want a picture, the helping professional may suggest that a photograph could be kept in the hospital files in case the parents change their minds at any time.

Whether to name the baby is another important decision, although the couple should not be pressured or rushed. The helping professional might suggest that it will be easier to talk about their baby and its death if they are able to call the baby by name. Also, a name has a symbolic importance; it says to the world that this baby was born and carries a place in the family memories. Some parents may feel that naming their baby will make them become too attached, so that they will feel greater pain while mourning their loss. The helping professional will need to point out that the parents have already become very attached, by virtue of having loved, wanted, and fantasized about their baby during the past months. The pain of loss is going to be there whether or not the baby has a name.

Parents who decide to name the baby also must decide what name to choose. Parents who had already chosen a name need to consider whether to use that name for their baby who has died. The helping professional might want to point out that, in a sense, the chosen name really does belong to this baby; if saved for a future child, it may carry memories of the baby for whom it was originally planned. A special name can be chosen for a future baby, just as the parents had chosen a particular name in anticipation of this baby.

Religious and personal beliefs will influence the couple's decision about having an autopsy performed. If the parents have a strong need to know what went wrong and whether the baby was healthy, an autopsy may provide some clues. Parents must be told, though, that an autopsy cannot always determine the cause of the stillbirth. If the parents plan to see the baby after the autopsy as part of a funeral service, they must be certain that the hospital and funeral director are both informed. The preliminary results of an autopsy may take one or two weeks; the full autopsy report will take several weeks longer. Once available, the results should be reviewed with a medical professional who can interpret the findings and answer the couple's questions. If the couple have questions after the autopsy conference, they should be encouraged to contact the medical professional for further clarification.

Whether to baptize the baby will depend on the couple's religious beliefs and need for personal comfort. The couple's religious leader or the hospital clergy may discuss this decision with the couple. Some denominations do not baptize children, while others baptize only the living. If religious comfort is important, however, the religious leader may suggest a range of options, including a prayer or a blessing for the baby.

Whether to have a service is also important to discuss. Again, this decision should not be rushed, except when the couple's religion encourages burial or cremation promptly after a death. Even if this is the case, the couple may decide to have a separate memorial service later. If possible, the service should be planned so that the mother can attend. In some cases, having the service in the hospital chapel will be preferred; in other circumstances, the service can be delayed until the mother has come home from the hospital. The helping professional will want to assist the couple in gathering information about burial and cremation and deciding which one is preferred. An important consideration may be whether the couple would like to have a memorial site to visit. It is important to ascertain whether the cemetery in which the baby will be buried allows for individualized markers, rather than having an anonymous plot in its infant section.

The service itself can be planned with the help of clergy, family, and close friends. The parents should be aware of the choices they can make, including what the baby will wear and whether they will take a part in dressing the baby or covering it with a blanket. Parents may want a special keepsake, doll, or other article placed in the casket or in the baby's hand. If the parents want to have some special involvement in the service, they should be encouraged to do so. The parents may wish to tape the service as one more way of preserving an important memory. If the baby will be viewed at the service, the couple may want to plan some private time with the baby before including loved ones in their expressions of shared sorrow. When family and close friends are included in the service, they will be better able to empathize with the couple's feelings in the months ahead. Many families find that sharing a meal with loved ones after the service can give emotional replenishment.

Regardless of the couple's choices about a service, some consideration will need to be given to notifying friends of the baby's birth and death. In some cases, the couple will prefer to call a few people and ask them to call others. For out-of-town friends and relatives, an announcement may be mailed. One such announcement, sent by parents of a stillborn son, was sensitively worded, "We are sad to tell you that our son [his name] was born and died on [date]. This baby meant so much to us. We hope you will understand and share in our sorrow and loss."

As they make plans for the mother to leave the hospital, both parents will have ambivalent feelings. On the one hand, the hospital, with all its reminders of the stillbirth and the intense feelings surrounding it, may have felt like a prison for the couple, who yearn to "get back to normal." On the other hand, the hospital offered something of a cushion against the realities of facing the world with empty arms, an empty nursery, and an ache in the heart. The mother may feel less bereft if she has a keepsake of the baby to carry out of the hospital with her as she leaves.

Returning Home

Once home, the mother will be still experiencing the physical aftermath of her delivery, whether it was vaginal or by Cesarean section. The discomforts associated with recovery—engorged breasts, a still-pregnant appearance, and a lack of energy —will not be cushioned by the joy of having a newborn to cherish. In addition to the physical discomforts, the mother also must adjust to her body's hormonal changes. Such changes may make her feelings of depression even more intense. During this time, a professional can help both the mother and father communicate about their sadness and their particular needs, since each will experience grief differently.

Arriving home with empty arms is painful, and this difficulty may be compounded by the appearance of the nursery or whatever area of the home had been set aside for the baby's homecoming. Some family members, wishing to spare the mother the pain of seeing the empty nursery, may have dismantled it and put away all reminders of preparations for the baby. If the mother was not consulted, she may feel robbed of the chance to make her own choices about how to deal with the baby's things; and the sight of the dismantled nursery may precipitate a fresh outburst of grief and anger.

> When I came home, I was shocked to find that all my careful preparations for the baby's arrival had been erased. It was as if I had never even been pregnant. The nursery had been turned back into my sewing room; the booties and blankets I had knitted had been hidden away; the gifts from the baby shower were nowhere to be seen. It was as if people expected me to get back to normal and forget that we had organized not just our home but our whole lives to be ready for the baby's arrival. Now our lives were shattered, and my relatives had robbed me of the chance to begin picking up the pieces myself.

If the nursery has not been touched, the parents can take time to decide what they want to do with the room. They need not feel that they are abnormal if they want to leave it as is for a while; after all, they have a great deal of grief to absorb, and there is no need to rush in such a private decision. If and when the couple decide to make changes in the room, they may want to ask a close friend or a relative to help or, perhaps, to do it for them. Some couples choose to leave the room as it is, to remind them that their hopes for another baby thrive, despite the tragedy of losing the baby for whom the nursery was originally assembled.

The couple may be tempted initially to get rid of all reminders of the nursery, as a way of banishing their pain. The professional might want to caution them against making too hasty a decision, especially if they may, at some later time, consider conceiving or adopting a baby. Their pain will be with them regardless of the visual reminders of the nursery, and even these reminders can be tucked away, either in their home or someone else's, until they can make a plan not influenced by the haste of trying to restore normalcy to their lives.

The mother, who nurtured the baby in her body, will feel a unique emptiness and may express the feeling that she has lost a part of herself. This is especially true with a stillbirth, because the parents have had no opportunity to get acquainted with their child as a person separate from the mother. The mother's associations with her baby, therefore, are those of the baby in utero; and she will feel the loss of her baby both as a bodily loss and as an emotional loss. There may also be feelings of shattered self-esteem, as the mother wonders why she—unlike many other women—was unable to give birth to a healthy baby. Such feelings are common in the infertility experience, but to have come so close to having a healthy baby and not to realize this dream leaves the parents' self-esteem particularly vulnerable.

The mother will need to make choices about how to spend the first days and weeks after the stillbirth. The professional should help her understand that the early months will be filled with an emptiness and a longing for the baby. Talking about the baby, both to her mate and to understanding loved ones, will probably be helpful; but she will also need some privacy for her grief. At this time, the helping professional might want to ask the woman what other losses she has sustained in her life and what methods of coping worked best for her during those difficult times. If the mother has not adequately mourned the earlier losses, she may need to grieve not only for her baby but also for the reawakened losses that the baby's death may represent for her.

The helping professional will want to encourage the woman to pamper herself and not to expect too much of herself too soon, either emotionally or physically. Food and exercise may be especially important to discuss at this time. The woman may not have the energy or the inclination to prepare and eat nutritionally well-balanced meals. The helping professional may need to explore at this time what food represents to her. Careful eating may be a poignant reminder of her concern about nutrition during pregnancy, and now she no longer feels entitled to take care of herself alone. Perhaps this is a woman who tends to undereat or overeat during times of stress. If so, the helping professional may help the woman see that her current attitude toward food is interrelated with her grief. Together, they may explore ways in which needs can be met apart from food, putting nutrition in its proper perspective.

The woman's physical appearance is likely to be of concern. The woman may feel that her body has been pulled out of shape "all for nothing," and she may feel anger about her physical appearance. Anger is a highly energizing emotion and may prompt the woman to consider how to begin getting her shape back. She should seek the approval of her physician or of a physical therapist before undertaking an exercise regimen, because it may be too taxing or inappropriate for the particular muscles that she hopes to tighten. She should be encouraged, however, to consider some form of regular, moderate exercise. The decision to exercise may enable the woman to get out of doors, join an exercise group, and get her mind off her sadness.

Rejoining the real world may hold special terrors for the woman who is still recovering from a stillbirth. If she still looks pregnant, she may dread the questions from well-meaning strangers. She may be amazed at how the stillbirth experience has altered her perspective of the world: the sight of pregnant women and infants may stimulate feelings of anger and jealousy; seeing baby food and diapers in the grocery store may cause tears to well up in her eyes; even a picture or an article in a magazine or a newspaper may remind the woman of her dashed hopes and dreams.

The helping professional can help the woman with these problems in several ways. Some women may feel guilty about their anger toward expectant parents or parents of small children because, they believe, "Nice people don't feel that way." The professional should inform the woman that these feelings are normal for someone who has experienced her particular sadness and reassure her that she is not a bad person for having such thoughts. When the woman has these feelings toward close friends or relatives, the situation is more delicate. The woman may want to explain to them that being with them is difficult in these early weeks and months, because she is reminded of the joy she had hoped they could share as their families grew together. She may, on the other hand, want to see her friends without their infants and children. In addition, the woman may want to ask for her family's understanding if she avoids family reunions with children, family christenings, baby showers, and other painful events.

The helping professional may want to explore with the woman how, or whether, to keep the lines of communication open with loved ones who currently serve as reminders of joyful parenthood. The woman may, in time, be able to take small steps toward incorporating these relationships back into her life, especially those with her most empathic and supportive friends and relatives. She may need help in distinguishing which friends and relatives are not capable of understanding her particular needs—namely, those who tell her that she should be over her sadness by now, make her feel guilty for choosing to remain away from a family affair, tell her that she is wallowing in her grief, or feel awkward with her no matter what her mood. People who cannot be helpful to her as she recovers emotionally should be avoided as much as possible; and, when necessary, the woman's mate should help protect her from being pressured to participate in events that she does not feel ready to handle.

Another problem that the woman may face has to do with structuring her time. If she has quit her job in anticipation of spending her days with her newborn, she may now feel unproductive and lacking in personal worth. In the first weeks, she may benefit from some time at home to pamper herself, absorb the shock of her loss, and gain physical strength and emotional equilibrium. If being at home is a difficult reminder of the infant who cannot share her days, however, then reentering the work force may be highly therapeutic. The time away from her previous job may give her the flexibility she needs to consider taking some courses, either for fun or for educational advancement, doing volunteer work, or exploring new career directions.

Returning to Work

If, rather than quitting her job, the woman has taken maternity leave, returning to work may cause problems. If the maternity leave is time limited, the woman may be pressured to return before she feels ready to undertake the demands of her job. In that case, the helping professional might explore with her such options as asking her employer for an extension or for fewer hours, returning on the expected date to see how she is able to manage, claiming a disability based on the emotional adjustment she needs to make following the stillbirth, or quitting her job altogether. Some jobs may be especially difficult for the woman to resume, especially if they require contact with infants, children, or pregnant women. Other difficult-to-resume jobs may be those with demanding hours or unpredictable work schedules. A woman who needs to have a sense of control over some aspects of her life may feel undue pressure if her job does not allow her to exert this control. The woman who does not have the financial flexibility to leave her job may need to become involved in counseling as she continues to balance her work with her need to mourn.

Whether in a familiar work setting or in a new undertaking, the woman will find unanticipated difficulties. Some colleagues will make insensitive remarks ("When are you going to try again?" "It's all for the best," "Glad to see you looking so cheerful"), some will avoid her out of feelings of awkwardness, and others will ignore altogether any reference to the stillbirth, effectively communicating their view of it as a nonevent.

> The worst recollection that I have as I think back was of people who knew of our son's stillbirth and said nothing. Nothing! Did they think that by ignoring our love for him they were shielding us from pain? Oh, we felt the pain all right, but it was made so much worse by their inability to acknowledge our tremendous loss!

The woman may want to think of times during the day or places where she can have the privacy to shed a few tears, as she will probably need to do. It may be difficult to encounter people whose lives are calm or who tend to complain about what seem like petty issues. The woman may feel out of place in the midst of the workplace gossip, which now seems irrelevant and unimportant compared with her own struggle to get through each day. If she has returned to work after originally having planned to take some time off to be with her baby, she may sense a feeling of unreality because she is working rather than being where she thinks she should be—at home taking care of her baby.

Other Children

If the stillborn infant was not the first child in the family, then both parents' need to grieve is complicated by other demands in their lives: the other child or children, the laundry, the shopping and cooking, and whatever other tasks at home need to be attended to regularly because of the needs of the other children. To the extent that they can, the parents should be encouraged to let their friends and relatives know in concrete ways how they can help. If money is not a problem, the couple should consider purchasing some of the services that would otherwise overburden them.

To combat any feelings of failure about the stillbirth, the woman may try to "do it all" on the home front, thereby tiring herself out and not leaving time for working through her grief. Much as she loves her other children, she will probably find herself becoming impatient more quickly. Concentrating may be difficult, as may be any readiness to make decisions. The parents may need the professional's support as they help their children understand the stillbirth and the feelings that have emerged in its aftermath. Parents may need to be reassured that they can share their tears with their children as they explain that they are sad about the baby's death and that their crying is one way of expressing their sadness. Parents may find helpful suggestions in books that explain a child's perspective on loss and death (Bernstein, 1983; Arnstein, 1978; Bluebond-Langner, 1977; Grollman, 1967; Jackson, 1965; Nagy, 1965; Ilse, Burns, and Erling, 1984).

Parents should be aware that most young children have ambivalent feelings at the prospect of a new baby arriving in the house. In the midst of their apprehensions about the impact that a new baby might have on their lives, children at one time or another may have expressed the wish that the baby not come into the family. Even if these thoughts have not been expressed, they probably have been on the minds of children in the family. Parents need to acknowledge to the children that it is normal for them to have wondered what changes in their lives the baby's arrival would bring and, even, to have wished that the baby would not come into the family at all. Parents will further need to point out to children that no one in the family caused the baby to die and that the death could not have been prevented by anyone in the family. Just as the whole family has joined together to anticipate the baby's birth, so it needs to draw together to mourn the baby's death. Secretive mourning by the adults in the family may cause the children to feel excluded and rejected, and may add further to any existing feelings of guilt that are present.

If the children are preschoolers, they are likely to be confused about what has occurred. They see family members grieving for a baby that never came home from the hospital. The children may associate hospitals with negative events, since their mother left them to go to the hospital, had a baby there who died, and then came home sad and crying. The parents will want to point out that hospitals, doctors, and nurses are helpful in many ways to people who need them. Preschoolers are also likely to be confused about the concept of death. They will not understand its permanence and may benefit from having the parent remind them of a plant or a pet that has died. Being dead should not be described as the same as going to sleep, because the children may become fearful that they could die in their sleep. Since preschoolers think in concrete rather than in abstract terms, they can be told that being dead means that you cannot see the person anymore. Even when the physical permanence of death is stressed, though, parents will probably want to assure their children that they are still entitled to have feelings for the baby that died. Parents should emphasize that, even though the baby's death has made them sad, they still love their remaining children very much.

Older children are more capable of understanding death,

partly because of their capacity to think more abstractly and partly because they may have had more experience with death. Despite their ability to grasp the concept of death more easily, though, there will still be many residual feelings with which they may need help. It is a good idea to inform the child's teacher of the loss the family is mourning, so that the teacher can be especially understanding of and responsive to the child during this difficult time. The teacher should be asked to draw to the parents' attention any problems that arise in school that perhaps should be discussed in more detail at home. An older child may feel anger at the baby for causing grief in the family or for usurping the parents' time. The child may use negative behaviors as a way of telling the parents, "Here I am. I'm alive and I need you!" Regressive behaviors, school phobias, and general separation anxieties are common responses for children in a family where a death is being mourned. If parents feel drained and incapable of giving special attention to their children, they should consider other resource people—clergy, counselors, close relatives, favorite teachers, or parents of friends—who might be helpful at this time, either for them or for their children.

The Father

As the father begins to face the world again, he may encounter special difficulties. Solicitous friends will inquire about his mate's condition, perhaps neglecting to recognize that he, too, has sustained a tremendous loss and deserves concern as well. A husband relates:

> People were forever asking how they could help or, worse still, suggesting things that I could do to make the experience less tormenting for Sally. Everyone seemed to assume that my role in all of this was to be the strong one. It would have meant so much for someone to have offered *me* a shoulder to lean on!

Just as the general subject of death is an awkward one for many people to respond to, the special nature of this death will cause both friends and acquaintances to be uncertain of the most supportive ways to extend themselves. Some people, in their awkwardness, will not even express their condolences, leaving the father to wonder whether these people view the stillbirth as a nonevent. The awkwardness of others can cause the father to wonder whether he is entitled to mourn, and it is in this area that the professional can be especially helpful.

The father may assume that his mate has sustained the greater loss, because she carried the baby in her body during the pregnancy, and that he should be emotionally strong to enable her to lean on him as she mourns.

> John seemed so preoccupied with comforting me that I began to wonder where his feelings were. He seemed to be getting back to normal at the very time I was falling apart. I found myself feeling furious that he could absorb such a tremendous loss with so little reaction. I began to hate it when he comforted me. What I really needed was for him to share the sadness he was hiding so effectively.

The professional can help him recognize that, even though he was not pregnant, he shared his wife's dreams for their child. He might be encouraged to discuss some of his fantasies about what the baby represented: the chance to be a parent; the opportunity to nurture a new life and to share it as the baby grew; the anticipation of birthday parties, developmental milestones, and sharing family traditions; the curiosity about family resemblances, inherited talents, and the investment in the name that he and his mate selected for this special child. In addition to helping the father recognize the loss that his baby's death represents to him, this discussion of his attachment to the baby will help him put into words the ache that he may be stoically enduring.

Once the father has been encouraged to accept his stake

in this baby, he may recognize that he has a right to grieve for all the losses represented by the baby's death. The helping professional may want to remind the father that neither he nor anyone else can protect his mate from the grief she will feel and that they might both be solaced if they share their sadness. Even though the parents may be at different stages in the mourning process, keeping the channels of communication open between them is vitally important.

Because males in American society are often socialized to be stoic in the face of disaster, to ignore their feelings in favor of getting on with life, and to keep their emotions to themselves, the helping professional needs to reassure the father that crying is a normal response to the devastating emotional blow he has experienced. Males who believe that crying is a sign of weakness can be told that it takes a brave person indeed to be in touch with painful feelings and to express them through crying. Crying can also be described as an excellent tension release. These statements may help the father reframe his attitudes about his crying and recognize that crying can have a therapeutic effect on his mate. The professional also can help the father think of other people whom he can talk to about his feelings—for example, a member of the clergy or another professional who is especially sensitive to the loss he has sustained. Since some men may still be more inclined to take action as an expression of their grief than to use talking as an outlet, the helping professional will want to discuss with the father whether certain efforts to memorialize his child would comfort him and other family members. Such efforts will be discussed later in this chapter.

The Couple

The strain of the loss on the couple's relationship will take a variety of forms. Initially, the couple will try to ascertain how much they can expect from each other by way of comfort, understanding, and responsibility for day-to-day tasks that now feel especially burdensome. The couple may benefit from concrete suggestions about ways to reconnect with geographically or emotionally distant family members. Perhaps they can ask family members to call more often than usual, even after the first weeks. Visits from some members of the family may be welcome, or perhaps the couple could travel to be with particularly supportive family members. The focus on the larger family network is appropriate at this time, because if the extended family is distant, the couple may find themselves totally dependent on one another for mutual comfort. When each is so bereft, it is not reasonable to expect that either could have the emotional strength to meet the needs of the other.

In some cases, family members will not be the most helpful comforters for the couple. The couple will need to anticipate which friends, clergy, or community professionals they can reach out to for comfort. If the community has a support group composed of other parents who have suffered pregnancy loss or the death of a child, the couple might be encouraged to contact such a group. RESOLVE and Compassionate Friends are national groups concerned about parents grieving a stillborn child, and they have chapters in many cities as well as publications available to the public.

The couple's sexual intimacy is likely to be affected by the sadness they feel over the loss of their baby. Some couples find that intimacy offers them a special closeness at a time when life has little joy. Others find that the irritations and tensions of the day intrude on their sexual relationship and prevent them from enjoying sex. They may even feel that pleasure of any kind is disloyal while they mourn their baby, or they may associate sexual relationships with fear because of the prospect of a new pregnancy. Conversely, one or both partners may feel a desperate need to achieve another pregnancy as soon as possible, thereby turning sexual intimacy into a procreative effort at the possible expense of the comforting pleasures otherwise associated with lovemaking. For other couples, memories of how their dead child was conceived may overshadow their reawakening sexual interest.

The tensions associated with sexual intimacy vary; they include impotence, sobbing during lovemaking, physical pain during intercourse, and loss of desire. In addition, the two partners may have very different feelings about their readiness to have intercourse. The woman will need to recuperate physically from childbirth, which many physicians believe takes about six weeks. Even after the six-week period, though, the woman may find that her vagina does not lubricate easily during lovemaking, which may contribute to pain during intercourse. The emotional readiness for intercourse may also be different for the partners. If one person is eager to resume lovemaking and the other is hesitant or opposed, the resulting tension can exacerbate the grieving process.

Open communication will be especially important at this time. The helping professional may encourage the couple to appreciate the many forms of sexual closeness and intimacy, since some couples tend to define sexual pleasure solely in terms of intercourse. The professional may also want to help the couple think of ways that they can separate their necessary grief from their efforts to be sexually intimate. They might, for instance, avoid discussing their baby in the bedroom or in whatever other part of the house they choose to make love; or they might set aside some time, long before lovemaking, to talk about their day and the way in which their grief has been helped or hurt by the events they have experienced. To begin lovemaking with these feelings unexpressed will make it difficult to focus on mutual pleasuring.

The helping professional may need to broach the subject of sexual intimacy with the couple, since many couples feel awkward about bringing up such a personal and sensitive subject. Once the couple understand that tensions around sexual intimacy are normal, they may feel comfortable about confiding any difficulties that they have been experiencing.

Memorializing the Baby

The word *memorialize* means "to commit to memory." Some parents who have experienced a pregnancy loss may want to have a lasting memorial to their child. Those who have buried their child may choose a small headstone for the grave. Those who did not have a service when their baby died may want to plan a service. Some parents have jewelry made, using their baby's birthstone, as a special keepsake. If the parents have a yard, they may want to plant a special flower or a tree.

Memorial gifts could include books for the public library, baby furniture for a day care center, or a scholarship for a preschooler to attend a nursery school. A donation to an organization that helps parents cope with the grief of a pregnancy loss may seem especially fitting.

At home, the parents may want to put in a special place all the keepsakes that they brought home from the hospital, perhaps adding to it a favorite baby outfit, blanket, or toy that was purchased or made especially for this baby. Parents may want to collect or write a scrapbook of poems that are especially meaningful. It may be comforting to keep a diary of the weeks and months after the baby's death, both as an outlet for feelings and, later, as a measure of how far along the parents have come in resolving their sadness.

Future Pregnancies

The decision to become pregnant again is fraught with emotion for most parents who have experienced a pregnancy loss. These couples often have mixed feelings or change their minds several times. Assuming that the woman has her physician's approval to try to conceive again, the couple may fear that they will be unable to conceive or carry a pregnancy to term, particularly if there has been a history of infertility; they may worry about whether the baby will be healthy; they may be unable to relax and enjoy a subsequent pregnancy as they did with the earlier pregnancy; and they may be besieged with emotional flashbacks of the earlier pregnancy. The professional may be especially supportive by helping the couple examine whether their readiness to try to conceive again is based on the wish to replace the child who has died or whether it is an outgrowth of their resolution of their baby's death. The pregnancy should not represent an effort to erase the loss of the stillborn baby but, rather, to acknowledge the couple's desire to build a family, incorporating their loss as integral to the fabric of that family.

If, for medical reasons or personal choice, the couple will not have another pregnancy, the helping professional's assistance may be especially important, since the couple will be mourning not only their dead child but also all the other birth children that they will not have. The decisions that the couple must face include whether to expand their family through adoption or to remain childfree and find other ways to channel their nurturing capacities.

The devastating emotions from surviving a stillbirth will touch the couple's lives for many months. The availability and support of a range of helping professionals may be very important during their period of mourning and, later, as they decide about their readiness to build their family (Lewis and Page, 1978). Although the initial shock of the stillbirth may cause the couple to be highly dependent on professionals, these individuals will assume less significant roles for the couple as they leave the hospital experience behind, plan a funeral or memorial service, and begin to pick up the fragments of their lives and move forward. All professionals who have interacted with the couple need to remember that time only gradually eases the pain of losing their baby. Therefore, even if the professional no longer has regular contact with the parents and sees them weeks or months after the stillbirth, he still should remember to ask how life has been since losing their baby, offer soothing memories of what was a highly stressful period, and determine whether there is any area in which they need help and support. Too often, friends and professionals forget that the mother and father may be silently struggling months after the most apparent sources of support have ceased and that an offer of help may be very important in their efforts to resolve their grief.

12

Conclusion:
The Persistent Legacy
of Infertility

Despite the success that an individual has in coming to terms with previous or ongoing infertility, "resolution" rarely means an end to the emotional twinges that occur from time to time. For some, the outcome of their struggle with infertility is a birth child; for others, adoption has provided a longed-for opportunity to build a family; and still others choose to remain child-free and to channel their energies in directions that do not involve raising children.

Whatever life choices an infertile person makes, the remnants of infertility are rarely banished forever but, rather, appear periodically, usually when least expected. As Menning (1977, p. 117) aptly reminds infertile people:

> My infertility resides in my heart as an old friend.
> I do not hear from it for weeks at a time, and then,
> a moment, a thought, a baby announcement or
> some such thing, and I will feel the tug—maybe
> even be sad or shed a few tears. And I think,
> "There's my old friend." It will always be part of
> me.

What are these remnants of infertility with which individuals must grapple? Although no empirical research has been done on this question, conversations with adoptive parents, long-time RESOLVE members, and former clients have highlighted several common themes.

Universal Remnants

Regardless of the life choices a person or a couple have made following "resolution," certain issues are fairly universal. The couple's sexual relationship is one. Infertile couples usually have a long history of trying to maximize their chances of conceiving by having sex during the woman's most fertile time of the month. Whether or not ovulation is controlled medically, couples experience some stress as they pinpoint the time of ovulation and doggedly try to conceive. Months or years of this behavior tend to take a toll on the sexual relationship. These couples begin to equate sex with procreation while forgetting the earlier days of sexual spontaneity and pleasure. Also, sex becomes associated with intercourse while other forms of sexual pleasuring may disappear from a couple's repertoire. Many couples feel anger about their sexual relationship because it seems to control them rather than leaving them free to grow through it. Thus, a couple with a history of infertility who, even years after resolution, complain about a void in their sexual relationship should be encouraged to explore the messages about sex that persist from that period of infertility when procreation was the primary concern.

Another issue that couples face is birth control. For couples who have tried steadfastly to conceive, the thought of practicing birth control often hits an irrational nerve. Some individuals consciously choose to practice birth control as a way to end that long period of uncertainty around conception. For such individuals, birth control represents an opportunity to exert some control in their current life around functions that were painfully out of control in the past. Other individuals, however, may need help in exploring what birth control represents for them. Are they fearful that their choice of birth control may limit future childbearing options? Are they still angry that, by using birth control before infertility was diagnosed, they may have wasted precious childbearing years? Are they resisting further intervention with their reproductive functions after extensive medical treatment for infertility?

Birth control can be problematic in other ways for some couples, especially when the method of choice is not highly reliable. Some couples are beleaguered by the fear that their method of contraception may fail, leaving them with an unintended pregnancy. Because of their earlier struggles with infertility, the couple may be emotionally resistant to considering the finality of sterilization of one partner as a way of practicing reliable birth control; yet the alternative of abortion may be totally unthinkable for the couple. The apprehension felt by one or both partners at the prospect of an unplanned pregnancy can wreak havoc on sexual relations and contribute to their feeling out of control reproductively, though in a far different way than experienced during the infertile period.

Infertile individuals who have succeeded in conceiving and bearing a child often find that their attitudes toward having children have changed as a result of their fertility struggle. A couple who initially wanted only a few children may revise this initial plan because of the increased value that their infertility caused them to attach to having children. This change in plans need not be a problem, assuming that both partners agree, but often one partner has moved beyond the original understanding of the desired number of children while the other partner has not. Another factor influencing this decision is likely to be the woman's experience during her pregnancy. If it was an anxiety-filled time, perhaps with medical complications, she may have rethought her original expectations for having more children. Likewise, if her partner experienced a great deal of worry for her health or the health of his unborn child, he may reconsider the original plan for family size.

Couples evaluating their attitudes about future pregnancies may need help in several areas. Would having more children fill a real wish for more children, or could it represent something else, such as a need to prove oneself reproductively, to prove one's capacity as a superparent, or to have repeated reassurance that the pain of infertility need never haunt them again? It is sometimes helpful to have the parents discuss their hopes and dreams for children currently in the family and then to weigh the impact of having more children on future hopes for the family. Perhaps the parents can be asked to figure out how much energy or money is being spent and to assess whether having more children would be a drain on these resources. Finally, people with a history of infertility are particularly vulnerable to viewing their lives entirely in terms of their children and their children's needs, often ignoring their own needs or their needs as a couple. Such issues should be explored with parents to help them develop a balanced perspective on life decisions that may have been skewed forever by their earlier struggle with infertility.

An unexpected surprise for many women is the anger that they feel on the day their menstrual period begins. This anger tends to be more pronounced and unanticipated for women who have given birth; they are surprised at the intensity of their feelings at the very time they are relishing their new roles as mothers. Menstruation serves as just one more reminder of the impact of their earlier infertility and their continuing feelings of reproductive uncertainty.

Many infertile individuals continue to have a general pervasive concern for their health. For some, the focus is on their reproductive health, either because of ongoing problems or because the earlier experience of body betrayal was difficult to manage. Depending on the extent of medical treatment, an infertile person's very image of self may have become redefined in medical terms, and moving past that experience often takes time. Couples who adopt or give birth to children may worry that they will not be healthy enough or live long enough to offer their children all they hope to give them over a lifetime. Although these are somewhat existential concerns, they may be underlying sources of stress for someone who has grappled with infertility. In some cases, simply bringing the concerns out into the open for exploration is sufficient to help the individual gain a sense of mastery; in other cases, especially where ongoing medical problems do exist, the individual can gain some sense of control by becoming knowledgeable about health matters and participating actively in health care decisions. Taking life for granted, however, does not come lightly after one has struggled with infertility, and the concern about mortality seems to remain one of the more persistent legacies of the infertility experience.

Impact of Infertility on Parenting

Whether infertile individuals give birth to children or adopt them, their early years as parents often are spent trying to balance the idealism of wanting children with the reality of having them. Parents with a history of infertility may feel undeserving of the joy now available to them as parents. It is as though they have endured so much psychological pain that they now feel unentitled to joy, for fear that too much rejoicing will invite some inexplicable disaster. They also may develop unrealistically high expectations for themselves in an effort to be "perfect parents." Such parents are unnecessarily hard on themselves, believing that every childrearing problem could have had a better outcome if only they had "tried harder," "known more," or "been better." Not only are such expectations unnecessarily harsh, but they rob the parents of the fun of relaxing with their children, being spontaneous, laughing at themselves, and growing and changing in response to mutual needs.

Aspiring parents often fail to realize the tremendous burden they place on their children, for the implicit message these children receive is that they are a reflection of their parents' adequacy or inadequacy. Children who feel unentitled to fail or make mistakes will develop their own set of problems, not the least of which may be an inability to separate their needs from those of the parents who depend so strongly on their children for validation of their identities.

The opposite aspect of expecting too much from one's children is not expecting enough. This aspect may be manifested in parental overindulgence. Overindulgent parents feel primarily responsible for fulfilling a child's needs for happiness. Instead, they should be encouraged to help their child develop his own resources—not by satisfying the child's every whim but by allowing him to delay gratification and to think of creative ways to achieve goals. In short, they should prepare the child to cope with the frustrations of life.

Overindulgent parents also are unable to set clear limits for their children. The confusion between setting limits and denying love is often at the root of this difficulty. Parents who want to see their children happy all the time are highly ambivalent about setting limits if they cause tantrums, sulkiness, or anger. A professional can help such parents by discussing with them the different ways that love can be expressed and by pointing out that parents who set clear and consistent limits are legitimately expressing their love.

Perhaps one of the most unspeakable fears that haunts the parent with a history of infertility is the fear of losing the child who is so precious. These parents are often highly protective of their children and always acutely aware of dangers or risks.

> It's a little humorous now, as I think of all the precautions I took to keep my child safe—checking her two or three times a night, keeping her in a car seat for an extra year, only using a few familiar sitters, never letting her ride in cars driven by other parents, taking her to the pediatrician the minute she developed a fever. . . . Since, deep down, I was terrified of losing her, I spent a lot of energy anticipating possible threats and protecting her against them.

Although there is nothing inherently wrong in being attentive to dangers that one's child might encounter, parents should not communicate inappropriate messages to their children. Parents should be encouraged to examine their own behaviors for indications of overprotectiveness, and they should be careful not to communicate a sense of insecurity or lurking danger to their children. Such messages can make children wary and suspicious in circumstances that do not warrant such feelings, and ultimately children who are preoccupied with the dangers of the world may choose to avoid the challenges of interacting with "outsiders" and instead invest all their energy in family relationships.

Another consequence for parents who fear losing a much-loved child is the need to conceive or to adopt another child soon. Birth parents may need to prove their continuing fertility; adoptive parents may feel a very real pressure to begin adoption proceedings promptly, given the uncertain waits associated with both agency and independent adoption. In both cases, the parents are unconsciously viewing the other child as a replacement for the possible loss that they silently dread. Professionals can help these parents by talking about the rational ways that they offer protection and security to their child and by encouraging them to look carefully at the effect of spacing on the child or children already in the family.

When the children of infertile parents reach adolescence, a whole new set of challenges arises (Shapiro and Seeber, 1983). Feelings about sexuality that were influenced by infertility, as well as resentment toward fertile people, can resurface when parents see their children entering their childbearing years. Even after the most painful feelings associated with infertility have been resolved, parents may find themselves jealous, resentful, anxious, or hopeful about their child's presumed ability to have children.

Infertility may have left some of these parents conflicted about their sexuality, and they may feel more than the expected awkwardness in discussing sexual matters with their adolescent. Parents may worry that such a discussion will lead to questions about their own infertility. Parents who are reluctant to discuss sexual matters may discourage their children from raising both moral and practical questions about their sexuality. The challenge that parents confront at this time is to face their feelings about their own sexuality, so that they may communicate openly with their child.

Birth control also is a difficult subject for most parents to discuss. If the parents have not practiced birth control since learning of their infertility, they may feel out of touch or uninformed. If the parents believe that their infertility was caused by a birth control method or by delaying pregnancy, they may find it difficult to promote their adolescent's responsible use of birth control when sexual activity warrants it. Adoptive parents may have a special problem in discussing birth control with their children, because they are aware that their child's birth parents did not use birth control effectively. The adoptive parents may have difficulty discussing the importance of responsible sexual behavior without speaking negatively of the child's birth parents. Conversely, they may imply that the child who was born out of wedlock has to take extra precautions in order to avoid repeating the "mistake" of the birth parents.

Just as birth control may be difficult to discuss, abortion is especially emotion laden. Couples who for years tried unsuccessfully to achieve a pregnancy or adopt an infant may feel intense anger at women who are able to become pregnant but have abortions. Discussing abortion with one's adolescent becomes an exercise in separating out intense personal feelings from the effort to encourage the child to weigh the ethical and emotional issues involved in the topic of abortion. Adopted children are painfully aware that their birth mother might have chosen that solution for her unplanned pregnancy. They may also oppose the idea of an abortion because they would thereby deny themselves any connection to a genetic relative. When adopted children feel strongly against abortion, parents should provide education about birth control and encourage the option of abstinence, so that the adolescent need not fear an unwanted pregnancy.

The rebellious behavior typical of adolescence will present a special challenge to parents who are trying to live up to standards of perfection in childrearing. Those adolescents sensing rigid or inflexible expectations may have a greater need to rebel than young people who perceive their parents as open to discussing and negotiating reasonable compromises. Since adolescence is a time when young people seek a sense of identity, the need to differentiate from one's parents may be particularly great. Parents with a history of infertility may feel a stronger need to see themselves reborn through their children and, therefore, may have more difficulty than other parents when their teenagers reject or question their values or their hopes and plans for the adolescent's future. Likewise, when the adolescent begins to move away from the family, either geographically or emotionally, parents may have a particularly difficult time letting go. This is understandable from several perspectives: first, many parents with a history of infertility define their parental roles more strongly than other roles in their lives. Thus, the re-definition of the parental role may be difficult to accept if it means less involvement with one's offspring. Second, since infertility and the concomitant childlessness were perceived so aversively in earlier years, parents may feel a resurgence of emptiness reminiscent of that difficult period. The efforts of young people to differentiate their identities tend in many families to coincide with the onset of menopause for the mother. The feeling of constant transition may revive feelings of loss of control and result in parents holding tightly to their children at the very time the children need an opportunity to experiment with autonomy.

Another issue related to the adolescent quest for identity is the effort that some adoptees make to find their birth parents. This need to search for parents buried in their past can be disconcerting for adoptive parents, who fear that their adolescent may be searching because the adoptive parents, somehow, have been lacking and have not given enough love. Adoptive parents also harbor the very real concern that the birth parents, once found, may do something to hurt their child emotionally. In any case, adoptive parents may need help in exploring the feelings aroused by their child's search. Once the feelings are identified, parents may be able to communicate more clearly with their adolescents about their own concerns. This, in turn, may enable their child to share forthrightly the roots of the need to search for birth parents, as well as the child's own special set of fears and apprehensions bound up in the search.

The Impact of Menopause

The cessation of menstruation presents adjustments for all women. For women with a history of infertility, the end to their childbearing years may revive many of the earlier feelings present in their struggle with infertility.

Even though our two adopted children were adolescents when my menopause began, I was unaware
that I would feel so strongly about the end of my

reproductive years. Bill and I had never used birth control, and, although I was past the point of crying each time my period came, I always felt a lingering "what if?" Now I really have to bring some closure to that tenuous hope for pregnancy, and it's hard to relinquish.

Feeling a loss of control is common as the woman struggles with the onset of menopause, which reminds her of body betrayal in the past and—especially—of the fact that options for expanding her family are now gone forever. That finality contrasts with behavior during the earlier period of infertility, when she showed a tenacity and determination to overcome reproductive barriers, whether by medical intervention or through adoption. Indeed, the revival of preoccupation with one's reproductive health can itself be an unwelcome reminder of the earlier infertile times.

Some of the impact of menopause may be related to a woman's motivation for having a family. Women whose needs were closely tied to the desire to be pregnant, give birth, and nurse a baby may feel a greater sense of reproductive letdown than those who simply wanted children and were satisfied to fill that need through adoption.

For women who have chosen childfree living, the onset of menopause revives the question of what they may have missed by not pursuing medical intervention or adoption. As these women look ahead to their needs in later years, the feelings of emptiness may be far greater than they were when the original decision was made to remain childfree. If the childfree years enabled the woman to develop important dimensions of herself, on the other hand, then feelings of loss associated with menopause may be minimal.

Some women regard menopause as the end of their struggle to achieve a pregnancy. The sense of loss can be substantial for these women and their partners, and they may need considerable time to mourn the loss of the birth child they can never have. For these couples in particular, and for all couples in this age group generally, the onset of menopause occurs at the same time that other losses are being experienced: children leaving home, parents dying or experiencing declines in health, career aspirations being reevaluated, friends moving away as lifestyles change, and the physical aging and loss of stamina that come with later years. Active mourning may be a highly appropriate and therapeutic response, although, ultimately, the couples must look ahead to those future life goals and hopes that need not be diminished by the passage of years.

Interacting with One's Adult Children

Pangs of emotion stemming from infertility sometimes return when children marry and contemplate having children. Parents may feel tempted to encourage their sons and daughters to have children as soon as possible.

> I would so love a grandchild. But both of our children are happy pursuing their lives without children at this point, so it's my need rather than theirs. Yet as they reach their thirties, I find myself feeling worried that they may experience some difficulties getting pregnant. My own infertility was bad enough, but I don't think I could stand to watch either of my children bear that pain!

In addition to ascertaining that their children are fertile, parents may also want to save their children the pain of infertility brought on by delaying efforts at childbearing until after the peak fertile years. Parents who had difficulty letting go of their own children may feel the need for grandchildren as a way of replacing their adult children. And because individuals with a history of infertility are typically older when they first become parents, they may want the pleasure of enjoying grandchildren while they are still energetic and healthy.

Adopted children sometimes have very mixed feelings about how to interact with their parents when a pregnancy does occur. This dilemma can be particularly pronounced between mothers and daughters. The daughter may be apprehensive that her ability to achieve a pregnancy will revive her mother's feelings of inadequacy or sadness. If rivalry or jealousy has been present in the mother-daughter relationship, the daughter's pregnancy may highlight her capacity to do something her mother never could. The mother, on the other hand, may find her old feelings of resentment toward pregnant women surfacing.

Another dilemma that occurs for the adopted daughter is the wish to turn to her mother for reassurance about pregnancy, labor, or delivery. Yet these are experiences that few adoptive mothers have had, so she may be no more knowledgeable than her daughter. In such a situation, the mother must give the daughter permission to seek advice from someone else; she can even learn with her daughter the various dimensions of pregnancy that she never had the chance to learn because of her infertility.

Parents whose efforts to have children resulted in pregnancy loss must show real restraint as they conceal their fears from their daughters and attempt to share in the positive aspects of the daughter's pregnancy.

Childfree Living

Couples who resolved their infertility by opting for childfree living may always wonder, "What would our lives have been like if . . . ?" Sometimes one partner more than the other embraced the choice of childfree living, and the remnants of yearning in the other partner can be troublesome. Even when both partners opted for childfree living as a clear preference, they may have had unrealistically high expectations for the life they would lead without children. As a result, they may be unprepared to deal with career disappointments, relationship problems, and financial strains.

Childfree couples also must frequently deal with questions or insensitive remarks about the absence of children in their lives (Faux, 1984; Shealy and Shealy, 1981). Many of these couples probably had to listen to awkward and insensitive questions from acquaintances and relatives while they were trying to resolve their infertility. Now, once again, they have to respond to other people's assumptions or value judgments about their private life. Some people will imply that the couple are being selfish to choose a childfree existence. Other comments are meant to be validating but serve only to point out the speaker's insensitivity: a relative who offers to trade in all of his children for one of the couple's vacations in the sun; a friend who complains that her children have held her back from pursuing career aspirations; an acquaintance who says, "You're lucky not to have kids. If I had it to do all over again, I'd be like you and enjoy my freedom." All these responses, offered freely to a childfree couple, only remind the couple of the option that was never theirs.

Another burden for some childfree couples is the awareness of their own parents' grief at not being able to become grandparents. Parents who had anticipated this role with zest may enter a mourning process similar to the one experienced by the infertile couple when they worked to resolve their infertility. They may also convey their disappointment that the couple did not choose adoption or a more aggressive pursuit of medical intervention. Children, even as adults, are highly vulnerable to such messages, and their parents' disapproval of their decision to live a childfree life may cause a permanent rift in the parent-child relationship. If the infertile couple are in therapy, they might ask their therapist to help them show their parents that they need support, not disapproval, from them. If the parents can be included in a limited number of counseling sessions, they and the couple can discuss this painful area and open up the relationship for improved future communication.

The choice to be childfree does not eliminate an individual's nurturing capacities. Therefore, many childfree individuals will seek creative ways of channeling their need to nurture (Harper, 1980; Burgwyn, 1981; Lindsay, 1981; Love, 1984). Some may decide to take care of foster children, although most infertile couples find the inevitable prospect of separating from foster children too painful. Some couples may adopt a pet, or do volunteer work with people of many ages and needs, or channel their energies into helping others who are more actively struggling with infertility or the pain of pregnancy loss; or, if they are artistically gifted, they may use their work as a way of enriching the lives of others.

Dealing with the Remnants of the Infertility Struggle

After infertile couples have reached some sense of resolution, they still may occasionally once again feel helpless, sad, and out of control. Perhaps even more upsetting is the realization that infertility is a part of their lives forever, affecting them at developmental milestones in ways they never could have anticipated.

It is natural to feel resentful at something that stays in one's life, unwelcome and uninvited, especially when so much hard work has gone into exorcising the demon of infertility years before. Perhaps it is most helpful for infertile individuals to be encouraged to view infertility as the "old friend" referred to at the beginning of this chapter. It is, in fact, a significant experience in the individual's life and deserves to be reckoned with. The fear that some people have is that their infertility will return to haunt and control them as it once did. Individuals with these fears can be encouraged to discuss the sense of mastery they have achieved over their infertility; they can be helped to anticipate times in the future when it may once again be a problem for them; and they can be encouraged to be insightful about their original struggle as a way of gaining a sense of ongoing learning about themselves and the impact of infertility on their lives.

RESOURCE A

Glossary

Abortion

Complete. A miscarriage in which all the products of conception have been expelled and the cervix is closed.

Habitual. A miscarriage occurring on three or more separate occasions.

Incomplete. A miscarriage in which only a portion of the products of conception have been expelled, usually requiring dilation and curettage.

Induced. Intentional termination of pregnancy.

Inevitable. A miscarriage that cannot be halted.

Missed. A miscarriage in which a dead fetus and other products of conception remain in the uterus for four or more weeks.

Selective. Often used to refer to intentional termination of pregnancy after a deformity of the fetus is found.

Spontaneous. A miscarriage or the unintended termination of a pregnancy before the twentieth week.

Therapeutic. Intentional termination of pregnancy for the purpose of preserving the life of the mother.

Threatened. Symptoms such as vaginal bleeding, with or without pain, which may end with a miscarriage or with continuation of a normal pregnancy.

Abruptio placentae. A condition in which the placenta detaches prematurely from the uterine wall, cutting off the supply of oxygen to the fetus.

This glossary is reprinted with the permission of Serono Symposia, USA.

201

Adhesion. An abnormal attachment of adjacent serous membranes by bands or masses of fibrous connective tissue.

Adrenal glands. Two glands near the kidneys that produce hormones, including some sexual hormones.

Agglutination of sperm. Sticking together of sperm.

Amenorrhea. The absence of menstruation.

Amniocentesis. A procedure for withdrawing a sample of amniotic fluid (by inserting a needle through the abdominal wall) from the uterus of a pregnant woman to obtain information about the fetus.

Amniotic fluid. The fluid that surrounds the fetus in the uterus and protects it during pregnancy and labor.

Ampulla. The upper end of the vas deferens in which sperm are stored.

Androgens. General class of male sex hormones. Testosterone is one example.

Andrology. The science of diseases of men.

Anomaly. A malformation or abnormality in any part of the body.

Anovulation. Total absence of ovulation. Not necessarily the same as "amenorrhea," since menses may still occur with anovulation.

Anovulatory bleeding. The type of menstruation often associated with failure to ovulate. May be scanty and of short duration or abnormally heavy and in irregular patterns.

Antibody. Substance that fights or otherwise interacts with a foreign substance in the body.

Artificial embryonation. Process by which artificial insemination of a woman results in an embryo. The embryo is then flushed out five days after conception and implanted in a second woman (the wife of the man who donated the sperm).

Artificial insemination by donor (AID). The instillation of donor semen into a woman's vagina for the purpose of conception.

Artificial insemination by husband (AIH). The instillation of a husband's semen into the wife's vagina for the purpose of conception.

Aspermia. The absence of semen and sperm.

Azoospermia. The absence of sperm in the ejaculate.

Basal body temperature (BBT). The temperature of the woman, taken either orally or rectally, upon waking in the morning before any activity. Used to help determine ovulation.

Bicornuate uterus. A congenital malformation of the uterus in which it is divided internally by a septum and appears to have two "horns."

Breech birth. Delivery of an infant's feet or buttocks first, instead of the head.

Capacitation. The alteration of sperm that takes place during their passage through the female reproductive tract and gives them the capacity to penetrate and fertilize the ovum.

Cautery. Sealing tissues together with heat.

Cervix. The lower section of the uterus that protrudes into the vagina and dilates during labor to allow the passage of the infant.

Cesarean section. The surgical removal of the fetus by means of an incision through the abdominal wall into the uterus.

Chromosomes. Rod-shaped bodies in a cell's nucleus which carry the genes that convey hereditary characteristics.

Cilia. Microscopic hairlike projections from the surface of a cell that are capable of beating in a coordinated fashion.

Clitoris. The small erectile sex organ of the female, located in front of the urethra and the vagina and similar to the penis of the male.

Clomiphene citrate (Serophene^R or Clomid^R). A synthetic drug used to stimulate the hypothalamus and pituitary gland to increase FSH and LH production. It is usually used to treat ovulatory failure caused by hypothalamic pituitary dysfunction.

Coitus. Sexual intercourse.

Conception. The fertilization of a woman's egg by a man's sperm, resulting in a new life.

Congenital. A characteristic or defect present at birth, acquired during pregnancy but not necessarily hereditary.

Contraception. The prevention of pregnancy by any means of birth control.

Corpus luteum. The special gland that forms in the ovary at the site of the released egg. This gland produces the hormone progesterone during the second half of the normal menstrual cycle.

Cryobank. A place where frozen sperm is stored.

Cryptorchidism. Undescended testicles.

Culdoscopy. Direct visualization of the ovaries, the exterior of the Fallopian tubes, and the uterus by means of an instrument inserted through a small incision in the vagina. A diagnostic study in the infertility workup.

Diethylstilbestrol (DES). A synthetic estrogen used occasionally as a "morning-after pill." Formerly thought to prevent miscarriage, it may have caused fertility problems in the offspring of women who took it.

Dilation and curettage (D & C). Dilation of the cervix to allow scraping of the uterine lining with an instrument (curette). Done as a therapeutic measure in infertility. Also, a means to induce abortion in the first trimester of pregnancy.

Dilation and evacuation (D & E). A method of induced abortion in which the cervix is dilated and the uterine contents removed by a suction device.

Down's syndrome. A genetic abnormality, formerly known as mongolism, which is characterized by the presence of an extra chromosome 21 and moderate to severe levels of retardation.

Dysgenesis. Faulty formation of any organ.

Dysmenorrhea. Painful menstruation.

Dyspareunia. Painful intercourse for either the woman or the man.

Ectopic pregnancy. A pregnancy in which the fertilized egg implants anywhere but in the uterine cavity (usually in the Fallopian tube, the ovary, or the abdominal cavity).

Egg donation. Surgical removal of an egg from one woman for deposit into the Fallopian tube or uterus of another woman.

Ejaculation. The male orgasm, during which approximately two to five cubic centimeters of seminal fluid and sperm are ejected from the penis.

Embryo. The term used to describe the early stages of fetal growth, from conception to the eighth week of pregnancy.

Embryo adoption. Process by which artificial insemination of a woman with donor sperm results in an embryo that is implanted into a second woman (also called artificial embryonation).

Embryo transfer. Introduction of an embryo into a woman's uterus after in vitro or in vivo fertilization.

Endocrine system. System of glands including the thymus, pituitary, thyroid, adrenals, testicles or ovaries, parathyroid, and pancreas.

Endocrinologist. A doctor who specializes in diseases of the endocrine glands.

Endometrial biopsy. The extraction of a small sample of tissue from the uterus for examination. Usually done to show evidence of ovulation.

Endometriosis. The presence of endometrial tissue (the normal uterine lining) in abnormal locations such as the tubes, ovaries, and peritoneal cavity, often causing painful menstruation.

Endometrium. The mucous membrane lining the uterus.

Endosalpinx. The tissue lining the Fallopian tube.

Epididymis. An elongated organ in the male, lying above and behind the testicles. It contains a highly convoluted canal, four to six meters in length, where, after production, sperm are stored, nourished, and ripened for a period of several months.

Epispadias. A congenital abnormality of the penis, in which the opening of the urethra is on the top of the shaft of the penis instead of at the end.

Erection. The enlarged, rigid state of the penis when aroused.

Estrogen. The primary female hormone, produced mainly in the ovaries from the onset of puberty and continuing until menopause.

Fallopian tubes. A pair of narrow tubes that carry the ovum (egg) from the ovary to the body of the uterus.

Fertilization. The penetration of the egg by the sperm.

Fetal death. The term often used to include both miscarriage and stillbirth.

Fetoscopy/placental aspiration. A technique for directly visualizing a fetus in the uterus and extracting a fetal blood sample.

Fetus. The developing baby from the ninth week of pregnancy until the moment of birth.

Fibroid tumor. A benign tumor of fibrous tissue that may occur in the uterine wall. An individual with such a tumor may be totally without symptoms, or the tumor may cause abnormal menstrual patterns or infertility.

Fimbriated ends. The fringed and flaring outer ends of the Fallopian tubes.

Follicle. The structure in the ovary that has nurtured the ripening egg and from which the egg is released.

Follicle-stimulating hormone (FSH). A hormone produced in the anterior pituitary that stimulates the ovary to ripen a follicle for ovulation.

Frigidity. The inability to become sexually aroused. Not a known cause of infertility.

Gamete. The male or female reproductive cells—the sperm or the ovum (egg).

Gamete intrafallopian transfer (GIFT). Procedure where clomiphene citrate, Pergonal^R, or Metrodin^R is used to stimulate ovulation. Then the egg is removed via laparoscopy and immediately mixed with fresh semen from the husband. This sperm-egg mixture is then transferred by laparoscopy into the Fallopian tubes.

Genes. Substances that convey hereditary characteristics, consisting primarily of DNA and proteins and occurring at specific points on the chromosomes.

Genetic. Pertaining to hereditary characteristics.

Genetic abnormality. A disorder arising from an anomaly in the chromosomal structure which may or may not be hereditary.

Genetic counseling. Advice and information provided, usually by a team of experts, on the detection and risk of recurrence of genetic disorders.

Gestation. The period of fetal development in the uterus from conception to birth, usually considered to be forty weeks in humans.

Gland. A hormone-producing organ.

Gonadotropin. A substance capable of stimulating the testicles or the ovaries.

Gonads. The glands that make the gametes (the testicles in the male and the ovaries in the female).

Gynecologist. A doctor who specializes in the diseases of the female reproductive system.

Hamster test. Used to determine the ability of a man's sperm to penetrate a hamster egg. Thought to be evidence of the sperm's general penetrating ability.

Hemorrhage. Excessive bleeding.

Hereditary. Transmitted from one's ancestors by way of the genes within the chromosomes of the fertilizing sperm and egg.

Hormone. A chemical, produced by an endocrine gland, which circulates in the blood and has widespread action throughout the body.

Hostility factor. The inability of sperm to survive in the vaginal or cervical area long enough to swim upward toward the ovum. The condition may be caused by an overacidic secretion or by an immunologic reaction that kills the sperm.

Human chorionic gonadotropin (hCG). A hormone secreted by the placenta during pregnancy that prolongs the life of the corpus luteum and thus preserves the pregnancy. This hormone accounts for pregnancy tests being positive. It may also be administered therapeutically in some infertility problems.

Human menopausal gonadotropin (hMG) (Pergonal[R]). A natural product containing both human FSH and LH. This material cannot be synthesized and must be extracted from the urine of postmenopausal women. It is used in the treatment of both male and female infertility.

Hydrocele. A swelling in the scrotum containing fluid.

Hydrosalpinx. A large fluid-filled, club-shaped Fallopian tube closed at the fimbriated end (the end nearest to the ovary). It is the cause of infertility.

Hydrospadias. A malformation of the penis in which the urethral opening is found on the underside rather than at the tip of the penis.

Hydrotubation. Lavage or "flushing" of the Fallopian tubes with a sterile solution that sometimes contains medication such as antibiotics, enzymes, or steroids. Thought by some doctors to dissolve adhesions or to maintain the opening of the tubes following surgery.

Hymen. A membrane that partially covers the virgin vagina.

Hyperplasia. Abnormal enlargement of an organ or tissue of the body.

Hypothalamus. A part of the base of the brain that controls the action of the pituitary.

Hysterectomy. The removal of the uterus. Can be total (including removal of the ovaries and tubes) or partial (just the uterus and sometimes the cervix).

Hysterosalpingogram. An X-ray study in which a contrast dye is injected into the uterus to show the delineation of the body of the uterus and the patency of the Fallopian tubes. Also called a tubogram or uterotubogram.

Hysterotomy. The surgical opening of the uterus for removal of tumors or repair of structural defects. The uterus is then sutured closed and remains in place. Also, a type of induced abortion used occasionally during the second trimester.

Immunologic response. The presence of sperm antibodies in the woman or man that tend to destroy sperm action by immobilizing the sperm or making them clump together.

Implantation. The embedding of the fertilized egg in the endometrium of the uterus.

Impotence. The inability of the male to achieve or maintain an erection for intercourse because of physical or emotional problems or combined factors.

Incompetent cervix. A weakened cervix that is incapable of holding the fetus within the uterus for the full nine months. Sometimes a cause of late miscarriage or stillbirth.

Infertility. The inability of a couple to achieve a pregnancy after one year of regular unprotected sexual relations, or the inability of the woman to carry a pregnancy to live birth.

Interstitial cells. The cells that produce the male hormone testosterone. Located between the seminiferous tubules of the testicles. Also called Leydig cells.

Intrauterine device (IUD). A device inserted into the uterus by a physician for the purpose of birth control. The device is about 90 percent effective.

In vitro (in glass) fertilization (IVF). A procedure in which an egg is removed from a ripe follicle and fertilized by a sperm cell outside the human body. The fertilized egg is allowed to divide in a protected environment for about two days and then is inserted back into the uterus of the woman who produced the egg. Also called "test-tube baby" and "test-tube fertilization."

In vivo fertilization. The fertilization of an egg by a sperm within the woman's body. In normal pregnancy, the woman in whom the egg is fertilized carries the pregnancy to term. In artificial embryonation or embryo adoption, the embryo is transferred from the woman in whom the fertilization took place to another woman.

Karyotype. Total characteristics of a cell, including size, form, and chromosome numbers. Used for genetic studies.

Klinefelter's syndrome. A congenital abnormality of the male wherein he receives an XXY genetic sex complement instead of XY. Most men with this condition are sterile and have secondary female characteristics and possible retardation.

Labia. Folds of skin on either side of the entrance of the vagina.

Laparoscopy. The direct visualization of the ovaries and the exterior of the tubes and uterus by means of inserting a surgical instrument through a small incision below the naval.

Laparotomy. Abdominal surgery.

Leydig cells. See Interstitial cells.

Libido. Conscious or unconscious sexual desire.

Luteal phase. The last fourteen days of an ovulatory cycle, associated with progesterone production.

Luteinized unruptured follicle syndrome (LUF). A condition where there are clinical indications that ovulation has occurred (blood hormonal changes, temperature rise on the BBT chart, and appropriate secreting endometrium found on endometrial biopsy) but the egg is not released from the ovary; the follicular sac is unruptured, and the egg is trapped.

Luteinizing hormone (LH). A hormone secreted by the anterior lobe of the pituitary during the entire menstrual cycle. The hormone peaks just before ovulation. May be given therapeutically in infertility situations.

Menarche. The onset of menstruation in girls.

Menopause. The cessation of menstruation as a result of aging or ovary failure. Most commonly occurs between the ages of forty and fifty. Surgical menopause is the abrupt cessation of menstruation caused by the removal of the ovaries (hysterectomy).

Menotropins (human menopausal gonadotropin, or hMG). The generic name for Pergonal[R], an extract of menopausal urine containing FSH and LH. The hMG is administered by injection to treat certain types of anovulation in women and azoospermia or oligospermia in men.

Menstruation. The shedding of the uterine lining by cyclic bleeding that normally occurs about once a month in the mature female, in the absence of pregnancy, until menopause.

Miscarriage. A spontaneous abortion of a fetus up to the age of viability.

Mittelschmerz. German for "middle pain," referring to the pain during ovulation that some women experience.

Morphology of sperm. The study of the shape of sperm cells. This evaluation is part of a semen analysis.

Motility of sperm. The ability of the sperm to move about.

Mumps orchitis. Inflammation of the testicle caused by mumps virus; frequently leads to sterility.

Mutagen. A substance that alters the genetic structure of the sperm or ovum before conception.

Myomectomy. A surgical removal of a tumor (myoma) in the uterine muscular wall.

Nidation. The implantation of the fertilized egg in the endometrium of the uterus.

Obstetrician. A doctor who specializes in pregnancy and childbirth.

Oligospermia. A scarcity of sperm in the ejaculate of the male.

Orchitis. An inflammation of the testes.

Ovaries. The sexual glands of the female, which produce the hormones estrogen and progesterone and in which the ova are developed. There are two ovaries, one on each side of the pelvis, and they are connected to the uterus by the Fallopian tubes.

Ovary retention. Failure of the egg to be released even though the follicle has ruptured.

Oviduct. Fallopian tube.

Ovulation. The discharge of a ripened egg, usually at about the midpoint of the menstrual cycle.

Ovum. The egg (reproductive) cell produced in the ovaries each month. (The plural of ovum is ova.)

Pap test. A simple swabbing of the cervix to determine the presence of cancerous tissue. The test should be done annually unless otherwise recommended by a physician.

Pelvic inflammatory disease (PID). Inflammatory disease of the pelvis, often caused by infection.

Penis. The male organ of intercourse.

Perinatal. Referring to the period of time from the twentieth week of pregnancy through the first twenty-eight days of life.

Pituitary. A gland located at the base of the human brain. Secretes a number of important hormones related to normal growth and development and fertility.

Placenta. A spongy organ attached to the wall of the uterus through which nourishment and oxygen pass from the bloodstream of the mother into the bloodstream of the fetus by way of the umbilical cord. Normally expelled after delivery of the fetus. Also called afterbirth.

Polycystic ovarian syndrome (PCO). Development of multiple cysts in the ovaries due to arrested follicular growth. This condition causes an imbalance in the amount of LH and FSH released during the ovulatory cycle. Infertility associated with PCO is often responsive to drug therapy (clomiphene citrate, urofollitropin).

Polyp. A nodule or small growth found frequently on mucous membranes, such as in the cervix or the uterus.

Postcoital test (Huhner test or P.K. test). A diagnostic test for infertility, in which vaginal and cervical secretions are obtained by vaginal examination following intercourse and then analyzed under a microscope. Normal test results show large numbers of motile sperm.

Premature ejaculation. Discharge of sperm from the penis prior to or immediately after entering the vagina.

Progesterone. A hormone secreted by the corpus luteum of the ovary after ovulation has occurred. Also produced by the placenta during pregnancy.

Prostaglandin. A hormone that induces labor when it is injected into the amniotic sac. It is often used in second-trimester abortions.

Prostate. A gland in the male that surrounds the first portion of the urethra near the bladder. It secretes an alkaline liquid that neutralizes acid in the urethra and stimulates motility of the sperm.

Pseudocyesis. A condition simulating pregnancy, in which a woman believes herself to be pregnant but is not. Also called false pregnancy.

Retrograde ejaculation. Discharge of sperm backward into the bladder rather than through the penis.

Retroverted uterus. Uterus that is flexed severely forward or backward.

Rubin test. Test in which a harmless gas such as carbon dioxide is blown into the uterus under pressure and will escape out of the Fallopian tubes if they are open. Used as a diagnostic test for infertility. Also called tubal insufflation or "blowing of the tubes."

Saline. A salt solution which, when injected into the amniotic sac, leads to the death of the fetus. Often used during second-trimester abortions.

Salpingitis. Inflammation of the Fallopian tubes.

Salpingolysis. Surgery to clear the Fallopian tubes of adhesions.

Salpingoplasty. Surgery to correct blocked Fallopian tubes.

Scrotum. The bag of skin and thin muscle that holds the testicles.

Secondary infertility. The inability to conceive or carry a pregnancy after having successfully conceived and carried one or more pregnancies.

Semen. The sperm and seminal secretions ejaculated during orgasm.

Semen analysis. The study of fresh ejaculate under the microscope to count the number of million sperm per cubic centimeter, to check the shape and size of the sperm, and to note their ability to move (motility).

Seminal vesicles. A pair of pouchlike glands above the prostate in the male. They produce a thick, alkaline secretion that is added to sperm during ejaculation.

Seminiferous tubules. The long tubes in the testicles in which sperm are formed.

Septum. An abnormality in organ structure present since birth, in which a wall is present where one should not exist.

Sperm (spermatozoa). The male reproductive cell.

Sperm bank. Place in which sperm (by donor or by husband) is stored frozen for future use in artificial insemination.

Spermatogenesis. The production of sperm within the seminiferous tubules.

Spinnbarkheit. The stretchability of cervical mucus. This is a rough measure of how easily sperm cells can enter and penetrate the cervical secretions.

Split ejaculate. A method of collecting a semen specimen so that the first half of the ejaculate is caught in one container and the rest in a second container. The first half usually contains most of the sperm. This first half is then used to inseminate the woman.

Stein-Leventhal disease. A condition characterized by hirsutism, menstrual dysfunction, and infertility with enlarged polycystic ovaries.

Stillbirth. Death before birth of a fetus that is of at least twenty weeks' gestation.

Surrogate carrier. A woman who gestates an embryo that is not genetically related to her and then turns over the child to its genetic parents.

Surrogate mother. A woman who becomes pregnant through insemination with the sperm of the husband of an infertile woman and then, following birth, turns the child over for adoption by the couple.

Teratogen. A substance that alters fetal growth and development and causes birth abnormalities.

Testicles. The male sexual glands, of which there are two. Contained in the scrotum, they produce the male hormone testosterone and the male reproductive cells, the sperm.

Testicular biopsy. Small surgical excision of testicular tissue to determine the ability of the cells to produce normal sperm.

Testosterone. The most potent male sex hormone, produced in the testicles.

Test-tube baby. Child born through in vitro fertilization.

Thyroid gland. A gland located at the front base of the neck. Secretes the hormone thyroid, found to be necessary for normal fertility.

"Tipped" uterus. A uterus tilted backward toward the woman's back, rather than the more common state of tilting toward the front of the abdomen. By itself, this should not be a cause of infertility.

Toxemia. Often referred to as pre-eclampsia, an abnormal condition of late pregnancy characterized by swelling, high blood pressure, and protein in the urine.

Trisomy 18. A genetic abnormality characterized by an extra chromosome 18, severe mental retardation, and physical anomalies.

Tubal insufflation. See **Rubin test.**

Tubogram. See **Hysterosalpingogram.**

Tuboplasty. Surgical repair of Fallopian tubes.

Turner's syndrome (ovarian dysgenesis). A congenital abnormality of the female wherein she receives an XO instead of an XX genetic sex complement. Women with this condition are sterile.

Ultrasound (pulse-echo sonography). A technique for visualizing the fetus in the uterus, which allows for estimating the size of the fetus and for detecting fetal abnormalities.

Umbilical cord. The lifeline through which nourishment, oxygen, and waste products pass between the placenta and the fetus.

Urethra. The tube that carries urine from the bladder to the outside. In men, it also carries semen from the prostate to the point of ejaculation during intercourse.

Urofollitropin. The generic name for Metrodin[R], a parenterally administered drug used to treat infertility in patients with polycystic ovarian syndrome who have an elevated LH:FSH ratio and are nonresponsive to clomiphene citrate.

Urologist. A doctor who specializes in diseases of the urinary tract in men and women, and the genital organs in men.

Uterotubogram. See Hysterosalpingogram.

Uterus. The hollow, muscular organ that holds and nourishes the fetus until the time of birth.

Vagina. The birth canal opening in the woman, extending from the vulva to the cervix of the uterus.

Vaginal septum. A wall dividing the vagina lengthwise or obstructing it with side-to-side placement.

Vaginismus. A spasm of the muscles around the opening of the vagina, making penetration during sexual intercourse either impossible or very painful. Can be organic or psychogenic in nature.

Varicocele. A varicose vein of the testicles, sometimes a cause of male infertility.

Vas deferens. A pair of thick-walled tubes (about forty-five centimeters long) in the male, leading from the epididymis to the ejaculatory duct in the prostate. During ejaculation, the ducts make wavelike contractions to propel sperm forward.

Vasectomy. Surgery to excise part of vas deferens to sterilize a man.

Vasogram. X ray of the sperm ducts.

Venereal disease (VD). Any infection pertaining to or transmitted by sexual intercourse. Most commonly known as gonorrhea and syphilis. VD is readily treatable if medical help is sought early. It is a major cause of infertility in both men and women if allowed to go untreated.

Viability (of a fetus). Capability of survival outside the uterus, usually after twenty weeks' gestation.

Vulva. The external genitalia of the female.

Wedge resection. A surgical procedure in which a small section is excised from an ovary.

Bibliography
of Infertility Publications

Books Overviewing Infertility—Medical

Amelar, R. D., Dubin, L., and Walsh, P. C. *Male Infertility.* Philadelphia: Saunders, 1977.

Bain, J., and others. *Treatment of Male Infertility.* New York: Springer-Verlag, 1982.

Barker, G. H., and Bronson, R. A. *Your Search for Fertility.* New York: Morrow, 1981.

Behrman, S. J., and Kistner, R. W. *Progress in Infertility.* Boston: Little, Brown, 1975.

Bellina, J. H., and Wilson, J. *You Can Have a Baby.* New York: Crown, 1985.

Cooke, C., and Dworkin, S. *Infertility: The Ms. Guide to a Woman's Health.* Cambridge, Mass.: Black and White Publishing Co., 1979.

Corson, S. L. *Conquering Infertility.* East Norwalk, Conn.: Appleton-Century-Crofts, 1983.

Decker, A., and Loebl, S. *Why Can't We Have a Baby?* New York: Dial Press, 1978.

Garcia, C.-R., and others. *Current Therapy of Infertility.* St. Louis: Mosby, 1984.

Glass, R. H., and Ericsson, R. J. *Getting Pregnant in the Nine-*

This bibliography is reprinted with the permission of RESOLVE, Inc.

teen Eighties: New Advances in Infertility Treatment and Sex Preselection. Berkeley: University of California Press, 1982.

Glezerman, M., and Jecht, E. W. (eds.). *Varicocele and Male Infertility II.* New York: Springer-Verlag, 1984.

Hammond, M. G., and Talbert, L. M. *Infertility: A Practical Guide for the Physician.* Oradell, N.J.: Medical Economics Books, 1985.

Hargreave, T. B. (ed.). *Male Infertility.* New York: Springer-Verlag, 1983.

Harkness, C. *The Infertility Book: A Comprehensive Medical and Emotional Guide.* San Francisco: Volcano Press, 1987.

Howard, J. T., and Schultz, D. *We Want to Have a Baby.* New York: Dutton, 1979.

Hunt, R. B. *Atlas of Female Infertility Surgery.* Chicago: Year Book Medical Publishers, 1986.

Johnston, P. I. *Understanding: A Guide to Impaired Fertility for Family and Friends.* Fort Wayne, Ind.: Perspectives Press, 1983.

Jones, H. W., and others. *In Vitro Fertilization.* Baltimore: Williams & Wilkins, 1986. (Highly technical medical text about all aspects of the IVF procedure.)

Kaufman, S. *You Can Have a Baby.* Nashville, Tenn.: Thomas Nelson, 1978.

Lipshultz, L. I., and Howards, S. S. *Infertility in the Male.* New York: Churchill Livingstone, 1983.

McIlhaney, J. S., and Nethery, S. *1250 Health-Care Questions Women Ask.* Grand Rapids, Mich.: Baker Book House, 1985.

Perloe, M., and Christie, L. G. *Miracle Babies and Other Happy Endings.* New York: Rawson Associates, 1986.

Silber, S. J. *How to Get Pregnant.* New York: Scribner's, 1980.

Stangel, J. J. *Fertility and Conception: An Essential Guide for Childless Couples.* New York: Paddington Press, 1979.

Swanson, J. M., and Forrest, K. (eds.). *Men's Reproductive Health.* New York: Springer-Verlag, 1984.

Warner, M. P. *Modern Fertility Guide: Practical Advice for the Childless Couple.* New York: Funk & Wagnalls, 1961.

White, R. D. V. (ed.). *Aspects of Male Infertility.* Vol. 4 of *In-*

ternational Perspectives in Urology. Baltimore: Williams &
Wilkins, 1982.

Books Overviewing Infertility—Emotional

Anderson, A. K. *Taste of Tears, Touch of God*. Nashville, Tenn.:
Oliver-Nelson Books, 1984.
Andrews, L. B. *New Conceptions: A Consumer's Guide to the
Newest Infertility Treatments*. New York: St. Martin's Press,
1984. (Focuses on legal aspects of new technologies.)
Blais, M. *They Say You Can't Have a Baby*. New York: Norton,
1979.
Castro, L. (ed.). *Song of Infertility*. South Charleston, W. Va.:
Jalamap Publications, 1985. (Book of poetry. Order from
Castro, 216 Maple Street, Summersville, W. Va. 26651; $3.95.)
Corea, G. *The Mother Machine: Reproductive Technologies
from Artificial Insemination to Artificial Wombs*. New York:
Harper & Row, 1985.
Erling, S. *A Rainbow After the Storm*. St. Paul, Minn.: S. Erling,
1983. (Self-published poetry collection. Order from Erling,
1515 N. Dale Street, St. Paul, Minn. 55117; $5.00.)
Fenton, J. A., and Lifchez, A. S. *The Fertility Handbook*. New
York: Clarkson N. Potter, 1980.
Halverson, K., and Hess, K. M. *The Wedded Unmother*. Min-
neapolis: Augsburg, 1980.
Harkness, C. *The Infertility Book: A Comprehensive Medical
and Emotional Guide*. San Francisco: Volcano Press, 1987.
Harrison, M. *Infertility: A Guide for Couples*. Boston: Houghton Mifflin, 1977.
Johnson, J., and others. *Trying to Conceive*. Omaha, Neb.: Cen-
tering Corp., 1986. (Order from P.O. Box 3367, Omaha, Neb.
68103; $2.45 plus $1.00 postage; booklet approximately 24
pp.)
Liebmann-Smith, J. *In Pursuit of Pregnancy*. New York: New-
market Press, 1987.
Love, V. *Childless Is Not Less*. Minneapolis: Bethany House,
1984.

Maitland, S. *The Languages of Love.* New York: Doubleday, 1980. (Fiction about an infertile couple's relationship.)

McGowan, J. Y. *Waiting: Hopes and Frustrations of a Childless Couple.* New York: Vantage Press, 1983.

Mazor, M. D., and Simons, H. F. (eds.). *Infertility: Medical, Emotional, and Social Considerations.* New York: Human Sciences Press, 1984.

Menning, B. E. *Infertility: A Guide for the Childless Couple.* Englewood Cliffs, N.J.: Prentice-Hall, 1977.

Mitchard, J. *Mother Less Child.* New York: Norton, 1985.

RESOLVE of Chicago. *Feelings About Infertility.* Chicago: RESOLVE of Chicago, 1983. (Poetry collection edited and published by RESOLVE of Chicago, 3043 W. Jerome, Chicago, Ill. 60645; $7.00.)

Salzer, L. P. *Infertility: How Couples Can Cope.* Boston: G. K. Hall, 1986.

Stigger, J. A. *Coping with Infertility.* Religion and Medicine Series. Minneapolis: Augsburg, 1983.

Stout, M. *Without Child: A Compassionate Look at Infertility.* Grand Rapids, Mich.: Zondervan, 1985. (A Christian account of one woman's experience with infertility.)

Van Regenmorter, J., Van Regenmorter, S., and McIlhaney, J. S. *Dear God, Why Can't We Have a Baby?* Grand Rapids, Mich.: Baker Book House, 1986.

Articles and Chapters Overviewing Infertility

Boston Women's Health Book Collective. *Our Bodies, Ourselves.* New York: Simon & Schuster, 1985. (This edition has a chapter on infertility.)

Clapp, D. N. "Emotional Response to Infertility: Nursing Interventions." *Journal of Obstetrics and Gynecologic Neonatal Nursing,* 1985, *14,* 6.

Clark, M., and others. "Infertility: New Cures, New Hope." *Newsweek,* Dec. 6, 1982, pp. 102–110.

Coman, C. "Trying (and Trying and Trying) to Get Pregnant." *Ms.,* May 1983, pp. 21–24.

Dalton, K. "The Sexual Disease You Never Hear About." *Self,* Nov. 1983, pp. 54–58. (About chlamydia.)
Harris, D. "What It Costs to Fight Infertility." *Money,* Dec. 1984, pp. 201–212.
Henig, R. M. "New Hope for Troubled Couples." *Woman's Day,* May 22, 1984, pp. 32–43.
Jacoby, S. "Men's Intimate Illnesses: What Every Couple MUST Know." *McCall's,* Sept. 1985, pp. 76–80, 160.
Mazor, M. "The Problems of Infertility." In *The Woman Patient.* New York: Plenum Press, 1978.
Mazor, M. "Barren Couples." *Psychology Today,* May 1979, pp. 101–112.
Menning, B. E. "Counseling Infertile Couples." *Contemporary Ob/Gyn,* 1979, *13* (2), 101–108.
Menning, B. E. "The Emotional Needs of Infertile Couples." *Fertility and Sterility,* 1980, *34* (4), 313–319.
Pogash, C. "This Story Has a Happy Ending." *Redbook,* Aug. 1982, pp. 81–86.
Yalof, I. "As the Sperm Turns." *Gentlemen's Quarterly,* March 1986, pp. 158–165.

Periodicals and Newsletters on Infertility

(Additional newsletters are published by RESOLVE, Inc., and its chapters.)
Fertility Review. Holman, J. F. (ed.). Can be ordered through Fertility Review, North Duke Professional Center, 4020 North Roxboro Road, Durham, N.C. 27704; $25 for six issues annually. Excellent critique of medical aspects of infertility.
Loving Arms. Pregnancy and Infant Loss Center of Minnesota, 1415 E. Wayzata Boulevard, Suite 22, Wayzata, Minn. 55391.
Stepping Stones. P.O. Box 11141, Wichita, Kans. 67211. (Free bimonthly newsletter for Christian infertile couples.)

Publications on Pregnancy Loss

Adler, J., and others. "Learning from the Loss." *Newsweek,* March 24, 1986, pp. 66–67.

Berezin, N. *After a Loss in Pregnancy: Help for Families Affected by a Miscarriage, a Stillbirth, or the Loss of a Newborn.* New York: Simon & Schuster, 1982.

Berg, B. J. *Nothing to Cry About: One Woman's Struggle to Have Her Own Baby.* New York: Seaview Books, 1981. (Fiction.)

Borg, S., and Lasker, J. *When Pregnancy Fails: Families Coping with Miscarriage, Stillbirth, and Infant Death.* Boston: Beacon Press, 1981.

Cohen, M. D. *The Limits of Miracles.* South Hadley, Mass.: Bergin & Garvey, 1985. (Poems about the loss of babies.)

DeFrain, J. *Stillborn: The Invisible Death.* Lexington, Mass.: Lexington Books, 1986.

Friedman, R., and Gradstein, B. *Surviving Pregnancy Loss.* Boston: Little, Brown, 1982.

Ilse, S. *Empty Arms.* Long Lake, Minn.: Wintergreen Press, 1982. (Order from Wintergreen Press, 4105 Oak Street, Long Lake, Minn. 55356; $4.50 plus postage.)

Ilse, S., and Burns, L. H. *Miscarriage: A Shattered Dream.* Long Lake, Minn.: Wintergreen Press, 1985. (Order from Wintergreen Press, 4105 Oak Street, Long Lake, Minn. 55356; $4.50 plus postage.)

Kotzwinkle, W. *Swimmer in the Secret Spa.* New York: Avon Books, 1975. (Fiction.)

Page, T. "Life Miscarried." *New York Times Magazine,* Jan. 27, 1985, p. 50.

Panuthos, C., and Romeo, C. *Ended Beginnings: Healing Childbearing Losses.* South Hadley, Mass.: Bergin & Garvey, 1984. (A guide for those experiencing pregnancy loss.)

Peppers, L. G., and Knapp, R. J. *How to Go On Living After the Death of a Baby.* Atlanta: Peachtree Publishers, 1985.

Pizer, H., and Palinski, C. O. *Coping with a Miscarriage.* New York: New American Library, 1980.

Schweibert, P. R., and Kirk, P. *Still to Be Born.* Portland, Ore.: Perinatal Loss, 1986. (Order from Perinatal Loss, 2116 N.E. 18th Avenue, Portland, Ore. 97212; $4.00.)

Seiden, O. J., and Timmons, M. J. *Coping with Miscarriage.* Blue Ridge Summit, Pa.: Tab Books, 1984.

Woods, J. R., and Esposito, J. L. (eds.). *Pregnancy Loss: Medi-*

cal *Therapeutics and Practical Considerations.* Baltimore: Williams & Wilkins, 1987.

Zehnder, G. G. *Feelings.* Cleveland: Cleveland Regional Perinatal Network, 1984. (Twenty-page pamphlet on grieving after a pregnancy or neonatal loss. Available from Cleveland Regional Perinatal Network, 2105 Adelbert Road, Cleveland, Ohio 44106.)

Publications on Adoption

Arms, S. *To Love and Let Go.* New York: Knopf, 1983. (Profiles of birth mothers experiencing loss after releasing an infant for adoption.)

Bolles, E. B. *The Penguin Adoption Handbook.* New York: Viking Penguin, 1984.

Canape, C. *Adoption: Parenthood Without Pregnancy.* New York: Holt, Rinehart & Winston, 1986.

de Hartog, J. *The Children.* New York: Atheneum, 1969. (Discussion of Korean adoptions.)

Gilman, L. *The Adoption Resource Book.* New York: Harper & Row, 1984.

Gilman, L. "Adoption: How to Do It on Your Own." *Money,* Oct. 1985, pp. 161–168.

Gradstein, B., Gradstein, M., and Glass, R. "Private Adoption." *Fertility and Sterility,* 1982, *37* (4), 548–552.

Hallenback, C. A. *Our Child: Preparation for Parenting in Adoption.* Wayne, Pa.: Our Child Press, 1984.

Hamm, W., and others. *Self-Awareness, Self-Selection and Success: Parent Preparation.* Washington, D.C.: North American Council on Adoptable Children, 1985. (On special needs adoption. Write North American Council on Adoptable Children, 810 18th Street, N.W., Suite 703, Washington, D.C. 20006.)

Holmes, P. *Supporting an Adoption.* Wayne, Pa.: Our Child Press, 1983. (Self-published thirty-page booklet of information and advice for family and friends. Order from Our Child Press, 800 Maple Glen Lane, Wayne, Pa. 19087; $4.75.)

Jewett, C. *Adopting an Older Child.* Boston: Harvard Common Press, 1978.

Johnston, P. I. (ed.). *Perspectives on a Grafted Tree.* Fort Wayne, Ind.: Perspectives Press, 1983. (Beautifully illustrated book of poetry on adoption. Order from Perspectives Press, 905 W. Wildwood Avenue, Fort Wayne, Ind. 46807; $12.95.)

Johnston, P. I. *An Adopter's Advocate.* Fort Wayne, Ind.: Perspectives Press, 1984. (Order from Perspectives Press, 905 W. Wildwood Avenue, Fort Wayne, Ind. 46807; $6.95.)

Klibanoff, S., and Klibanoff, E. *Let's Talk About Adoption.* Boston: Little, Brown, 1973.

Kline, D. "He's Ours . . . He's Really Ours." *McCall's,* March 1984, pp. 56–67.

Krementz, J. *How It Feels to Be Adopted.* New York: Knopf, 1982.

Lovenheim, B. "The Baby Brokers." *Redbook,* Oct. 1983, p. 102.

Machol, L. "Report on Adoption, 1982." *Contemporary Ob/ Gyn,* 1982, *19* (2), 65–91.

McNamara, J. *The Adoption Advisor.* New York: Dutton (Hawthorn Books), 1975.

Martin, C. *Beating the Adoption Game.* La Jolla, Calif.: Oak Tree Publications, 1980. (Currently out of print. Order from Martin, 457 Westbourne, La Jolla, Calif. 92037; $15.00.)

Mason, M. M. *The Miracle Seekers: An Anthology of Infertility.* Fort Wayne, Ind.: Perspectives Press, 1987. (Excellent collection of short stories depicting a variety of personal struggles with infertility. Write Perspectives Press, 905 W. Wildwood Avenue, Fort Wayne, Ind. 46807; $14.95 plus $1.80 postage and handling.)

Nelson-Erichsen, J., and Erichsen, H. R. *Gamines: How to Adopt from Latin America.* Minneapolis: Dillon Press, 1981. (A 350-page volume with extensive resources.)

Plumez, J. H. *Successful Adoption.* New York: Crown (Harmony Books), 1982.

Smith, J., and Miroff, F. I. *You're Our Child.* Lanham, Md.: University Press of America, 1981.

Sorosky, A. D., Baron, A., and Pannor, R. *The Adoption Triangle.* New York: Doubleday (Anchor Press), 1978. (Addresses the interrelation of birth parents, adoptive parents, and adopted child.)

Viguers, S. T. *With Child: One Couple's Journey to Their Adopted Children.* San Diego, Calif.: Harcourt Brace Jovanovich, 1986.

Publications on Artificial Insemination by Donor

Alexander, N. J., and others. *Artificial Insemination.* Portland: Oregon Health Sciences University, 1981. (Booklet about AID.)

Atallah, L. "Report from a Test Tube Baby." *New York Times Magazine,* April 18, 1976, p. 16. (AID daughter conceived in the 1950s.)

Beck, W., and Wallach, E. "When Therapy Fails—Artificial Insemination." *Contemporary Ob/Gyn,* 1981, *17* (1), 113–129.

Curie-Cohen, M., and others. "Current Practice of Artificial Insemination by Donor in the United States." *New England Journal of Medicine,* 1979, *300* (11), 585–590.

Harvey, B., and Harvey, A. "How Couples Feel About Donor Insemination." *Contemporary Ob/Gyn,* 1977, *9* (6), 93–97.

Robinson, S., and Pizer, H. E. *Having a Baby Without a Man: The Woman's Guide to Alternative Insemination.* New York: Simon & Schuster, 1985.

Schlaff, W., and Vercollone, C. F. *Understanding Artificial Insemination: A Guide for Patients.* Arlington, Mass.: RESOLVE, Inc., 1987.

Snowden, R., and Mitchell, G. D. *The Artificial Family: A Consideration of Artificial Insemination by Donor.* London: Allen & Unwin, 1981.

Snowden, R., Mitchell, G. D., and Snowden, E. M. *Artificial Reproduction: A Social Investigation.* London: Allen & Unwin, 1983.

Wallis, C., and others. "The New Origins of Life." *Time,* Sept. 10, 1984, pp. 46–53.

See also Andrews, *New Conceptions* (in "Overview—Emotional" section).

Books on Childfree Living and Decision-Making Issues

Bombardieri, M. *The Baby Decision: How to Make the Most Important Choice of Your Life.* New York: Rawson Associates, 1981. (Order from Merle Bombardieri, 26 Trapelo Road, Belmont, Mass. 02178; $9.95 paper, $13.95 cloth.)

Burgwyn, D. *Marriage Without Children.* New York: Harper & Row, 1981.

Fabe, M., and Wikler, N. *Up Against the Clock: Career Women Speak on the Choice to Have Children.* New York: Random House, 1979.

Faux, M. *Childless by Choice: Choosing Childlessness in the Eighties.* New York: Doubleday, 1984.

Fox, G. L. *The Childbearing Decision: Fertility Attitudes and Behaviors.* Newbury Park, Calif.: Sage, 1982.

Lindsay, K. *Friends as Family.* Boston: Beacon Press, 1981.

Shealy, C. N., and Shealy, M. C. *To Parent or Not?* Norfolk, Va.: Donning Co., 1981.

Whelan, E. M. *A Baby? . . . Maybe.* Indianapolis: Bobbs-Merrill, 1975.

Pregnancy and Parenting Concerns

Boston Women's Health Book Collective. *Ourselves and Our Children.* New York: Random House, 1978.

Freeman, R. K., and Pescar, S. C. *Safe Delivery.* New York: Facts on File, 1982.

Friedland, R., and Kant, C. (eds.). *The Mother's Book.* Boston: Houghton Mifflin, 1981. (Chapters on foster and adoptive parenting, pregnancy after infertility, miscarriage, and stillbirth.)

Kitzinger, S. *The Complete Book of Pregnancy and Childbirth.* New York: Knopf, 1980.

McCauley, C. *Pregnancy After 35.* New York: Dutton, 1976.

Milunsky, A. *How to Have the Healthiest Baby You Can.* New York: Simon & Schuster, 1987.

Nance, S. *Premature Babies: A Handbook for Parents.* New York: Arbor House, 1982.

Procaccini, J., and Kiefaber, M. W. *Parent Burnout*. New York: Doubleday, 1983.

Special Topics

Ballweg, M. L. *Overcoming Endometriosis*. New York: Congdon & Weed, 1987.

Beauchamp, T. L., and Childress, J. F. *Principles of Biomedical Ethics*. New York: Oxford University Press, 1983.

Bichler, J. *DES Daughter: A True Story of Tragedy and Triumph*. New York: Avon Books, 1981.

Elias, S., and Annas, G. J. *Reproductive Genetics and the Law*. Chicago: Year Book Medical Publishers, 1987.

Fertility and Pregnancy Guide for DES Daughters and Sons. New Hyde Park, N.Y.: DES Action National, 1984.

Fletcher, J. C. *Coping with Genetic Disorders: A Guide for Counseling*. San Francisco: Harper & Row, 1982.

Gindoff, P. R., and Jewelewicz, R. "Reproductive Potential in the Older Woman." *Fertility and Sterility*, 1986, *46* (6), 989–1002.

Graham, K. M. *An Adopted Woman*. New York: Remi Books, 1983. (A true story of her search and her discoveries.)

Hales, D., and Creasy, R. K. *New Hope for Problem Pregnancies*. New York: Harper & Row, 1982.

Johnson, J. "When Things Go Wrong: What to Do If Your Newborn Dies." *Mothering*, Spring 1986, pp. 26–29.

Machol, L. "How Fecund Are Women over 30?" *Contemporary Ob/Gyn*, 1982, *20* (2), 201–206.

McKaughan, M. "The Ectopic Epidemic." *Woman's Day*, April 3, 1984, pp. 62–65.

Menken, J., Trussell, J., and Larsen, U. "Age and Infertility." *Science*, Sept. 1986, *233*, 1389–1394.

Older, J. *Endometriosis*. New York: Scribner's, 1983.

Orenberg, C. L. *DES: The Complete Story*. New York: St. Martin's Press, 1981.

Reproductive Outcomes in Women Exposed In Utero to Diethylstilbestrol: A Review of the Literature, 1978 to 1984. New Hyde Park, N.Y.: DES Action National, 1986.

Schwartz, D., and Mayaux, B. A. "Female Fecundity as a Function of Age." *New England Journal of Medicine*, 1982, *306* (7), 404–406.

Shepard, T. *Catalog of Teratogenic Agents*. (5th ed.) Baltimore: Johns Hopkins University Press, 1986.

U.S. Congress, Office of Technology Assessment. *Reproductive Health Hazards in the Workplace*. Washington, D.C.: U.S. Government Printing Office, 1985.

Fertility Awareness for Infertile Couples

Nofziger, M. *A Cooperative Method of Natural Birth Control*. Summertown, Tenn.: The Book Publishing Company, 1976.

Nofziger, M. *The Fertility Question*. Summertown, Tenn.: The Book Publishing Company, 1982. (On monitoring your ovulatory cycle.)

Books on Hysterectomy

Dennerstein, L., Wood, C., and Burrows, G. *Hysterectomy: How to Deal with the Physical and Emotional Aspects*. New York: Oxford University Press, 1982. (Order from Oxford University Press, 1600 Pollitt Drive, Fair Lawn, N.J. 07410.)

Morgan, S. *Coping with a Hysterectomy*. New York: Doubleday (Dial Press), 1982.

Publications on In Vitro Fertilization

Blake, J. "Children of Love, Children of Science." *Boston*, Dec. 1984, pp. 194–197.

Clapp, D. N., and Bombardieri, M. "Easing Stress for IVF Patients and Staff." *Contemporary Ob/Gyn*, 1984, *24* (4), 91–99.

Fadiman, A. "Small Miracles of Love and Science." *Life*, Nov. 1982, pp. 44–52.

Jones, H. W., and others (eds.). *In Vitro Fertilization—Norfolk*. Baltimore: Williams & Wilkins, 1986. (A 319-page volume, $65.00.)

Machol, L. "In Vitro Fertilization: The Work Continues." *Contemporary Ob/Gyn*, 1982, *19* (5), 40–61.
Perloe, M., and Christie, L. G. *Miracle Babies and Other Happy Endings: For Couples with Fertility Problems.* New York: Rawson Associates, 1986.
Phillips, M. "One Woman's Courage." *American Health*, Nov. 1985, pp. 76–90.
Singer, P., and Wells, D. *Making Babies: The New Science and Ethics of Conception.* New York: Scribner's, 1985.
Tilton, N., Tilton, T., and Moore, G. *Making Miracles: In Vitro Fertilization.* New York: Doubleday, 1985.
See also Andrews, *New Conceptions* (in "Overview—Emotional" section).

Publications on One-Child Families

(For those experiencing secondary infertility or infertility for the second time around.)
Hawke, S., and Knox, D. *One Child by Choice.* Englewood Cliffs, N.J.: Prentice-Hall, 1977.
Kappelman, M. *Raising the Only Child.* New York: New American Library, 1977.

Publications on Surrogate Mothers

(National RESOLVE has many of these articles on file.)
Fox, G. L. "Surrogate Motherhood: Implications for the Family." Paper presented at an interdisciplinary symposium on surrogate motherhood, Wayne State University Schools of Medicine and Law, Detroit, Nov. 20, 1982.
Gelman, D., and Shapiro, D. "Infertility: Babies by Contract." *Newsweek*, Nov. 4, 1985, pp. 74–76.
Gorney, C. "For Love and Money." *California Magazine*, Oct. 1983, pp. 88–96, 150–155.
Hirsh, B. D. "Parenthood by Proxy." *Journal of the American Medical Association*, 1983, *249* (16), 2251–2252.
Keane, N. P., and Breo, D. *The Surrogate Mother.* New York: Everest House, 1981.

"Other Mothers: The Surrogate Debate." Roundtable discussion. *Public Welfare*, Fall 1983, pp. 7-12.

Parker, P. J. "Surrogate Motherhood: The Interaction of Litigation, Legislation and Psychiatry." *International Journal of Law and Psychiatry*, 1982, *5*, 341-354.

Parker, P. J. "Motivation of Surrogate Mothers: Initial Findings." *American Journal of Psychiatry*, 1983, *140* (1), 117-118.

Parker, P. J. "Surrogate Motherhood, Psychiatric Screening and Informed Consent, Baby Selling, and Public Policy." *Bulletin of the American Academy of Psychiatry and the Law*, 1984, *12* (1), 21-39.

Rushevsky, C. A. "Legal Recognition of Surrogate Gestation." *Women's Rights Law Reporter*, 1982, 7 (2), 107-142.

Winslade, W. J. "Report from America." *Journal of Medical Ethics*, July 1981, pp. 153-154.

See also Andrews, *New Conceptions* (in "Overview—Emotional" section).

On Coping and Mourning

Bowers, S. A., and Bowers, G. H. *Asserting Yourself.* Reading, Mass.: Addison-Wesley, 1976.

Broderick, C. *Couples: How to Confront Problems and Maintain Loving Relationships.* New York: Simon & Schuster, 1979.

DeRosis, H. A., and Pellegrino, V. Y. *The Book of Hope: How Women Can Overcome Depression.* New York: Macmillan, 1976.

Hanes, M. *Beyond Heartache.* Wheaton, Ill.: Tyndale House, 1984. (Coping with loss as a result of infertility or miscarriage.)

Johnston, P. I. *Understanding.* Fort Wayne, Ind.: Perspectives Press, 1983. (Guide for couples and their families affected by infertility. Order from Perspectives Press, 905 W. Wildwood Avenue, Fort Wayne, Ind. 46807; $3.50.)

Kushner, H. *When Bad Things Happen to Good People.* New York: Schocken Books, 1981.

Linn, D., and Linn, M. *Healing Life's Hurts.* Ramsey, N.J.: Paulist Press, 1978.

Pincus, L. *Death and the Family.* New York: Random House, 1976.
Rubin, T. I. *The Angry Book.* New York: Macmillan, 1970.
Rubin, T. I. *Reconciliations: Inner Peace in an Age of Anxiety.* New York: Viking Penguin, 1980.
Sheehy, G. *Pathfinders.* New York: Morrow, 1981.
Tatelbaum, J. *The Courage to Grieve.* New York: Harper & Row, 1980.
Tubesing, D. A. *Kicking Your Stress Habits.* Duluth, Minn.: Whole Person Associates, 1981. (Order from Whole Person Associates, P.O. Box 3151, Duluth, Minn. 55803.)
Westberg, G. E. *Good Grief.* Philadelphia: Fortress Press, 1962.
Yalom, I. D. *Existential Psychotherapy.* New York: Basic Books, 1980.

RESOLVE Publications

(The following is a list of fact sheets that can be obtained from RESOLVE, Inc. They are listed alphabetically by topic.)

- Adoption
- Artificial Insemination (husband or donor)
- AID: Views on AID (Collection)
- Clomiphene Citrate (Clomid, Serophene)
- DES: Its Impact on Infertility
- Endometriosis
- hMG (Pergonal) and hCG
- Immunologic Infertility (sperm antibodies)
- In Vitro Fertilization: An Overview
- Laparoscopy: What to Expect
- Luteal Phase Defects
- Medical Management of Male Infertility
- Microsurgical and Laser Techniques for Tubal Repair
- Miscarriage: Emotional Impact
- Miscarriage: Medical Facts
- Overview of the Infertility Work-Up and the Tests Used
- Pinpointing Ovulation
- Polycystic Ovarian Disease (Stein-Leventhal Syndrome)

- Prolactin Problems (Parlodel, etc.)
- Religious Perspectives on Infertility (Collection)
- Semen Analysis
- Surrogate Mother Programs
- T-Mycoplasma
- Understanding Health Insurance
- Varicocele: Surgical and Medical Treatment
- What Is an Infertility Specialist

Governmental Publication

U.S. Congress, Office of Technology Assessment. *Infertility: Medical and Social Choices*, OTA-BA-358. Washington, D.C.: U.S. Government Printing Office, May 1988. This 402 page report costs $16 and can be ordered from the Superintendent of Documents, Dept. 36-AW, Washington, D.C. 20402-9325.

RESOURCE C

Educational, Self-Help, and Support Group Resources

American Association of Sex Educators, Counselors, and Therapists
5010 Wisconsin Avenue N.W., Suite 304
Washington, D.C. 20016

Publishes booklets on sexual concerns for physically disabled patients. Also can give referrals to local therapists affiliated with the organization.

American Fertility Society
2131 Magnolia Avenue, Suite 201
Birmingham, Ala. 35256

Publishes *Fertility and Sterility* monthly; has list of physicians who are members of the society.

Compassionate Friends
(National Office)
P.O. Box 1347
Oak Brook, Ill. 60521
(312) 323-5010

Has chapters throughout the country and provides support and information to couples who have experienced pregnancy loss.

DES Action
2845 24th Street
San Francisco, Calif. 94110
(415) 826-5060

Has national newsletter and local chapters.

This material is reprinted with the permission of RESOLVE, Inc.

Endometriosis Association
P.O. Box 92187
Milwaukee, Wis. 53202

Has over forty chapters and an excellent newsletter.

Hysterectomy Educational
  Resources and Services
501 Woodbrook Lane
Philadelphia, Pa. 19119
(215) 247-6232

Publishes a newsletter dealing with surgery, estrogen replacement, and postsurgery information.

IUD Litigation Information
  Service
National Women's Health
  Network
224 7th Street, S.E.
Washington, D.C. 20003

Will advise women on legal action if infertility was caused by IUD, especially Dalkon Shield.

North American Council on
  Adoptable Children
  (NACAC)
810 18th Street, N.W.,
  Suite 703
Washington, D.C. 20006
(202) 466-7570

Has information on placement of older children, publishes a newsletter, and has a network of parents' groups.

OURS, Inc.
3307 Highway 100 North,
  Suite 203
Minneapolis, Minn. 55442
(612) 535-4829

Publishes a newsletter, has listing of agencies doing international adoptions.

Parents for Private Adoption
P.O. Box 7
Pawlet, Vt. 05761

Publishes a newsletter and provides information on the subject of legal private adoption.

Pregnancy and Infant Loss
   Center
1415 E. Wayzata Boulevard,
   Suite 22
Wayzata, Minn. 55391
(612) 473-9372

Publishes newsletter and other
materials for professionals and
families who have experienced
this kind of tragedy.

RESOLVE, Inc.
5 Water Street
Arlington, Mass. 02174
(617) 643-2424

Provides telephone counseling, referral to medical and related services, support groups,
and public education through
newsletters, fact sheets, and
chapter activities in over forty-
five cities.

References

Abarbanel, A. R., and Bach, G. "Group Psychotherapy for the Infertile Couple." *International Journal of Fertility*, 1959, *4*, 151–160.

Alberti, R., and Emmons, M. L. *Your Perfect Right: A Guide to Assertive Behavior.* San Luis Obispo, Calif.: Impact, 1974.

Andrews, L. B. *New Conceptions: A Consumer's Guide to the Newest Infertility Treatments.* New York: St. Martin's Press, 1984.

Arnstein, H. S. *What to Tell Your Child: About Birth, Illness, Death, Divorce and Other Family Crises.* Westport, Conn.: Condor, 1978.

Bennis, W. G., and Shepherd, H. A. "A Theory of Group Development." *Human Relations*, 1956, *9*, 415–437.

Berelson, B., and Steiner, G. A. *Human Behavior.* San Diego, Calif.: Harcourt Brace Jovanovich, 1964.

Berezin, N. *After a Loss in Pregnancy: Help for Families Affected by a Miscarriage, a Stillbirth, or the Loss of a Newborn.* New York: Simon & Schuster, 1982.

Bernstein, J. E. *Books to Help Children Cope with Separation and Loss.* (2nd ed.) New York: Bowker, 1983.

Bloom, L., Coburn, K., and Pearlman, J. *The New Assertive Woman.* New York: Dell, 1975.

Bluebond-Langner, M. "Meanings of Death to Children." In H. Feifel (ed.), *New Meanings of Death.* New York: McGraw-Hill, 1977.

Bolles, E. B. *The Penguin Adoption Handbook.* New York: Viking Penguin, 1984.

235

Bombardieri, M. *The Baby Decision: How to Make the Most Important Choice of Your Life.* New York: Rawson Associates, 1981.

Borg, S., and Lasker, J. *When Pregnancy Fails: Families Coping with Miscarriage, Stillbirth, and Infant Death.* Boston: Beacon Press, 1981.

Bowers, S. A., and Bowers, G. H. *Asserting Yourself.* Reading, Mass.: Addison-Wesley, 1976.

Burgwyn, D. *Marriage Without Children.* New York: Harper & Row, 1981.

Callahan, B. N. *Assertiveness Training.* Boston: Resource Communications, 1980.

Clapp, D. N., and Bombardieri, M. "Easing Stress for IVF Patients and Staff." *Contemporary Ob/Gyn,* 1984, *24* (4), 91–99.

Compassionate Friends. *Grieving, Healing, Growing.* Oak Brook, Ill.: Compassionate Friends, 1982.

Dauten, D. A. *Quitting: Knowing When to Leave.* New York: Walker & Co., 1980.

DeFrain, J. *Stillborn: The Invisible Death.* Lexington, Mass.: Lexington Books, 1986.

Drake, T. S., and Grunert, G. M. "A Cyclic Pattern of Sexual Dysfunction in the Infertility Investigation." *Fertility and Sterility,* 1979, *32,* 542–545.

Faux, M. *Childless by Choice: Choosing Childlessness in the Eighties.* New York: Doubleday, 1984.

Fensterheim, H., and Baer, J. *Don't Say Yes When You Want to Say No.* New York: Dell, 1975.

Fleming, J. "Infertility as a Chronic Illness." *Resolve Newsletter,* Dec. 1984, p. 5.

Fox, E. F., Nelson, M. A., and Bolman, W. M. "The Termination Process: A Neglected Dimension in Social Work." *Social Work,* 1969, *14* (2), 53–63.

Freese, A. *Help for Your Grief: Turning Emotional Loss into Growth.* New York: Schocken Books, 1977.

Friedman, R., and Gradstein, B. *Surviving Pregnancy Loss.* Boston: Little, Brown, 1982.

Garland, J. A., Jones, H. E., and Kolodny, R. "A Model for

Stages of Development in Social Work Groups." In S. Bernstein (ed.), *Explorations in Group Work.* Boston: School of Social Work, Boston University, 1965.

Garvin, C. D. *Contemporary Group Work.* Englewood Cliffs, N.J.: Prentice-Hall, 1981.

Garvin, C. D., and Glasser, P. H. "Social Group Work: The Preventative and Rehabilitative Approach." In P. Glasser, R. Sarri, and R. Vinter (eds.), *Individual Change Through Small Groups.* New York: Free Press, 1974.

Gilman, L. *The Adoption Resource Book.* New York: Harper & Row, 1984.

Ginsburg, J. E. "International Adoption." In M. D. Mazor and H. F. Simons (eds.), *Infertility: Medical, Emotional, and Social Consequences.* New York: Human Sciences Press, 1984.

Goodman, K., and Rothman, B. "Group Work in Infertility Treatment." *Social Work with Groups,* 1984, 7 (1), 79–96.

Grollman, E. A. (ed.). *Explaining Death to Children.* Boston: Beacon Press, 1967.

Guastella, G., and others. "Gamete Intrafallopian Transfer in the Treatment of Infertility: The First Series at the University of Palermo." *Fertility and Sterility,* 1986, 46 (3), 417–423.

Hackman, J. R., and Morris, C. G. "Group Tasks, Group Interaction Process, and Group Performance Effectiveness: A Review and Proposed Interpretation." In L. Berkowitz (ed.), *Advances in Experimental Social Psychology.* Orlando, Fla.: Academic Press, 1975.

Hare, A. P. *Handbook of Small Group Research.* New York: Free Press, 1962.

Harper, K. *The Childfree Alternative.* Brattleboro, Vt.: Stephen Greene Press, 1980.

Hartford, M. E. *Groups in Social Work.* New York: Columbia University Press, 1971.

Hotchner, T. *Pregnancy and Childbirth.* New York: Avon Books, 1984.

Ilse, S., Burns, L. H., and Erling, S. *Sibling Grief . . . After Miscarriage, Stillbirth or Infant Death.* Wayzata, Minn.: Pregnancy and Infant Loss Center, 1984.

Ilse, S., and Leininger, L. *Grieving Grandparents . . . After Miscarriage, Stillbirth or Infant Death.* Wayzata, Minn.: Pregnancy and Infant Loss Center, 1985.

Jackson, E. N. *Telling a Child About Death.* New York: Dutton (Hawthorn Books), 1965.

Jackson, P. L. "Chronic Grief." *American Journal of Nursing,* July 1974, *74,* 1288–1291.

Jakubowski-Specter, P. *An Introduction to Assertiveness Training Procedures for Women.* Washington, D.C.: American Personnel and Guidance Association, 1973.

Janis, I. L., and Mann, L. *Decision Making.* New York: Free Press, 1977.

Johnston, P. I. *An Adopter's Advocate.* Fort Wayne, Ind.: Perspectives Press, 1984.

Kennedy, J. F. "Maternal Reactions to the Birth of a Defective Baby." *Social Casework,* July 1970, *51,* 410–416.

Kraft, A., and others. "The Psychological Dimensions of Infertility." *American Journal of Orthopsychiatry,* 1980, *50,* 618–627.

Kübler-Ross, E. *On Death and Dying.* New York: Macmillan, 1969.

Lalos, A., and others. "The Psychosocial Impact of Infertility Two Years After Completed Surgical Treatment." *Acta Obstetricia et Gynecologica Scandinavica,* 1985a, *64,* 599–604.

Lalos, A., and others. "Psychological Reactions to the Medical Investigation and Surgical Treatment of Infertility." *Gynecologic and Obstetric Investigation,* 1985b, *20* (4), 1–9.

Lamb, E. J., and Leurgans, S. "Does Adoption Affect Subsequent Fertility?" *American Journal of Obstetrics and Gynecology,* 1979, *134* (2), 138–144.

Lazarus, A., and Fay, A. *I Can if I Want To: The Direct Assertion Therapy Program to Change Your Life.* New York: Morrow, 1975.

Lebow, G. H. "Facilitating Adaptation in Anticipatory Mourning." *Social Casework,* 1976, *57* (7), 458–465.

Leitko, T. A., and Greil, A. L. "Involuntary Childlessness, Gender, Female Employment and Emotional Distress." Paper presented at meeting of the American Sociological Association, Washington, D.C., Aug. 1985.

Levine, B. *Group Psychotherapy.* Englewood Cliffs, N.J.: Prentice-Hall, 1979.

Lewis, E., and Page, A. "Failure to Mourn a Stillbirth: An Overlooked Catastrophe." *British Journal of Medical Psychology,* 1978, *51,* 237–241.

Lindemann, E. "Symptomatology and Management of Acute Grief." In H. J. Parad (ed.), *Crisis Intervention: Selected Readings.* New York: Family Service Association of America, 1965.

Lindsay, K. *Friends as Family.* Boston: Beacon Press, 1981.

Love, V. *Childless Is Not Less.* Minneapolis: Bethany House, 1984.

Mahlstedt, P. "The Psychological Component of Infertility." *Fertility and Sterility,* 1985, *43* (3), 335–346.

Malloy, D., and others. "A Laparoscopic Approach to a Program of Gamete Intrafallopian Transfer." *Fertility and Sterility,* 1987, *47* (2), 289–294.

Mann, R. *Interpersonal Styles and Group Development.* New York: Wiley, 1967.

Matson, P. L., and others. "The In Vitro Fertilization of Supernumerary Docytes in a Gamete Intrafallopian Transfer Program." *Fertility and Sterility,* 1987, *47* (5), 802–806.

Mazor, M. D. "Emotional Reactions to Infertility." In M. D. Mazor and H. F. Simons (eds.), *Infertility: Medical, Emotional, and Social Consequences.* New York: Human Sciences Press, 1984.

Melges, F. T., and DeMaso, D. R. "Grief-Resolution Therapy: Reliving, Revising, and Revisiting." *American Journal of Psychotherapy,* 1980, *34,* 51–61.

Menning, B. E. *Infertility: A Guide for the Childless Couple.* Englewood Cliffs, N.J.: Prentice-Hall, 1977.

Menning, B. E. "The Emotional Needs of Infertile Couples." *Fertility and Sterility,* 1980, *34* (4), 313–319.

Menning, B. E. "RESOLVE: Counseling and Support for Infertile Couples." In M. D. Mazor and H. F. Simons (eds.), *Infertility: Medical, Emotional, and Social Consequences.* New York: Human Sciences Press, 1984.

Mosher, W. D., and Pratt, W. F. *Fecundity and Infertility in the United States, 1965–82.* Advance Data from Vital and Health

Statistics, No. 104. DHHS Pub. No. (PHS)85-1250. Hyatts-
ville, Md.: National Center for Health Statistics, Public Health
Service, 1985.

Nagy, M. "The Child's View of Death." In H. Feifel (ed.), *The
Meaning of Death.* New York: McGraw-Hill, 1965.

Nance, S. *Premature Babies: A Handbook for Parents.* New
York: Arbor House, 1982.

Notman, M. T. "Psychological Aspects of AID." In M. D. Mazor
and H. F. Simons (eds.), *Infertility: Medical, Emotional, and
Social Consequences.* New York: Human Sciences Press,
1984.

Pizer, H., and Palinski, C. O. *Coping with a Miscarriage.* New
York: New American Library, 1980.

Rapaport, L. "The State of Crisis: Some Theoretical Considerations." *Social Service Review,* 1962, *36,* 211–217.

Reid, W. J., and Epstein, L. *Task-Centered Casework.* New
York: Columbia University Press, 1972.

Rhodes, S. "A Developmental Approach to the Life Cycle of
the Family." *Social Casework,* 1977, *58* (5), 301–311.

Rose, S. *Group Therapy: A Behavioral Approach.* Englewood
Cliffs, N.J.: Prentice-Hall, 1977.

Rosenfeld, D. L., and Mitchell, E. "Treating the Emotional Aspects of Infertility: Counseling Services in an Infertility Clinic." *American Journal of Obstetrics and Gynecology,* 1979,
135, 177–180.

Salzer, L. P. *Infertility: How Couples Can Cope.* Boston: G. K.
Hall, 1986.

Schwartz, W. "Social Group Work: The Interactionist Approach." In *Encyclopedia of Social Work.* Vol. 2. New York:
National Association of Social Workers, 1971.

Seibel, M. M., and Taymor, M. L. "Emotional Aspects of Infertility." *Fertility and Sterility,* 1982, *37* (2), 137–145.

Seligman, M. *Helplessness: On Depression, Development and
Death.* New York: W. H. Freeman, 1975.

Shapiro, C. H. "Termination: A Neglected Concept in the Social
Work Curriculum." *Journal of Education for Social Work,*
1980, *16* (2), 13–19.

Shapiro, C. H. "The Impact of Infertility on the Marital Relationship." *Social Casework,* 1982, *63* (7), 387–393.

Shapiro, C. H. "Is Pregnancy After Infertility a Dubious Joy?" *Social Casework*, 1986, *67* (5), 306-313.

Shapiro, C. H., and Seeber, B. "Sex Education and the Adoptive Family." *Social Work*, 1983, *28* (4), 291-296.

Shealy, C. N., and Shealy, M. C. *To Parent or Not?* Norfolk, Va.: Donning Co., 1981.

Shepherd, C. *Small Groups*. Novato, Calif.: Chandler & Sharp, 1964.

Simos, B. *A Time to Grieve*. New York: Family Service Association, 1979.

Smith, M. *When I Say No I Feel Guilty*. New York: Bantam Books, 1975.

Snowden, R., and Mitchell, G. D. *The Artificial Family: A Consideration of Artificial Insemination by Donor*. London: Allen & Unwin, 1981.

Solnit, A. J., and Stark, M. H. "Mourning and the Birth of a Defective Child." In *Psychoanalytic Study of the Child*. Vol. 16. New York: International Universities Press, 1961.

Sommer, R. *Personal Space*. Englewood Cliffs, N.J.: Prentice-Hall, 1969.

Soules, M. R. "The In Vitro Fertilization Pregnancy Rate: Let's Be Honest with One Another." *Fertility and Sterility*, 1985, *43* (4), 511-513.

Stringham, J. G., Riley, J. H., and Ross, A. "Silent Birth: Mourning a Stillborn Baby." *Social Work*, 1982, *27* (4), 322-327.

Tatelbaum, J. *The Courage to Grieve*. New York: Harper & Row, 1980.

Thomas, E. J. *Marital Communication and Decision Making*. New York: Free Press, 1977.

Times, R. *Living with an Empty Chair: A Guide Through Grief*. Amherst, Mass.: Mandala Press, 1977.

Trout, M. D. "Birth of a Sick or Handicapped Infant: Impact on the Family." *Child Welfare*, July-Aug. 1983, *62*, 337-348.

Valentine, D. (ed.). *Infertility and Adoption*. New York: Haworth Press, 1988.

Walker, H. E. "Sexual Problems and Infertility." *Psychosomatics*, 1978, *19* (8), 477-484.

Worden, W. *Grief Counseling and Grief Therapy*. New York: Springer, 1982.

Yalom, I. D. *The Theory and Practice of Group Psychotherapy.*
New York: Basic Books, 1975.

Ziller, R. C. "Toward a Theory of Open and Closed Groups."
Psychological Bulletin, 1965, *63,* 164–182.

Index